# CORREIO AÉREO

A History of the Development of Air Mail Service in Brazil

William Victor Kriebel

*To Steve — with appreciation for your encouragement and support — [signature] NAPEX '97*

The American Air Mail Society

# ACKNOWLEDGEMENTS

I would like to acknowledge the following who were instrumental in providing information for this study: the American Air Mail Society, *The Airpost Journal, The American Air Mail Catalogue*, The American Philatelic Research Library, *The American Philatelist*, The Air and Space Museum of the Smithsonian Institution, LUFTHANSA airlines and VARIG airlines.

A special thank you is extended to the following individuals who provided their expertise and encouragement: Dan Barber, R. E. G. Davies, Ted Eckhardt, Harry Eisenstein, John Hawkins, Douglas Kelsey, Thomas Knapp, Jay Levin, Gerard Marque, Stephen Neulander, Stephen Reinhard, John Paul do Rio Branco, Stephen Rose, Lais Scutto, the late Don Thomas, Karlheinz Wittig, and the late Anthony DeBellis and Alfred Hillel who first ignited my interest in this area. If I have missed the name of anyone else who has helped, my sincere apologies.

I am grateful for the support and encouragement from the Publications Committee of the American Air Mail Society and its Chairman, Robert Lana, and former President, Cheryl Ganz.

Finally, my love, appreciation and thanks to my wife Marjorie, who tolerates my philatelic interests and edited the final draft of this work.

Library of Congress Catalog Card Number: 96-78591

ISBN: 0-939429-19-5

Cover: A LUFTHANSA airline Dornier Do 18 Wal receives a catapult start at 150 km/hr. from the deck of the *Ostmark* (c. 1936).
Back cover: Evening on the Rio Potingi, near Natal, Brazil. A Junkers W 34, of the SYNDICATO CONDOR airline, moored on the river bank (left of palm tree).

# CONTENTS

Correio Aéreo: A History of the Development of Air Mail Service in Brazil

# PREFACE

This study was started in mid-1980 as a result of research into the, then, relatively limited resources, in English, relating specifically to the development of air mail services in Brazil. I had assumed the role of editor of *Bull's Eyes*, the quarterly journal of the Brazil Philatelic Association, and the study served as a basis for an 18-part series that continued over the next four and one-half years. It started with limited resources in both information and, alas, philatelic examples. It was written as material was acquired and as members of the Association contributed their knowledge. This current work is an attempt to revise, update, and expand the original and present it in a single volume format where it, hopefully, will serve as a much needed reference.

The format of the original has been maintained—each of the airlines (most formed before World War II) are treated in alphabetical order, as separate, but contributing, entities and, therefore, some of the historical information may overlap in time.

This study is restricted to Brazil and the fledgling efforts to maintain communications within and without of the country and, in turn, to develop the aerial lines and ground/sea facilities necessary for those services. R.E.G. Davies' excellent, monumental work, *Airlines of Latin America since 1919*, did not appear until the original series was almost complete—had it appeared sooner, that work might never have happened. The primary thrust of the present study is air mail and the philatelic consequences—perhaps irrelevant to some, but very important historically (and financially at the time) to those early pioneers!

The development of lighter-than-air craft and airships—in particular, zeppelins—has been the subject of many books and numerous articles, both in and out of the philatelic press. Although some background information is necessary, I will attempt to limit my discussion to their development as it relates to Brazil and her air mail services. The same is true for several other airlines, for example, LUFTHANSA, which has its own illustrious history outside of Brazil.

I include (redrawn and expanded from the original series) views of some of the aircraft involved—all at the same scale—for comparison purposes. Charles Lindbergh's Ryan NYP, better known as the *Spirit of St. Louis*, probably the most familiar airplane to aircraft enthusiasts, is shown (below) for reference.

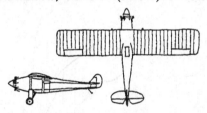

It is recognized that certain data, especially dates, are often in dispute. I have attempted to include information that has been confirmed by more than one source, including postal markings. No claim to infallibility is made, and I hope I have been able to catch all the proper accent marks as well as the errors.

Readers who can elaborate, modify and/or correct the information contained herein are requested to write to the author in care of the American Air Mail Society. Alternative source information, references, diagrams, philatelic or period illustrations and/or related items are also desired.

◊

Opposite: The DEUTSCHE LUFT HANSA Dornier Wal *Munsun* (D-2069) approaches a "drag sail" at the stern of the base-ship *Westfalen* preparatory to being hauled aboard, serviced and sent on its way in a 1933 trial flight. (All photographs, unless noted otherwise, are courtesy of LUFTHANSA German Airlines.)

South America (c. 1927) with the major cities on Brazil's "Southern Coast."

# INTRODUCTION

## CORREIO AÉREO

The birth of commercial airline development in the world is easily traced to the end of World War I. Wartime research and development had improved the performance of the airplane to a practical, although somewhat imperfect, means of transport.

In the 1920s Brazil—3,300,000 square miles, half the area of South America, and larger than the contiguous United States—was ripe for the introduction of the airplane and the connective links that it offered.

Many areas of the country were undeveloped—or even unknown, except on maps. Roads, for the most part, were "under improved." The railroad "system," where it existed, usually involved non-connecting or even non-compatible track beds. Of the 25,000 miles of navigable waterways, over 80% was unused. Development was, for the large part, limited to a coastal strip less than 50 miles wide, and even that did not include the entire 5,000 miles of coastline. Most of the population and wealth was concentrated in the southeastern part of the country—the capital in Rio de Janeiro, the neighboring states of Minas Gerais and São Paulo, and the southernmost, Rio Grande do Sul. Its ten neighboring countries were as remote physically as they were linguistically—Brazil's origins are with the Portuguese, not the Spanish, French, or Dutch—although each of those nations had an interest in Brazil, at some point(s) in time, that was not necessarily in support of the interests of Brazil.

The airplane had proved capable of delivering relatively high-speed performance over somewhat formidable geographical barriers at a comparatively low investment-per-mile of route. This factor alone made it highly suitable to the terrain of South America where, unfortunately, there existed no airplane manufacturing facilities and little capital to develop any. Possible investors showed little interest in potentially risky flying ventures. The governments, although they were often unwilling or unable to provide the necessary subsidies, were aware of the advantages of air travel and were therefore eager to grant franchises.

The United States and Europe found themselves with an oversupply of the very facilities that Latin America lacked: a surplus of military airplanes, a quantity of trained personnel, and waiting manufacturing and supply facilities. The immediate military needs of the Allies had been reduced with the conclusion of World War I. Most of the nations were anxious to maintain a military air capability and, apparently, some had planned expansion and development of services and communication links while the war was still in progress.

The United States expressed a general lack of interest in South America at this time.[1] Between 1918 and 1926 scheduled air transport service within the nation was operated by the Post Office Department, which was heavily involved in the technical problems of operating a domestic line. Private capital had little interest in projects that did not have government support and profitable operations were virtually impossible without substantial government subsidy. The U.S. Post Office Department turned the domestic air mail over to private companies by competitive bidding in 1926-27 and many air transport companies were formed.[2] Public enthusiasm and general attitudes heightened with the Lindbergh flight in May 1927 and the booming stock market speculation of 1928-29 channeled many dollars into aviation securities making it relatively easy to finance almost any aeronautical venture, however sound.

Germany, by the terms of the Versailles Treaty, was barred from engaging in any form of military aviation activity, but not commercial development. She was also barred as a subscriber to the International

| AIRLINE COMPANY CROSS REFERENCE | Founded | See |
|---|---|---|
| **AIRLINE COMPANY CROSS REFERENCE** | **Founded** | **See** |
| Aero Geral | 1942 | VARIG |
| Aero Transporte Vitória | 1955 | bankrupt |
| Aerolloyd Iguassú S.A. | 1932 | VASP |
| Aerovias Brasil | 1942 | REAL |
| Air France | 1933 | AÉROPOSTALE |
| Central Aérea Ltda. (CENTRAL) | 1948 | NACIONAL |
| **COMPAGNIE GÉNÉRALE AÉROPOSTALE (C.G.A.)** | 1927 | |
| Companhia Aeronautica Brasileira (CAB) | 1930 | AÉROPOSTALE |
| Companhia Aeropostal Brasileira (CAB) | 1930 | AÉROPOSTALE |
| Companhia Itaú de Tranportes Aereos (ITAÚ) | 1947 | NACIONAL |
| Companhia Meridional de Transportes (Meridional) | 1944 | bankrupt |
| Compagnie Génerale d'Enterprises Aeronautiques (C.G.E.A.) | 1927 | AÉROPOSTALE |
| Condor Syndikat | 1924 | CONDOR |
| Consorcio Nacional de Transportes Aereos (NACIONAL) | 1947 | REAL |
| Correio Aéreo Militar (CAM) | 1931 | CAN |
| **CORREIO AÉREO NACIONAL (CAN)** | 1941 | |
| Correio Aéreo Naval (CAN) | 1934 | CAN |
| **DEUTSCHE LUFTHANSA A.G. (LUFTHANSA)** | 1926 | |
| **DEUTSCHE LUFTSCHIFFBAU ZEPPELIN G.m.b.H. (ZEPPELIN)** | 1898 | |
| Deutsche Zeppelin-Reederei | 1935 | ZEPPELIN |
| Empresa de Transportes Aérovias Brasil (AEROVIAS) | 1942 | REAL |
| Empresa de Transportes Aéreos Catarinense S.A. (TAC) | 1950 | CRUZEIRO |
| Empresa de Transportes Aéreos Norte do Brasil (AERONORTE) | 1949 | AEROVIAS |
| **EMPRESA de TRANSPORTES AÉREOS Limitada (ETA)** | 1928 | NYRBA |
| Les Lignes Aeriennes Latécoère (LATÉCOÈRE) | 1919 | AÉROPOSTALE |
| **LINEE AEREE TRANSCONTINTALI ITALIANE S.A. (LATI)** | 1939 | |
| Linha Aérea Transcontinental Brasileira (LATB/TCB) | 1944 | REAL |
| Linhas Aéreas "Natal" S.A. | 1946 | VITA |
| Linhas Aéreas Paulistas (LAP) | 1943 | LOIDE |
| Linhas Aéreas Wright | 1947 | REAL |
| Loide Aéreo Nacional S.A. (LOIDE) | 1949 | VASP |
| **NAVEGAÇÃO AÉREA BRASILEIRA S/A. (NAB)** | 1940 | LOIDE |
| **NEW YORK, RIO & BUENOS AIRES LINE (NYRBA)** | 1929 | PAN AMERICAN |
| NYRBA do Brasil | 1929 | PANAIR |
| Organizção Mineira de Transportes Aéreos (OMTA) | 1946 | NACIONAL |
| Panair do Brasil (PANAIR) | 1930 | CRUZEIRO |
| **PAN AMERICAN WORLD AIRWAYS, Inc. (PAN AM)** | 1927 | bankrupt |
| Paraense Transportes Aéreos | 1955 | bankrupt |
| Redes Estaduais Aereas Limitada (REAL) | 1945 | VARIG |
| **S.A. EMPRESA DE VIAÇÃO AÉREA RIO GRANDENSE (VARIG)** | 1927 | |
| S.A. Viação Aérea Gaucha (SAVAG) | 1946 | CRUZEIRO |
| Servição Postal Aéreo Militar (SPAM) | 1930 | CAN |
| Serviços Aéreos Condor (CONDOR) | 1941 | CRUZEIRO |
| Serviços Aéreos Cruzeiro do Sul (CRUZEIRO) | 1942 | |
| **SYNDICATO CONDOR, Ltda (CONDOR)** | 1927 | CONDOR |
| Transportes Aéreos Bandeirantes (TABA) | 1936 | AEROVIAS |
| Transporte Aero-Brasileiro (TAB) | 1937 | did not operate |
| Transportes Aéreos, Ltda (TAL) | 1947 | CRUZEIRO |
| Transportes Aéreos Nacional, LTDA. (NACIONAL) | 1947 | REAL |
| Transportes Aéreos Salvador (TAS) | 1949 | SADIA |
| Transportes Aéreos Sul-Americanos (TASA) | 1948 | bankrupt |
| Transportes Carga Aerea (T.C.A.) | 1947 | LOIDE |
| Universal Transportes Aéreos (Universal) | 1947 | bankrupt |
| Viação Aérea Arco Iris | 1945 | bankrupt |
| Viação Aérea Bahiana | 1946 | bankrupt |
| Viação Aérea Brasil S.A. (VIABRAS) | 1946 | NACIONAL |
| Viação Aérea Santos Dumont (VASD) | 1944 | NACIONAL |
| **VIAÇÃO AÉREA SÃO PAULO, S.A. (VASP)** | 1933 | |
| Viação Interstadual de Transportes Aereos (VITA) | 1946 | LATB/TCB |

Convention on Air Navigation. Subscribers to the Convention granted each other transit rights with a minimum of restrictions and, in turn, could easily discriminate against non-subscribers. To avoid these difficulties, Germany formed "national companies" in other European nations, particularly in the Baltic, which, in turn, obtained rights in other countries in which Germany might have otherwise been denied. South America, relatively free from French and English domination and already harboring a large German population which provided a sympathetic atmosphere, was ripe for the development of local "national" air transport facilities.[3]

Although seeming somewhat haphazard, the German projects in South America appear to follow a careful design. Nationally incorporated companies were regarded sympathetically by the local governments, in particular, Colombia, Bolivia and Brazil, which granted them concessions more freely than foreign incorporated lines. The first successful airline in South America, SOCIEDAD COLOMBO-ALEMANA DE TRANSPORTES AÉREOS (SCADTA), was formed in Colombia in 1919.[4] Although no German government funds were directly involved, SCADTA did receive help from the German aircraft industry. LLOYD AÉREO BOLIVIANO (LAB) was established in Bolivia in 1925 with the obvious help and support of the German Junkers aircraft industry.[5]

The force which fostered the development of the intercontinental airlines of Great Britain, the Netherlands and France—the desire to link up with scattered territories—was not a factor in the development of the lines to and in South America, since the European nations had few important colonies there. National prestige combined with a desire to spread national propaganda—political, cultural and, of course, commercial—was more likely the cause. However, France's anxiety to establish air communication with its overseas territories in the Orient and Africa led to the development of the western coast of Africa and suggested the "leap" across the Atlantic and access to the developing countries there, in particular the most prosperous, Argentina, and its capital, Buenos Aires, "Paris of South America."

In 1925 the French started survey flights within, to and from Brazil with the aims of reaching the major cities of the east coast of South America and further expansion west.[6] The most formidable barrier to any development of a real service to South America was the 1,800 miles of ocean between the westward bump of Africa at Dakar and the eastward shoulder of Brazil at Natal. With the first crossing by airplane in 1922, another in 1926 and at least five in 1927, including the first non-stop crossing (see Appendix A), it was clear that the trip over the seas was becoming routine, but also that bigger, better and faster aircraft would be needed. In the meantime, aircraft combined with ships would provide the first air mail services across the South Atlantic.

Those first air/ship efforts were made by the French AÉROPOSTALE, soon to be followed by the Germans with LUFTHANSA and ZEPPELIN. In between, and subsequently, many "nationals" with a collection of lines, including CONDOR, ETA and VARIG, and finally the American contingent, with NYRBA and PAN AM—more than 50 companies in all (partial list opposite)—affected the development of the aerial links internally (national) and externally (international) in Brazil between the wars. Some died aborning, some died from political or economical pressures, and some live on today.

It was realized early on that, at least at the beginning, few were ready to risk life-and-limb to be the "first" flying passengers or, more importantly, had the finances necessary to do so. Mail, then, was the answer to development and survival. Contracts for transport—exclusive, if possible—would be the source of subsidy. As in many other countries, Brazil, with no airline of its own, had no need for airline facilities—landing fields, seaplane bases, refueling points, service facilities, hangars, etc.—but would be willing to endorse those companies that offered to provide such facilities and, at the same time, provide the necessary communication links.

For the government, mail contracts were the least expensive alternative to obtain the services that they had become convinced they wanted or, more importantly, needed. Brazil had been the second country in the world—first in the Western Hemisphere—to issue postage stamps. It could not afford to not develop its lines of communications and air was the answer.

This, then, is a story of the development of those services—Correio Aéreo (Air Mail)—told from the viewpoint of each of the major lines, a story which starts after one World War and ends, for many of the participants, before or during the next.

◊

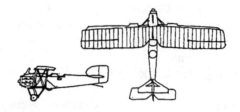

BREGUET 14

14-15 January 1925: Rio de Janeiro - Buenos Aires, Argentina
A cover from the first survey flight between Brazil and Argentina (no air mail postage).

# THE AIRLINES

## COMPAGNIE GÉNÉRALE AÉROPOSTALE

During World War I Toulouse industrialist Pierre-George Latécoère had been commissioned by the French government to build some war planes. After the war, now pilot Latécoère crossed the Pyrenees for the first time, 25 December 1918, in an airplane of his own design. This link, Toulouse to Barcelona, was extended to Rabat, French Morocco, on 8-9 March 1919. Latécoère and his pilot presented Marshal Lyautey with a bouquet of violets and the previous day's edition of *Le Temps*, the Paris newspaper. Impressed by the man and his goal, Marshal Lyautey helped Latécoère obtain encouragement and subsides from the French government to establish LES LIGNES AÉRIENNES LATÉCOÈRE (The Latécoère Air Line Services) and by September 1919 regular weekly mail service was established between Toulouse and Casablanca. The aim was to extend "The Line" down the west coast of Africa to Senegal and, eventually, across to Brazil and down the coast of South America to Buenos Aires. In April 1921 LATÉCOÈRE officially became COMPAGNIE GÉNÉRALE d'ENTREPRISES AERONAUTIQUES (C.G.E.A.). It was formally incorporated the following year, however, both names continued in use.[1]

In 1924 a Latécoère advance party traveled to Brazil and attempted to gain flying concessions and authorization to carry mail from the Brazilian government. Unfortunately, as much as the government may have wanted to provide support, there was no mechanism to do so. This was taken into account and the "rules" were contained in the first Civil Air Navigation Regulations (Law No. 4,911) of 12 January 1925, promulgated by Presidential Decree in July and placed under the administration of the Ministry of Transport and Public Works. Chapters related to air space, civilian aircraft, ground support, traffic and transport. "While inevitably to be amended and improved later, it was admirably comprehensive for its time."[2]

While these negotiations were being held, some test or "survey" flights did occur using tiny Breguet 14s between Brazil and Argentina (with the route: Rio de Janeiro - São Paulo - Florianópolis - Porto Alegre - Pelotas - Montevideo - Buenos Aires) and especially designed multi-colored envelopes (opposite page), featuring the flags of France and the three South American countries, were prepared for these flights with special cachet/postmarks.[3] The outbound flight was 14 January 1925; the return was 21 January arriving in Rio two days later. Covers exist between points on the route. Similar envelopes, with different text, were used for an additional survey flight which was attempted on 5 February 1925, by pilot Paul Vachet, between Rio de Janeiro and Recife with stops at Victoria, Caravelas and Bahia.[4] The flight ended at Bahia as the result of an accident.[5]

Another, and successful, flight was made on 5 March 1925 with a stop only at Bahia on 7 March. The return flight was on 9 March. Rio de Janeiro used the same black cachets as previously, Bahia used a similar cachet and two different rectangular cachets, but Recife used a new oval cachet both as a receiving mark and for the return flight. Covers are reported from Recife to Santos and São Paulo.[6]

In compliance with the law, Latécoère created a Brazilian affiliate, COMPANHIA BRASILEIRA DE EMPREENDIMENTOS AERONÁUTICOS, which received authorization (Decree No. 17,055) on 1 October 1925 to operate a route between Recife and Pelotas, with the rights to extend to Natal, Fernando de Noronha, and the Rocks of St. Peter and St. Paul.[7] However, the authorization was not approved by the Law Courts and new negotiations were entered into. Part of the French problem securing authorization, may have been related to the Germans who were rapidly expanding their own efforts in the area. By December 1926, a discouraged Latécoère sought help from a fellow countryman who had already established business and financial interests in Brazil: Marcel Bouilloux-Lafont.

Marcel Bouilloux-Lafont (1871-1944)

Marcel Bouilloux-Lafont, born in Angoulême, France, and trained as a lawyer, joined his father's business and became a wealthy banker with large property holdings in France and Brazil. His business interests required trips to South America and he longed for an alternative to ship travel. He was aware of the German efforts in airline development in South America and, as a true French patriot with bitter memories of the recent war, wanted the French to succeed. In a meeting between Latécoère and Bouilloux-Lafont, the latter declared, "I have never before invested a sou in aviation; but you are French, I am French, all my resources are at your disposal."[8]

Finally, on 9 March 1927, the Brazilian government granted the concession as outlined in October 1925, but without the extensions (Aviso No. 197).

However, eight days later, on 17 March 1927, Dr. Victor Konder, the Minister for Air Transportation and Public Works, signed the: "Instructions Approved by Executive Order of this Date for the Execution of the Transportation of Mail by Air".[9]

In brief, this lengthy document provided for an air mail service, with rates, to be executed within Brazil only be "domestic airlines"—fully responsible for the mail between post offices—who were required to issue their own stamps, the fees of which paid for the air service. In addition, normal government postage would cover the land costs. Further provisions established the rules for International Service, directly affecting C.G.E.A. as it soon had mail contracts with Argentina and Uruguay. International carriers—C.G.E.A. was the only one on the horizon—could not issue their own stamps, but would be provided with stamps by the government. These stamps accounted for the airlines' fees, with no part going to the post office whose fees were derived from regular postage as in the domestic lines.[10]

On 14 November 1927 test flights were made between Rio de Janeiro and Natal and Natal - Rio de Janeiro - Buenos Aires. No special markings are known by this writer. On 27 December 1927 a special cancel marked the flight from Rio de Janeiro to Natal—and the first use of the government overprinted stamps.

Rio de Janeiro (violet)

On 11 April 1927 Bouilloux-Lafont had purchased C.G.E.A. Latécoère maintained a small amount of stock and returned to building aircraft—new designs, including flying boats, which would be used by the line—near Bordeaux. On 30 April C.G.E.A. became COMPAGNIE GÉNÉRALE AÉROPOSTALE (C.G.A.) or, as it was more simply known, AÉROPOSTALE.

Bouilloux-Lafont clearly realized that revenues would not come from passengers, who had to be both wealthy and obviously adventurous—this was 1928, not 1996! The answer would be in mail contracts. He already had the French and Brazil service as part of the acquisition and he would obtain other contracts, the first with Argentina in June 1927, establishing AEROPOSTA ARGENTINA on 5 September of that year.[11] France was, and would soon prove to be, a strong contender in the South Atlantic mail service. The LINE was ready!

Since 1 June 1925 service between Paris and Dakar had been in full operation. On 1 March 1928 a new service was to begin. Starting out in Buenos Aires, the famous French pilot Jean Mermoz flew northward—Rio Grande - Rio de Janeiro - Natal—the mail was transferred to a borrowed French navy ship, ferried across 3,000 kilometers of ocean to Dakar, then flown northward to Paris in a transit time of eight days. Starting from Toulouse on 2 March 1928, pilot Elisée Négrin, would bring the southbound mail.[12]

| Tentative timetable for September 1927[13] | | |
|---|---|---|
| From - To | Distance (kms) | Time |
| Paris - Casablanca | 1,850 | 13 hours |
| Casablanca - Dakar | 3,000 | 1.5-2 days |
| Dakar - Cape Verde (Porto Praia) | 800 | 5 hours |
| Cape Verde - Fernando de Noronha | 2,200 | 3 days |
| Fernando de Noronha - Natal | 600 | 4 hours |
| Natal - Rio de Janeiro | 2,200 | 16 hours |
| Rio de Janeiro - Buenos Aires | 2,000 | 15 hours |
| Total | 12,650 | 8 days |

In spite of this great achievement, the trip was still not non-stop. Pilots flew from Buenos Aires—usually at night, often in terrible weather, and in open-cockpit, single-engine, monoplanes—to Natal where the mail they were carrying was loaded onto the ships—two obsolete destroyers (*avisos*), *le Peronne* and *le Luneville*.[14] After the crossing, the mail was transferred to other planes and flown on to France. The company looked for the day when the whole route could be traveled by air.

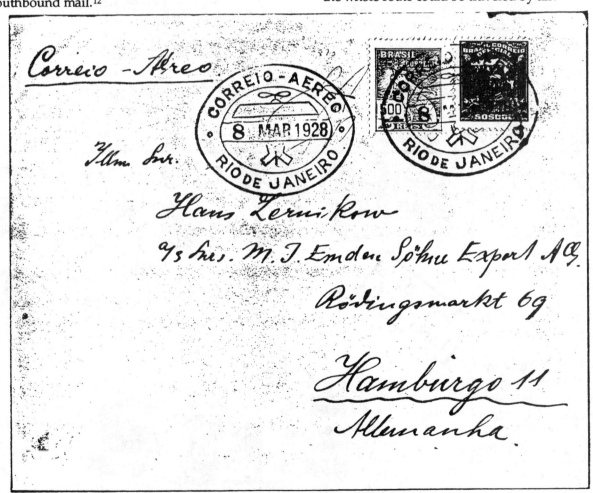

8 March 1928: Rio de Janeiro - Natal - Hamburg, Germany
500 rs. postage + 5,000 rs. air mail

C.G.A. also provided regular service—Rio de Janeiro - Montevideo - Buenos Aires. The cover (above) was posted by a major stamp dealer who once produced a philatelic catalogue and who also dealt with other collectibles: postcards money and medals.

A 1928 cover (right and far right) to Uruguay bears the Rio de Janeiro home office backstamp which reads "AERO-POSTAL," which is the Portuguese version of AÉROPOSTALE.

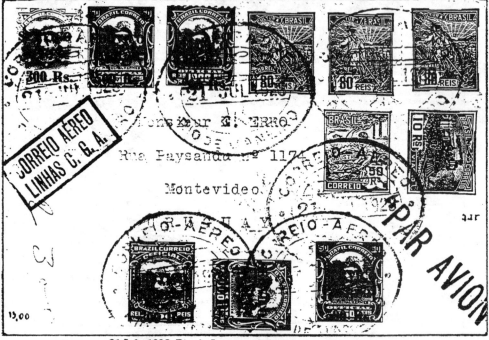

21 July 1928: Rio de Janeiro - Montevideo, Uruguay
300 rs. postage + 2,000 rs. air mail

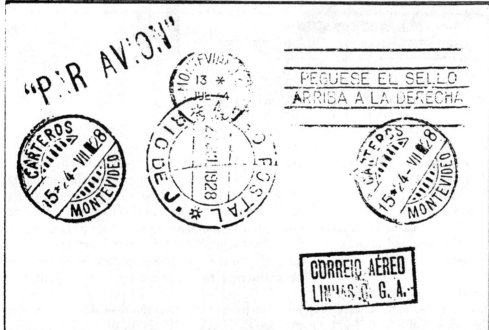

Reverse of cover (opposite page) showing "AEROPOSTAL" backstamp.

A cover (above) from a 7 April 1928 flight—Rio de Janeiro - Santos - São Paulo—illustrates the straight line and boxed cachets that C.G.A. developed.

Note the markings "Via Aerea Linhas C.G.A." and "Via Santos." Santos was the seaport connection for São Paulo, suggesting that seaplanes were used. To my knowledge C.G.A. had none, but perhaps had a "field" for landing the land planes (see next page).

31 January 1929: Bahia - Montevideo, Uruguay
200 rs. postage + 1,000 rs. air mail
"Os aviões da C.G.A. encurtam as distancias" = "C.G.A. airplanes shorten distances."

Unlike its domestic line competition, CONDOR, which used large seaplanes capable of carrying up to eight passengers, C.G.A. initially used small, single-engine land planes intended for mail. At the time, their largest airplane, the Latécoère 25 R 2 (shown over Rio harbor on the postcard above), could carry only four passengers.

To comply with Brazilian domestic regulations, AÉROPOSTALE established a subsidiary, COMPANHIA AERONAUTICA BRASILEIRA, (CAB) authorized on 14 February 1930 (Decree No. 19,115) to carry mail and passengers within Brazil with headquarters in Recife.[15]

The airline inaugurated flights from Recife to Natal on 29 April of that year, the return flight taking place on 1 May. Shown here (opposite page) are covers from the two legs of this first flight, the one (top) using a company envelope addressed to the Secretary General of the State government and the other (bottom) a pre-printed yellow envelope with black lettering. Flown covers are difficult to find.

This enterprise was short-lived—CAB's name was changed to CIA AEROPOSTAL BRASILEIRA on 11 July 1930 (Decree No. 19,280) and no other flights are known.

top: 29 April 1930: Recife - Natal
100 rs. postage + 350 rs. air mail

bottom: 1 May 1930: Natal - Recife
300 rs. postage + 350 rs. air mail

The first "commercial" crossing of the South Atlantic was reserved for AÉROPOSTALE in the form of, again, pilot Jean Mermoz, who was assisted by co-pilot/navigator Jean Darby and radio-operator Leopold Gimie. They used a Latécoère 28, single-engine float-plane, *Comte de la Vaulx*, to fly from St. Louis, Senegal, to Natal, Brazil, in 19 hours, 35 minutes.[16] The entire route ran from Paris to Rio de Janeiro on 10-14 May 1930.

Finally, on 8 July, the *Comte de la Vaulx* lifted off with its crew of three (and a new collection of mail bound for Europe from Argentina, Brazil, Chile, Paraguay and Uruguay) en route to Senegal. But the return flight was not to be—the plane was forced down about 400 miles from St. Louis. The *Comte de la Vaulx* was lost and the crew was picked up and transported ashore by the supply ship, *le Phocée*. On 6 June 1980 in honor of the flight's 50th Anniversary Brazil issued a stamp (picturing the aircraft) and a commemorative cover (opposite, above).

AÉROPOSTALE issued a propaganda cachet for the Third International Samples Fair held in Rio de Janeiro, 9 August-10 September 1930. About this time a green promotional label was produced.

Natal (black)  Rio de Janeiro (violet)

Mermoz and his crew attempted a return flight on 8 June 1930. Mail had been dispatched from several South American countries and special cachets were applied. On some, the rectangular cachet was pre-printed. The flight was delayed and, after several abortive attempts, the mail was sent by the air-sea route already established (arrived 18 June 1930).

Rio de Janeiro (purple)          Propaganda label

7 June 1930: Rio de Janeiro - Natal - Toulouse - Paris - (ship) - Jacksonville, FL
500 rs. postage + 2,500 rs. air mail

6 June 1980: First Day Cover of Brazil stamp honoring the 50th anniversary of the Mermoz flight.

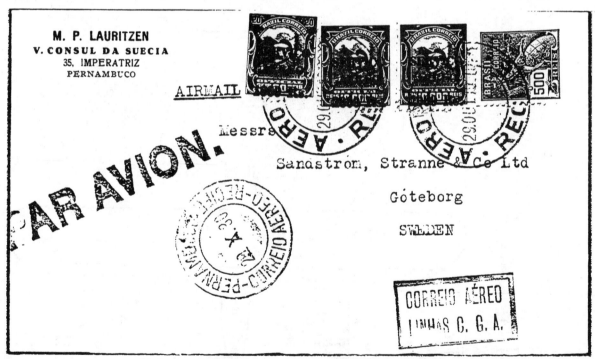

29 October 1930: (Swiss Vice Counsul) Recife - Goteborg, Sweden
500 rs. postage + 5,000 rs. air mail

It is interesting to note that the cover for the return flight (opposite page) bears only 2,500 rs. air mail postage (as do all the other covers I have for this flight), but the rate to Europe was actually 5,000 rs. for this fast service (see page 11 and above). Perhaps there was a special rate offered for this special flight! (?)

Airplane drawings all to the same scale ~ 1 inch = 30 feet

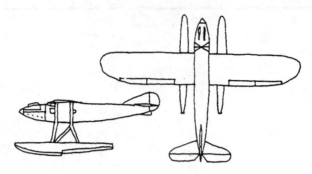

LATÉCOÈRE 28

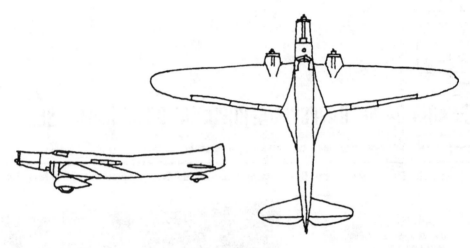

COUZINET 70

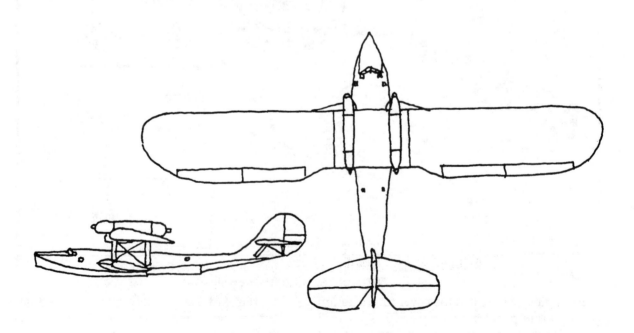

LATÉCOÈRE 300

With the loss of the *Comte de la Vaulx*, the French government, considering the single-engine plane somewhat inadequate for the treacherous South Atlantic, ordered two different four-engine flying-boats, the Blériot 5190 and the Latécoère 300, with the idea that, if necessary, forced mid-ocean landings would be possible.

AÉROPOSTALE had developed ambitious plans for expansion in South America, soon after extending "The Line" from Buenos Aires to Santiago in 1929. It was particularly interested in the West Coast up to Peru and the East Coast from Natal to the French West Indies. The French government became concerned about reports of over-expansion and in 1931 withheld the postal subsidy. A management and political intrigue ensued and the company approached bankruptcy, suspending service on some parts of "The Line." AEROPOSTA ARGENTINA was taken over by the Argentine Post Office Department.[17]

The French had achieved the linking of four continents—Europe, Asia, Africa and South America— and routes had been planned to China, Madagascar and North America. At the same time, however, French air transport was suffering from excessive competition. The French government decided to regroup the existing lines. SOCIETE GENERALE DES TRANSPORTES AERIENS (Farman), COMPAGNIE INTERNATIONALE DE NAVIGATION AERIENNE (CIDNA), AIR UNION and AIR ORIENT were all joined with AÉROPOSTALE in an amalgamated company, 25% of whose stock was held by the French government. The new company was called AIR FRANCE; the year was 1933.

American pilot Wiley Post flew solo around-the-world in the Lockheed Vega, *Winnie Mae*, during 15-21 July 1933. Five weeks later, AIR FRANCE absorbed the remains of the heavily embattled AÉROPOSTALE.

29 August 1931: Rio de Janeiro - Vila Alemana, Chile
200 rs. postage + 1,500 rs. air mail

Correio Aéreo: A History of the Development of Air Mail Service in Brazil

"THE WORLD'S GREATEST AIRWAY. — The routes covered by the COMPAGNIE AIR FRANCE, showing the airway from London, Berlin, Bordeaux and Toulouse to Madrid, Tangier, Casablanca, Dakar, Natal, Pernambuco, Rio de Janeiro, Montevideo, Buenos Ayres, and Santiago de Chile."—*Jane's All the World's Aircraft*, 1934.

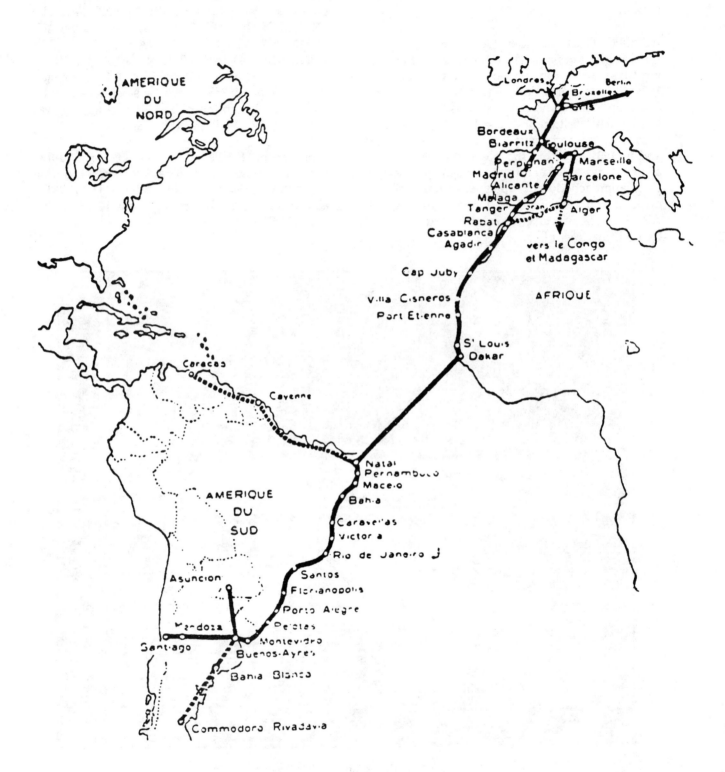

Correio Aéreo: A History of the Development of Air Mail Service in Brazil

While the four-engine flying boats, the Blériot 5190 and the Latécoère 300, were under development, M. Rene Couzinet developed a land-plane capable of making the trip. On 16 January 1933 the Couzinet 70, *Arc-en-Ciel* (*Rainbow*), was flown by Mermoz and his crew, including Couzinet as the first passenger, from St. Louis, Senegal, to Natal, Brazil, in a record time of 14 hours, 27 minutes.[18] After some modifications, the plane was put into regular postal service as the Couzinet 71 on 28 May 1934.

Financial problems had delayed the construction and delivery of the Blériot flying boat and it was actually beaten into service by a Latécoère 300, the *Croix-du-Sud* (*Southern Cross*), which made its first crossing on 3 January 1934. The Blériot model was named the *Santos Dumont*, after the Brazilian air pioneer, making its first crossing on 27 November 1934.[19]

AIR FRANCE initiated all-air, weekly flights between Brazil and Europe on 5 January 1936, and the 100th crossing was commemorated on 21 July that year with a color postcard (left, below) picturing a Latécoère 300 and the company flag.

On 7 December 1936, four hours out of Dakar, the *Croix-du-Sud*, together with the famous Mermoz and his crew, lost radio contact and disappeared without a trace, an unfortunate, but frequent, fate of the early aviation pioneers.

AIR FRANCE commemorated the 7th anniversary of the first commercial transatlantic crossing on 15 May 1937. The 10th Anniversary of service across the South Atlantic was commemorated on 12 May 1940. The 500th crossing of the South Atlantic by air was on 3 June 1940. Soon thereafter, AIR FRANCE services were suspended due to the war in Europe.

The Paris-Buenos Aires link was re-established on 23 June 1946 following a test flight encompassing Paris, Rio de Janeiro, Buenos Aires and Santiago. The 20th anniversary of the air mail service between France and South America was commemorated with a cachet (below) on 18 March 1948 .

On 30 July 1958 AIR FRANCE completed its 1,000th direct flight across the South Atlantic. AIR FRANCE continues today to service Brazil with bigger and faster airplanes than were ever imagined seventy years ago.

◊

CENTENARIO DA TRAVESSIA
DO ATLANTICO SUL COM CORREIO
TOTALMENTE AEREO
BRASIL – EUROPA EM 2 DIAS

POR CIMA DE
RIOS, VAL...

O

CORREIO ...D MILITAR

LEVARÁ VOSSA CORRESPONDENCIA,
MAIS DEPRESSA QUE O PROPRIO
VENTO

# CORREIO-AEREO MILITAR
## LINHA RIO-S.PAULO-GOIAZ

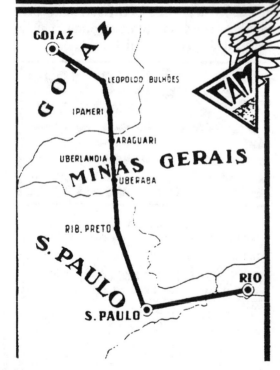

PONTOS DE ESCALA:
**S.PAULO**
**RIBEIRÃO PRETO**
**UBERABA**
**UBERLANDIA**
**ARAGUARI**
**IPAMERI**
**LEOPOLDO BULHÕES**
**GOIAZ**

| IDA | VOLTA |
|---|---|
| *Partida de São Paulo:* | *Partida de Goiaz:* |
| *Ás Terças-feiras, ás 11 horas* | *Ás Quartas-feiras, ás 11 horas* |
| *Chegada a Goiaz:* | *Chegada a São Paulo:* |
| *Ás Quartas-feiras, ás 13 horas* | *Ás Quintas-feiras, ás 14 horas* |

Preço da correspondencia: **500 RÉIS** por 10 gramas

AS CARTAS SÃO DEPOSITADAS NAS AGENCIAS DO CORREIO NACIONAL

A Correio Aéreo Militar (CAM) advertising poster of the period (c.1931).

Correio Aéreo: A History of the Development of Air Mail Service in Brazil

# CORREIO AÉREO NACIONAL

Dissidence, and even governmental disdain, was the lot of those in the Brazilian armed forces who wanted to create aeronautical services. In spite of innumerable obstacles, the men, in what was then called "military aviation" with training limited to the skies around Rio de Janeiro's military airfield, *Campo dos Afonsos*, eventually accomplished feats worthy of mention, using precarious equipment and venturing into unknown territory—the interior of the country. The resulting benefits accrued to Brazilian aviation and its air mail service.

Prior to World War I the potential of the airplane was recognized by writers in the national press but by only a few members in Brazil's government. On 13 January 1913 the Minister of War, General Vespasiano Albuquerque, signed an agreement with a group of Italian pilots which formed the basis of the Brazilian School of Military Aviation. Hangars and shops were built at *Campo dos Afonsos*, and a few Blériot monoplanes and Farman biplanes were acquired. In August 1916 the Naval School of Aviation was founded on the Ponta do Galeão. The Military School of Aviation was officially dedicated on 10 July 1919. Additional aircraft, including Nieuport trainers, Breguet 14 spotter craft and Spad S.VII fighters, were purchased. The years passed and many pilots were trained.

It was, perhaps, the transatlantic crossing by Cabral and Coutinho in 1922 (see Appendix A), which coincided with the Centenary of Brazil's Independence, which inspired further development. In 1927 the Directory of Military Aviation was established, headed by a staff general in direct contact with the Minister of War. Additional aircraft arrived at *Campo dos Afonsos*.

There was no question of the difficulties of transportation at this time in such a vast country. Roads were poor, railways were few and not inter-connected, and ship travel was slow. Most of the coastal shipping was on foreign ships. Trade with the interior—whose population was cut off from the more developed coastal centers of culture and production—was almost non-existent. A journey from Rio de Janeiro to Belém took twenty days. A letter could take months to arrive at its destination. Something had to be done.

In 1931, under the leadership of then-Major Eduardo Gomes, who, by 1949, was the Lieutenant General of the Air, an idealistic group approched General Jose Fernandez Leite de Castro, the Minister of War who had industrialized the Army.[1] The result was the formation of the Mixed Aviation Group with Gomes in command. Its equipment, mostly aging Curtiss "Fledgling" biplanes, was obtained from the Aviation School. A tiny, two-seat, open-cockpit biplane, the "Fledgling," was a training plane and a limited one at that. Its cruising speed was 75 mph and it could stay in the air for about five hours. Its cargo "hold" was in the tail with a capacity of 33 pounds—pilot's luggage, tools and mail bags. Gomes had his work cut out for himself and his men.[2]

The experiment was named the Military Postal Air Service, SERVIÇÃO POSTAL AÉREO MILITAR (SPAM), which was soon changed to Military Air Mail, CORREIO AÉREO MILITAR (CAM). The first survey flight took place on 12 June 1931, with Lieutenants Casimiro Montenegro Filho and Nelson Freire Lavenère-Wanderley flying a Curtiss "Fledgling," K-253, nicknamed "Frankenstein," from Rio de Janeiro to São Paulo (350 kms) in about three hours. A "Rio Correio Aéreo" cachet/cancel was reportedly applied, but no air fee was charged. The return flight was 15 June 1931. The official inauguration ceremony, however, was held in connection with the festivities commemorating the anniversary of the *Campo dos Afonsos*, 10 July 1931.

Flight covers are reported from Rio de Janeiro to São Paulo on 26 June and 26 August (a cover from this later date is shown, below).

The *Departmento dos Correios e Telegrafos* (Post and Telegraphs Department) Decree No. 527 of 25 July 1931 specified the regulations governing the service. The Decree was modified on 28 April 1933 and, again, on 11 May 1934. One of the peculiarities of the service was that the Military Air Mail rates for letters were the same as the Post Office's rates for surface mail. In order to mail a letter by the air service, all the sender had to do was to specify so on the envelope. Therefore, there exist many letters bearing the rubber-stamp legend, "By Military Air Mail" or "Military Air."

Four months after the first tests, the frail "Fledgling" attempted to break the isolation of Goiás, situated in the populated outskirts of the woodlands. With no accurate maps nor landing fields along the route, the first official flight was intended to be 12 October 1931 (the anniversary of the discovery of America)—Rio de Janeiro - São Paulo - Goiás—again with Montenegro and Lavenère-Wanderley, but it ended in a forced land-ing before reaching São Paulo. A flight—Ribeirão Preto - Araquari—scheduled for the following day was canceled. A week later, on 21 October, this time with Lieutenants Araripe and Lavenère-Wanderley at the helm, CAM opened the route—Rio de Janeiro - São Paulo - Ribeirão Preto - Uberaba - Araquari - Ipameri - Leopoldo Bulhões - Goiás. Regular service over this first route started on 1 November 1931.

These first air services were carried out with many difficulties: tiny Curtiss and Waco planes, inadequate ground installations (most "airports" were little more than primitive landing strips), poor instrumentation, unreliable maps and few or no landmarks, and no protection from the weather while in the air. But, over time and with experience, things improved. In mid-1932 new aircraft, Waco CSOs, were acquired.

Services were curtailed or halted between July and October during the 1932 São Paulo revolution, but by the end of that year additional routes had been opened—São Paulo - Ponta Grosso - Curitiba, Paraná State, and São Paulo - Bauru - Campo Grande, Mato Grosso State.

26 August 1931: Rio de Janeiro - São Paulo
200 rs. postage + 350 rs. air mail

23 November 1933 (backstamp): ? - Rio de Janeiro
200 rs. postage + 100 rs. required sur-tax
The "CORREIO AÉREO NACIONAL (Eagle) AVIAÇÃO MILITAR" cachet serves as cancellation device.

The following year, on 15 February 1933, an almost straight line northward—Rio de Janeiro - Belo Horizonte - Curvelo - Petrolina - Fortaleza—reached the Atlantic, without using the coastal routes of the other airlines, in two days. In December a westward branch reached Terezina. In 1934 newer model Waco planes—with enclosed cabins—replaced some of the older craft and the same route, making the same stops, was executed in one long day.

On 28 April 1933 Decree No. 22,673 modified the existing regulations: uniform postal rates were established—intra-state, inter-state, and international—based on weight, and air mail services were now administered by the Director General of Posts and Telegraphs in consort with the Minister of Transportation and Public Works.

Decree No. 24,603 of 6 July 1934 authorized CAM to provide air mail services under the same conditions as the commercial lines. Meanwhile, other services were opened—Belém - Rio de Janeiro—on 16 May 1934, into Rio Grande do Sul State in June/July and the western frontier of Mato Grosso State in August.

Military Air Mail proved itself; not only did it enable the aviators to perfect their skills and gain more experience—until then they had been confined to local, narrow flight paths—but it also reached the small, remote settlements, bringing closer together the unifying sentiments of the homeland. "The Military red aeroplanes also distributed propaganda material chiefly connected with health, and ambulance service with doctor was of great value in sparsely populated districts."[3]

## SERVIÇO POSTAL AEREO MARINHA DO BRASIL

In 1934 Naval Air Mail, SERVIÇO POSTAL AÉREO MARINHA DO BRASIL, was formed behind the driving force of the then-commander of the Galeão Air Base in Rio de Janeiro (now a civilian airport), Brigadier of the Air (1949) Fernando Vitor do Amaral Savaget. The original plan behind this service was to link the coastal cities with the Amazon River areas, however, only the southern routes were extended. The inaugural flight followed the coast line—Rio de Janeiro - Santos - Paranaguá - Florianópolis—utilizing a Waco CSO outfitted with pontoons. Official mail bore no stamps or postmark.

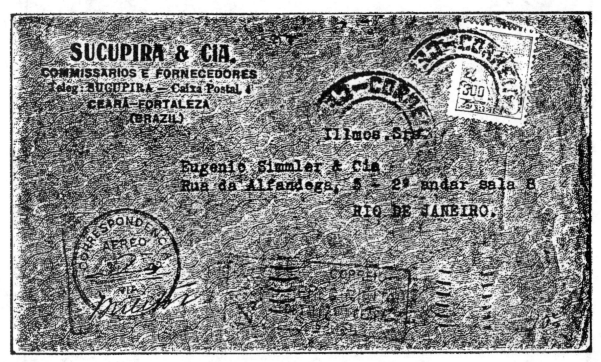

13 October 1934 (backstamp): Fortaleza - Rio de Janeiro
300 rs. postage
A circular NYRBA cachet has been altered after "VIA" by pen "Militar" also with a faint "CORREIO AEREO MILITAR FORTALEZA CEARA BRAZIL" with "CAM" in a point-down triangle, all in a boxed rectangle (violet) at bottom center.

| CORREIO AÉREO NACIONAL STATISTICS[4] | | | |
|---|---|---|---|
| Year | Route kms | Total Flown kms | Mail grams |
| 1931 | 1,565 | 54,888 | 340,045 |
| 1932 | 3,695 | 31,810 | 130,445 |
| 1933 | 6,880 | 206,310 | 3,834,132 |
| 1934 | 9,105 | 615,786 | 10,428,406 |
| 1935 | 11,560 | 916,632 | 18,355,877 |
| 1936 | 11,743 | 1,080,939 | 23,907,282 |

The line was further extended in 1936 to Porto Alegre and Rio Grande. Secondary routes extended from some of these points for the collection of mail from neighboring towns:

| Santos - | Ubatuba - São Sebastiao | (to the north) |
|---|---|---|
| | Iguapa - Cananeia | (to the south) |
| Florianópolis - | Tijuca - Itajai - Joinville - | |
| | São Francisco | (to the north) |
| | Laguna - Tubarao - Arangua | (to the south) |
| Rio Grande - | Pelotas | (to the north) |
| | Jaguarao - Santa Vitória | |
| | do Palmar | (to the south) |

The Ministry of Aeronautics was created on 21 January 1941 (Decree No. 2961) and the army and navy air services were placed under one authority, the new Minister, Dr. Joaquim Pedro de Salgado Filho. Article 16 of the Decree states: "The patrimony of the Ministry of Aeronautics will, initially, comprise the movable and real properties of the Military Air Arm, the Fleet Air Arm and the Department of Civil Aviation." CORREIO AÉREO MILITAR (CAM) and CORREIO AÉREO NAVAL (CAN) had become CORREIO AÉREO NACIONAL (CAN), the National Air Mail.

In contrast to other agencies, both foreign and domestic, which carried the mails, this new service was not subject to the postal rates set by the Post Office Department. As the volume of mail relegated to this new National service grew, many post offices used special cachets to identify the mail flown in this manner.

Six Beechcraft C-43s arrived in Rio on 31 December 1941, followed by nine more the following year. In 1943 15 more were added, as well as five Lockheed "Lodestar" twin-engined transports, the third generation of the "Electra."

Shortly after the attack on Pearl Harbor, Brazil broke diplomatic relations with Germany, Italy and Japan. In August 1942 five Brazilian commercial ships were sunk off the coast. Brazil and the U. S. formed a joint defense board and organized the then somewhat haphazard censorship of the mails—officially decreed on 9 December 1942. In addition, the Brazilian Expeditionary Force (FEB) was organized and eventually found service in Italy with the U. S. Fifth Army.[5]

18 July 1945: First Day Cover of Brazil stamps honoring the Brazilian Expeditionary Force and the U. S. Fifth Army.

Airplane drawings all to the same scale ~ 1 inch = 30 feet

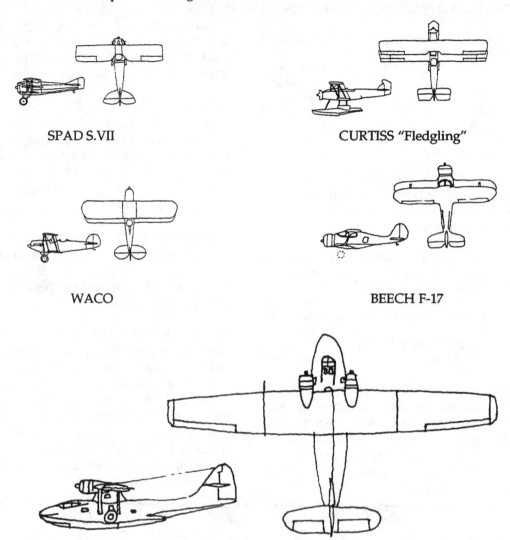

SPAD S.VII

CURTISS "Fledgling"

WACO

BEECH F-17

CONSOLIDATED PBY-5A "Catalina"

Photos (left to right above): Lt. Casimiro Montenegro Filho prior to his first flight of 12 June 1931; Brigadier General Nelson Freire Lavenère-Wanderly (the other pilot, then a Lieutenant, on the first flight) standing in front of a replica of the aircraft, K263; and Marshal of the Air Eduardo Gomes, Patron of CORREIO AÉREO NACIONAL. (Courtesy of CO FI).

As a result of Law No. 6437 of 26 April 1944, postal agencies in air bases used special cachets to frank military personnel mail—a free-franking privilege came into effect during the war—which bore the words "Postal Franking Soldier's Correspondence." Law No. 6438 of 26 April 1944 created the Postal Service of the Brazil Expeditionary Force. Its installations and maintenance were paid for by the War Ministry and its operations were under the joint control of the War Ministry and the Ministry of Transportation and Public Works. On this service, the National Air Mail worked closely with the Post Office. Along its routes, it collected all the mail destined for army units belonging to the FEB. Mail was transported abroad on military aircraft.

Mail from the southern and central regions of the country went to MAIL COLLECTOR SOUTH (*Correio Coletor Sul*) facilities in Rio de Janeiro, and mail from the rest of the country went to MAIL COLLECTOR NORTH (*Correio Coletor Norte*) in Natal. MAIL COLLECTOR facilities also handled censorship, which was noted on the mail by means of special cachets in black or green. Censor "tape" was also used.

Following the end of World War II, CORREIO AÉREO NACIONAL improved its services with the twin-engine Douglas DC-3/C-47, which first arrived in 1944, capable of carrying heavier loads and landing on "immature" airfields. It also utilized the war proven, Consolidated PBY "Catalina" flying boats along the Amazon and her tributaries. The plane was "called the 'Angel of Space' by the river people, and more familiarly 'Slow Duck' by Air Force personnel, continues in full service, thanks to assiduous and efficient maintenance."[6]

CORREIO AÉREO NACIONAL is now part of the *Força Aérea Brasileira* (Brazilian Air Force) and still services more than 200 Brazilian towns with two and four-engined planes. On 12 June 1956 Brazil issued a stamp for CAN's 25th anniversary.

In December 1977 Brazil issued a set of three stamps commemorating the integration of the national units: the Amazon flotilla, the construction battalion and CAN; the latter pictured the tail end of K263, the insignia, and a newer aircraft (below).

On 10 June 1981 Brazil issued a stamp honoring the 50th anniversary of the founding of CAN (below).

CORREIO AÉREO NACIONAL: "Anxious to work for the even greater unity of their vast homeland, the Brazilian soldiers created this service which is at the same time a [sic] anonymous heroism, spirit of cooperation, eagerness to serve well, proudness of being useful to society, a service that has undoubtedly helped the country's progress and the tender approach of its children: the Military Air Mail service!"[7]

◊

*Junkers Ganzmetall-Flugzeug F13*

"The JUNKERS F13, the world's first strut-free all-metal low-wing monoplane with a closed cabin, was the work-horse of the LUFT HANSA fleet between 1926 and 1932. More than 40 of them operated as land planes when equipped with wheels or skis, or seaplanes when fitted with pontoons. The heated cabin provided four passenger seats equipped with safety belts." (LUFTHANSA caption) Top: On the ground in Berlin. Bottom: An F13 is worked over by a "cleaning brigade."

# DEUTSCHE LUFTHANSA A.G.

Following the Treaty of Versailles, at the end of World War I, the so-called "Nine Rules," designed to prevent intensive military aeronautical development, were imposed upon Germany. Curiously, if not ironically, these restrictions imposed by the Allies worked, in part, to the actual benefit of Germany, at the same time hampering development of the Allies' own aviation equipment and routes.

The air provisions of the 1919 peace treaties fell into two groups: (1) military aircraft and (2) civilian aircraft. Basically, Germany's air force was abolished and a special commission was established to oversee the dismantling of material and the disbanding of personnel. A temporary regime (until 1 January 1923) was established to "administer" the air rights, unilaterally in favor of the Allies, while details were worked out at the Paris Convention without the participation of Germany.

In 1922 the "Nine Rules" were imposed, restricting the specifications (type, power, speed, performance, etc.) of civil aircraft; requiring registration of aircraft, factories and pilots; and limiting the number of engines and pilots to "reasonable" requirements. These "Rules" were apparently designed to hamper German aircraft/aeronautical development. In fact, they worked in reverse.

One of the "Rules," which permitted foreign private aircraft to use, upon payment, any airport facilities open to use by national aircraft, could, and did, allow the contracting states to require regular international airlines crossing their territory, with or without intention to land, to obtain prior approval. Such authorization could be—and by Germany often was—refused without any stated reason. States were also not required to act uniformly in their dealings.

Therefore, if the most direct routes to the East were to be developed, a principal difficulty was the necessity to fly over German territory. The Germans stood firm and denied transit to Britain and France, blocking the access to the Near East and forcing France to fly the high altitudes of Switzerland (requiring expensive, high-powered aircraft). At the same time, the Germans, with keen business sense, continued to urge international cooperation. Soon the Allies were looking, especially independently, for ways of bridging or aborting the Treaty provisions and/or making other concessions to the Germans. By 7 May 1926 Franco-German agreements had been signed for mutual air rights. Thus, the French gained access to Berlin, Czechoslovakia, and down to Constantinople (Istanbul), the air gateway to the East.

Meanwhile, as other countries worked to convert military aircraft to civilian use, Germany, barred from military activity, was forced to start afresh. New designs, new materials, and the elimination of many aircraft manufacturers, allowed those remaining—primarily Junkers Flugzeug und Moterwerke A. G.—to concentrate on a few selected projects and specific goals.

Junkers developed Europe's first all-metal-cabin aircraft, a two-crew, four-passenger, single-engine monoplane, the F13.[1] Not originally allowed in Germany by the Commission, the F13 was marketed in other countries—over 13 years, 322 planes were flying for 30 airlines in 12 nations—and it was extensively used by almost all European nations, South Africa, Canada, Colombia and Brazil.

Junkers had obtained control of other companies in Europe by providing machines, taking shares of stock in payment, and eventually controlling or supervising the management. It formed a conglomerate, EUROPA UNION, consisting of the parent and 20 other lines—the largest air traffic combination in the world—in May 1925.[2] The other major airline in Germany, DEUTSCHER AERO LLOYD, was exclusively an air transport company which used the most suitable, German-made, aircraft for the task at hand. In 1926, in an effort to eliminate the wasteful and expensive competition between the majors, an amalgamation was formed and the result was DEUTSCHE LUFT HANSA A.G.(DLH).[3]

The shareholders in the new company, LUFT HANSA, founded on 6 January 1926, consisted of the government (36%); the two previous companies, EUROPA UNION and DEUTSCHER AERO LLOYD, (27%); various provinces (19%); and private industry (18%). Allowing time to reorganize the administration of the new company and because no scheduled air services were flown during the winter in those days, the new company actually started operating on 6 April 1926. In the first year, four million miles were flown.

LUFT HANSA's "assistance" helped start several lines in South America, including SYNDICATO CONDOR and VARIG, and a base was established on the island of Fernando de Noronha, off the coast of Brazil northeast of Natal, as the first "stepping stone" on the west side of the Atlantic.

On the east side, routes between Berlin and Barcelona and, eventually, Madrid were explored with IBERIA, the Spanish line, which at the time was partially (24%) owned by the German company. The route was carried further, to the Canary Islands, using the small Dornier Wals. All that was missing was the aircraft to cross the ocean itself.

With the improvement in airline efficiency, the German post office decided that special flights for mail only should be initiated.[4] Most of these flights were at night. In 1929 experiments were started on the North Atlantic with a catapult installed on the liner *Bremen* and utilizing a small Heinkel float plane. Additionally, a mail connecting service was established between Berlin and Cherbourg, France, last port-of-call for transatlantic liners in Europe. In similar fashion, with connecting flights on both sides of the South Atlantic, transit time from Rio de Janeiro to Berlin was reduced to 11 days!

The first air-sea run was made on 21 March 1930: the mail was carried by CONDOR to Fernando de Noronha, Hamburg-Amerika's liner *Cap Arcona* on to the Canary Islands, and DLH aircraft to Germany

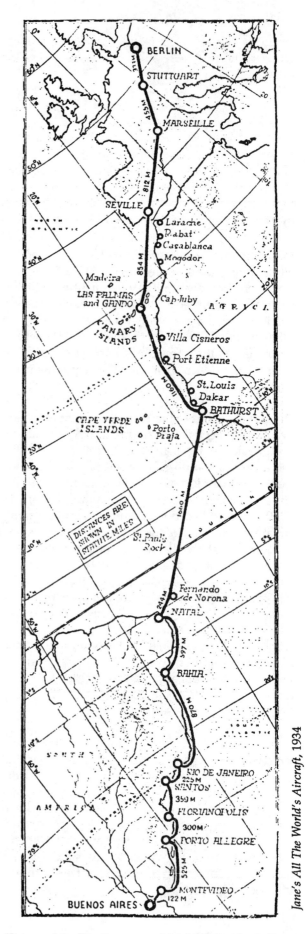

Jane's All The World's Aircraft, 1934

Correio Aéreo: A History of the Development of Air Mail Service in Brazil

(see SYNDICATO CONDOR). Further experiments were made, but soon other options and developments would end them.

The *Graf Zeppelin* made its first trip to Brazil that May and regular service was to follow. When the Zeppelin flights started, DLH provided connecting flights (*anschlussflug*), while at the same time attempting to develop an alternative, heavier-than-air solution. The range of the seaplanes to date was too short and in-flight refueling was not to be developed for some years. LUFT HANSA turned again to the seaplane and catapult combination. The steamer *Westfalen*, outfitted with refueling and catapult equipment, conducted the first experiment on 2 June 1933 with the Dornier-Wal *Monsun* launched mid-Atlantic toward Bathurst, British Gambia.[5] After the sixth experiment, 21 days later, the *Westfalen* returned to Germany for some modifications. No mail was officially taken on these flights.

On 3 February 1934 regular catapult service was inaugurated. A Heinkel He 70 flew the mail from Stuttgart to Seville; a Junkers Ju 52 carried it to Las Palmas, Canary Islands, refueled, and went on to Bathurst. There it was transferred to the Dornier-Wal *Taifun* which carried it—at a cruising altitude of about 30 feet—out to the *Westfalen*; then, hauled aboard, refueled and made ready to go on the catapult. "Captain Cramer von Clausbruch claimed that the ocean transfer involved a 'double-refueling'—a strong drink for the pilot as well as one for the aircraft."[6] At Natal the mail was taken over by CONDOR's *Tiete*, a Junkers W 34 aircraft, to complete the delivery, reaching Buenos Aires in a little more than 24 hours after leaving Natal on 7 February. The first return flight was 8-12 February 1934 (cover below). Flights were made twice monthly until July 1934, when they increased to weekly.[7]

First Flight: 8 February 1934: Rio Grande Norte - Kessel, Germany (Backstamped Stuttgart 12 February 1934)
1,400 rs. postage/registration + 4,200 rs. air mail/registration

The Dornier Wal *Monsun* (D-2069) is loaded aboard and then catapulted from the base-ship *Westfalen* on 6 June 1933.

Correio Aéreo: A History of the Development of Air Mail Service in Brazil

The Dornier Wal *Monsun* (D-2069) taxiing on smooth seas.

## LUFTHANSA CATAPULT FLIGHTS FROM BRAZIL

| da.mo.yr | 03.01.35 | 08.08.35 | 05.03.36 | 07.10.36 | 13.05.37 | 28.10.37 | 14.04.38 | 06.10.38 | 23.03.39 |
|---|---|---|---|---|---|---|---|---|---|
| 08.02.34 | 10.01.35 | 15.08.35 | 12.03.36 | 22.10.36 | 20.05.37 | 04.11.37 | 21.04.38 | 13.10.38 | 30.03.39 |
| 22.02.34 | 17.01.35 | 22.08.35 | 19.03.36 | 10.12.36 | 27.05.37 | 11.11.37 | 28.04.38 | 20.10.38 | 06.04.39 |
| 08.03.34 | 24.01.35 | 29.08.35 | 26.03.36 | 17.12.36 | 03.06.37 | 18.11.37 | 05.05.38 | 27.10.38 | 13.04.39 |
| 22.03.34 | 31.01.35 | 05.09.35 | 02.04.36 | 24.12.36 | 10.06.37 | 25.11.37 | 12.05.38 | 03.11.38 | 20.04.39 |
| 05.04.34 | 07.02.35 | 12.09.35 | 09.04.36 | 31.12.36 | 17.06.37 | 02.12.37 | 19.05.38 | 10.11.38 | 27.04.39 |
| 19.04.34 | 14.02.35 | 19.09.35 | 16.04.36 | 07.01.37 | 24.06.37 | 09.12.37 | 26.05.38 | 17.11.38 | 04.05.39 |
| 03.05.34 | 21.02.35 | 26.09.35 | 23.04.36 | 14.01.37 | 01.07.37 | 16.12.37 | 02.06.38 | 24.11.38 | 11.05.39 |
| 17.05.34 | 28.02.35 | 03.10.35 | 30.04.36 | 21.01.37 | 08.07.37 | 23.12.37 | 09.06.38 | 01.12.38 | 18.05.39 |
| 12.07.34 | 07.03.35 | 10.10.35 | 07.05.36 | 28.01.37 | 15.07.37 | 30.12.37 | 16.06.38 | 08.12.38 | 25.05.39 |
| 02.08.34 | 14.03.35 | 17.10.35 | 14.05.36 | 04.02.37 | 22.07.37 | 06.01.38 | 23.06.38 | 15.12.38 | 01.06.39 |
| 16.08.34 | 21.03.35 | 24.10.35 | 21.05.36 | 11.02.37 | 29.07.37 | 13.01.38 | 30.06.38 | 22.12.38 | 08.06.39 |
| 30.08.34 | 28.03.35 | 07.11.35 | 28.05.36 | 18.02.37 | 05.08.37 | 20.01.38 | 07.07.38 | 29.12.38 | 15.06.39 |
| 13.09.34 | 04.04.35 | 12.12.35 | 04.06.36 | 25.02.37 | 12.08.37 | 27.01.38 | 14.07.38 | 05.01.39 | 22.06.39 |
| 27.09.34 | 18.04.35 | 19.12.35 | 11.06.36 | 04.03.37 | 19.08.37 | 03.02.38 | 21.07.38 | 12.01.39 | 29.06.39 |
| 11.10.34 | 02.05.35 | 26.12.35 | 18.06.36 | 11.03.37 | 26.08.37 | 10.02.38 | 28.07.38 | 19.01.39 | 06.07.39 |
| 25.10.34 | 16.05.35 | 02.01.36 | 25.06.36 | 18.03.37 | 02.09.37 | 17.02.38 | 04.08.38 | 26.01.39 | 13.07.39 |
| 08.11.34 | 30.05.35 | 09.01.36 | 09.07.36 | 25.03.37 | 09.09.37 | 24.02.38 | 11.08.38 | 02.02.39 | 20.07.39 |
| 15.11.34 | 13.06.35 | 16.01.36 | 23.07.36 | 01.04.37 | 16.09.37. | 03.03.38 | 18.08.38 | 09.02.39 | 27.07.39 |
| 22.11.34 | 27.06.35 | 23.01.36 | 30.07.36 | 08.04.37 | 23.09.37 | 10.03.38 | 25.08.38 | 16.02.39 | 03.08.39 |
| 29.11.34 | 11.07.35 | 30.01.36 | 13.08.36 | 15.04.37 | 30.09.37 | 17.03.38 | 01.09.38 | 23.02.39 | 10.08.39 |
| 06.12.34 | 18.07.35 | 06.02.36 | 27.08.36 | 22.04.37 | 07.10.37 | 24.03.38 | 08.09.38 | 02.03.39 | 17.08.39 |
| 20.12.34 | 25.07.35 | 20.02.36 | 10.09.36 | 29.04.37 | 14.10.37 | 31.03.38 | 15.09.38 | 09.03.39 | 24.08.39 |
| 27.12.34 | 01.08.35 | 27.02.36 | 24.09.36 | 06.05.37 | 21.10.37 | 07.04.38 | 22.09.38 | 16.03.39 | 31.08.39 |

The Dornier Wal seaplane, *Monsun,* preparing to be launched from the catapult on board the base-ship *Westfalen.*

Correio Aéreo: A History of the Development of Air Mail Service in Brazil

In August 1934 another converted freighter, *Schwabenland*, was added and the service was slightly modified: the mail was loaded on a Wal onboard one of the ships, transported out about 100 miles and then shot on its way without a mid-ocean stop. The aircraft alternated with the *Graf Zeppelin* until that October—the end of her season—when the DLH schedule was adjusted to maintain weekly service.

Cachets for the ZEPPELIN and DLH flights in this period are the same and it is necessary to study the dates (opposite, above for DLH) related to the postmarks involved to ascertain which craft carried the mail. Most, if not all, Zeppelin mail bears a significant receiving mark. (See DEUTSCHE LUFTSCHIFFBAU ZEPPELIN and SYNDICATO CONDOR LIMITADA.)

westbound cachet

eastbound cachet

During the period 10-29 November 1934, Bathurst was quarantined (yellow fever) and the route was altered to Porto Praia, Cape Verde Islands. In April 1935 the *Graf Zeppelin* resumed its role, but, by July, DLH shaved a day off the trip and assumed the rights to first class mail. Mail leaving Germany every Thursday arrived at Natal on Saturday of the same week. After the seventh flight of 1935 the *Graf*'s mail was relegated to printed matter, small packages and parcel post. Collector's mail items—covers and cards—were continued to be carried as they were a major source of income for Zeppelin. In July DLH cooperated with AIR FRANCE to produce bi-weekly service. On 25 August the 100th regular flight left Stuttgart—4 million letters; 850,000 miles; and 1 1/2 years since the service began.

From 10 November to 4 December 1935 the catapult ships were out-of-service for maintenance overhaul and the *Graf Zeppelin*, already on her 16th flight of that year, operated a shuttle service to Bathurst. During 1936 a third ship, *Ostmark*, especially built as a catapult ship, joined in service to allow for ship maintenance rotation. However, in September 1936 the *Schwabenland* was moved to the Azores for North Atlantic service.

In April 1936 the German terminal was changed from Stuttgart to Frankfurt-am-Main with new facilities for both DLH and the *Graf Zeppelin* which again operated together and were now joined in service by the *Hindenburg*. After the end of the Zeppelin service in 1937, DLH continued operations until August 1939—a total of 482 flights in 5 years.

LUFTHANSA in 1938, the last complete pre-war year, carried 287,000 passengers on 52,619 flights within Germany and 13,483 outside the country—a total of 15,000,000 miles. World War II abruptly ended her future as a commercial airline. For almost six years, operations were connected to the war effort. LUFTHANSA felt a patriotic duty to connect Germany with friendly or neutral countries. Some disagreed with the Nazi policies, but that is not the subject of this study. On 6 May 1945 Canadian troops captured the operational facility, which had been moved several times, in Flensburg in northern Germany and, for all intents and purposes, the war, particularly LUFTHANSA's participation, was over. After the war all civilian aviation activities were under the control of the occupation forces.

DEUTSCHE LUFTHANSA was formerly dissolved on 1 January 1951. After almost ten years of negotiation, a new company was formed on 6 August 1954 assuming the proud name of the former company, but, except for legal purposes, known today as simply LUFTHANSA.

◊

The *Graf Zeppelin* (LZ 127) first crossed the South Atlantic in May 1930. After three trips in 1931, it started regular service in March 1932. A new era of transport for both passengers and mail had been opened.

The airplane drawings throughout this book are all drawn to the same scale of approximately 1"=30'. This circle (at right) represents the largest diameter of the *Graf Zeppelin*'s structure drawn to that scale for comparison purposes. In length, the *Graf* would be three times the width of this page!

# DEUTSCHE LUFTSCHIFFBAU ZEPPELIN G.m.b.H.

Zeppelin! A name that will live forever in the minds of air mail stamp collectors and flying enthusiasts everywhere.[1] Count Ferdinand von Zeppelin, born 8 July 1838, did not live to see his country's defeat in 1918. Some twenty years before he had formed the "Joint Stock Company for the Promotion of Motor Airship Flight" and the first Luftschiff Zeppelin (LZ.1) was born.[2] DEUTSCHE LUFTSCHIFFBAU ZEPPELIN G.m.b.H. (German Zeppelin Airship Construction Company), was housed in a floating shed at Manzell, near Friedrichshafen, on Lake Constance.

The young economist Hugo Eckener (1868-1954) had witnessed the second trial flight of the LZ.1 as a reporter for a news journal and, as an experienced sailor, was able to make suggestions relative to the design/wind considerations. The Count ignored most of the criticism from the "inexperienced" onlooker. Modifications, new models, and more test flights followed. Eckener continued reporting. When the LZ.4 burned in August 1908 it was Eckener, now a part-time publicity officer in the Zeppelin company, whose skillful manipulating of the media saved the company. Sympathetic contributions from across Germany poured in and the "Zeppelin Foundation for the Promotion of Aerial Navigation" was formed to administer the funds relatively free from impending government control.

Zeppelin had conceived the idea of the airship as a useful device in time of war, having developed his interests as an aerial (balloon) observer in the U. S. during the Civil War. When the German Army lost interest in the LZ.6 during the summer of 1909 Zeppelin's company was again threatened. Although originally dubious of the commercial value of airships as passenger carriers, Eckener became convinced that there was no alternative and, in turn, convinced the Count.

On 16 November 1909 Frankfurt witnessed the birth of the "world's first airline," DEUTSCHE LUFTSCHIFFARHTS AKTIEN GESELLSCHAFT (DELAG) (the German Airship Transport Company, Ltd.), founded in cooperation with, and with the financial support of, the Hamburg-Amerika shipping line (HAPAG). The mayors of Frankfurt, Cologne, Dusseldorf, Baden-Baden, Munich, Dresden, Leipzig, and Hamburg also contributed and became Directors.[3] Ten days later DELAG ordered its first airship, which was completed the following May, the LZ.7, *Deutschland*.

Losing a battle with strong winds the LZ.7 was destroyed on its sixth flight, 28 June 1910, fortunately without loss of life. Hugo Eckener was appointed Director of Flight Operations and he worked to—and finally did—develop a weather forecasting and reporting network to predict hazardous flying conditions. Airship development continued and more carriers were added to the Company.[4]

The German Navy ordered a model, L.1 (LZ.14), which was completed in September 1912 and had the dubious distinction of ending its career with the first zeppelin fatalities—crashing at sea in a down current, carrying fourteen people to a watery grave—ironically, a few hours after her sister ship, L.2 (LZ.18), made her maiden flight out of Friedrichshafen, 16 August 1913. On her 10th flight, 17 October 1913, the L.2 went up in flames killing most of the remaining, experienced airship crewmen.[5] Seemingly undaunted, an order for yet another airship was placed the following March and the L.3 (LZ.24) made her maiden flight on 11 May 1914.

DELAG's civilian operations ended with the Great War, but Zeppelin had more than enough to do with military demands. Airship activity was common to both sides during the war, although, at least at the outbreak, Germany was better equipped than either Britain, France or Russia. The Italians started work on airships somewhat belatedly in mid-1915. By war's end Germany had 15 operational zeppelins, mostly built in 1917-1918, seven of which were sabotaged some seven months after the Armistice. The remaining ships were taken by the Allies as reparations.

Two months after the Armistice the Company, now under Baron Gemmingen, the nephew of the Count, who died in 1917, with Hugo Eckener in charge of flight operations, formed DEUTSCHE LUFT-REED-EREI (DLR) with the backing of the industrial giant, Allgemeine Elektricitäts Gesellschaft (AEG), also known as Germany's "General Electric Company" and, again, with the cooperation of the Hamburg-Amerika shipping line. Services commenced on 5 February 1919 between Berlin and Weimar.[6]

Germany was prohibited from building large aircraft or airships for military use under terms of the Allied Commission. There was, however, no specific prohibition of the construction of lighter-than-air craft for civilian use. Accordingly, little time was wasted and the first post-war commercial zeppelin, the LZ.120, *Bodensee* (*Lake Constance*), made her first flight on 24 August 1919. She soon entered service between Berlin and Friedrichshafen. She was to be followed into service in January 1920 by LZ.121, the *Nordstern* (*North Star*). However, the Inter-Allied Commission finally decided to end these operations—the LZ.120 was sent to Italy, and the LZ.121 and the older LZ.72 were given to France. Again the company faced trouble.[7]

The United States Navy was also interested in airships and had started construction of the ZR-1 in August 1919 based on the design of the L.49 (LZ.96), which had been captured in France in October 1917. The destruction in August 1921 of the ZR-2, purchased from Britain as the R.38, delayed completion of the ZR-1 until 4 September 1923. She made her first flight as the *Shenandoah* (*Daughter of the Skies*).[8]

In lieu of paying the American share of war retributions—$800,000 in gold—Eckener offered to build an airship for the U.S. Navy. It was an effort to not only satisfy the "debt," but an attempt to keep the company in operation and the men working. The ploy worked—and the U.S. even put up an additional $100,000—but the project was delayed because England and France objected to the

increased size—a size deemed necessary for a ship capable of crossing the ocean—because it would be larger than the craft they possessed. They finally relented and in October 1924 the LZ.126 crossed to Lakehurst, New Jersey, with Eckener in command, and became the ZR-3, *Los Angeles*.

The Zeppelin Company was back in business, working with funds acquired again by public subscription and some help from the German government. Plans were forged for even bigger airships capable of regular ocean crossings. On 8 July 1928 the daughter of the late Count christened the newest airship with a name selected by Eckener. The LZ.127 was now the *Graf Zeppelin*.

The *Graf Zeppelin* flew to Lakehurst in October 1928 and again in August 1929. It then departed on its famous round-the-world flight. Eckener's next goal was a flight to South America. The primary financing for this flight would come from stamp collectors.[9] While in the U. S. in early 1930 accepting a Gold Medal from the National Geographic Society for his flight around-the-world, Eckener was apparently able to persuade the U. S. postal administration to issue the now famous "Zepps." Argentina, Bolivia, Brazil and Germany also issued stamps for the flight. The Brazil stamps were actually issues of the company printed in Germany and, "by arrangement," did not need to have the designs approved by the Brazilian government (see Appendix C).

Since these were an issue of the Zeppelin company itself, Eckener did not have to defer to the objections of the over-sensitive Post Office bureaucrats. At last he got the design he wanted. There, for all to see, was the comparison he had longed for, the comparison that Herbert Hoover had had the good sense to make: the likeness of the Graf Zeppelin to the Santa Maria and—by implication—of Eckener to Columbus.[10]

These stamps were sold in Brazil by SYNDICATO CONDOR who also provided interconnecting mail flights.

CONDOR etiquette advertising the service (enlarged).

# Special U. S. and Foreign Stamps

## For the First Europe—Pan-American Flight of the Airship

# "GRAF ZEPPELIN"

### ITINERARY OF VOYAGE:

On or after May 10th, 1930, the "Graf Zeppelin" will start from Friedrichshafen, Germany, on her first Europe Pan-American Round Flight. The first stop will be Sevilla, Spain, then Pernambuco, Brazil, then Rio de Janeiro, Brazil, and back to Pernambuco, where she will refuel. From Pernambuco the ship will then sail for the Naval Air Station at Lakehurst, N. J., U. S. A., where she will refuel before her return trip to Friedrichshafen, Germany, via Sevilla, Spain.

### SPECIAL U. S. STAMPS:

In commemoration of this first Europe Pan-American Round Flight the U. S. Post Office Department has announced the issue of three special stamps, designed and printed for this occasion. Only a limited amount will be printed and the plates will be subsequently destroyed. These stamps will be for the following values: $2.60, $1.30 and 65c. Each stamp will carry a reproduction of the airship and will have an inscription of about the following character: Graf Zeppelin—Europe Pan-American Round Trip Flight—May 1930. By special arrangements with the German Post Office Department letters and cards mailed at the New York Post Office in time to be dispatched by the steamer "Albert Ballin", sailing from New York May 1st, will be taken to Friedrichshafen on arrival at the German seaport of Hamburg-Cuxhaven. They will then also be postmarked by the Friedrichshafen Post Master and dispatched by the airship "Graf Zeppelin" for Lakehurst via Pernambuco. The rates for this round-trip mail from New York to New York will be $2.60 for each letter and $1.30 for each postal card. Furthermore United States Mail will be dispatched on the last leg of the round-trip from Lakehurst to Sevilla and from Lakehurst to Friedrichshafen rates for letters $1.30, each, postal cards 65c. By special arrangement with the German Postal Authorities all mail addressed to a mailing address within the United States and being taken off in Friedrichshafen at the end of the round-trip will be forwarded by next steamer from a German port back to the United States of America. All mail matter for round trip from United States to United States must be marked: "via Friedrichshafen and Graf Zeppelin to Lakehurst," and after being properly prepaid must be sent under cover to the New York Postmaster. If special issue Zeppelin stamps are desired and not obtainable at, office of mailing, money order for proper amount should be sent under same cover to Postmaster in New York and be mailed in time to reach the New York Postmaster by noon, April 30th, 1930.

### SPECIAL GERMAN, SPANISH AND BRAZILIAN STAMPS:

The "Graf Zeppelin" will also carry between all stops on this round-trip mail by special arrangement with the German, Spanish and Brazilian Postal Authorities at the following rates:

| | | |
|---|---|---|
| Friedrichshafen to Friedrichshafen, Round Trip | | |
| German Stamps—Reichsmark 12.- | ($3.00) | |
| Friedrichshafen to Sevilla, Round Trip | | |
| German Stamps—Reichsmark 12.- | ($3.00) | |
| Friedrichshafen to Sevilla, Round Trip | | |
| German Stamps—Reichsmark 2.- | ($ .50) | |
| Friedrichshafen to Pernambuco | | |
| German Stamps—Reichsmark 4.- | ($1.00) | |
| Friedrichshafen to Rio de Janeiro | | |
| German Stamps—Reichsmark 4.- | ($1.00) | |
| Friedrichshafen to Lakehurst | | |
| German Stamps—Reichsmark 10.- | ($2.50) | |
| Sevilla to Sevilla, Round Trip | | |
| Spanish Stamps—Peseta 24.- | ($3.00) | |
| Sevilla to Friedrichshafen, Round Trip | | |
| Spanish Stamps—Peseta 24.- | ($3.00) | |
| Sevilla to Pernambuco | | |
| Spanish Stamps—Peseta 8.- | ($1.00) | |
| Sevilla to Rio de Janeiro | | |
| Spanish Stamps—Peseta 8.- | ($1.00) | |
| Sevilla to Lakehurst | | |
| Spanish Stamps—Peseta 20.- | ($2.50) | |
| Sevilla to Friedrichshafen, via return trip from Lakehurst | | |
| Spanish Stamps—Peseta 4.- | ($ .50) | |
| Rio de Janeiro to Pernambuco | | |
| Brazilian Stamps—Milreis 5.- | ($ .60) | |
| Rio de Janeiro to Lakehurst | | |
| Brazilian Stamps—Milreis 10.- | ($1.20) | |
| Rio de Janeiro to Sevilla via Lakehurst | | |
| Brazilian Stamps—Milreis 20.- | ($2.40) | |
| Rio de Janeiro to Friedrichshafen via Lakehurst | | |
| Brazilian Stamps—Milreis 25.- | ($3.00) | |
| Pernambuco to Lakehurst | | |
| Brazilian Stamps—Milreis 10.- | ($1.20) | |
| Pernambuco to Sevilla via Lakehurst | | |
| Brazilian Stamps—Milreis 20.- | ($2.40) | |
| Pernambuco to Friedrichshafen via Lakehurst | | |
| Brazilian Stamps—Milreis 25.- | ($3.00) | |
| Lakehurst to Sevilla | | |
| Lakehurst to Friedrichshafen | | |
| American Stamps—$1.30 | | |
| American Stamps—$1.30 | | |
| New York to New York by steamer to Germany and then via Zeppelin from Friedrichshafen to Lakehurst | | |
| American Stamps—$2.60 | | |
| New York to Germany by steamer, Round Trip Friedrichshafen to Friedrichshafen via Zeppelin and back by steamer to U. S. A. | | |
| American Stamps—$3.90 | | |

### ALL POSTAL CARDS AT HALF RATE:

The German Post Master has agreed to provide either for special stamps or special inscription for the "Graf Zeppelin's" Europe Pan-American Round Trip. The Spanish Post Master and Postal Authorities have agreed to do likewise.

This office has made arrangements with the consent of the U. S. Postal Authorities to collect, list and number letters and postal cards which are addressed to be forwarded via "Graf Zeppelin" from ports of call outside the United States and to apply foreign stamps prior to dispatch. The flight will start between May 10th and May 15th. All letters and postal cards that are to be dispatched via "Graf Zeppelin" from any of the following ports: Friedrichshafen, Sevilla, Pernambuco or Rio de Janeiro and to carry postal stamps of the countries where these ports are located, should be marked: via "Graf Zeppelin" from.........................(place of departure) to .........................(place of arrival). They should carry a proper mailing address and also the address of the sender.

All letters and postcards for mailing at foreign postal offices should be sent to the undersigned office under cover enclosing certified check or money order to pay the rates applicable. This office will then assort, list and number letters and cards and dispatch them to their agents at ports of call. The respective agents will apply the proper stamps and deliver the mail to the postal authorities in charge at such places.

This arrangement has been made as a matter of convenience to stamp collectors and the dispatch by the airship "Graf Zeppelin" is not guaranteed. Mail to be dispatched via "Graf Zeppelin" with German stamps at Friedrichshafen, Germany, or Spanish stamps at Sevilla, Spain, should be mailed to reach this office not later than Monday, April 28th. Mail to be placed aboard the "Graf Zeppelin" at Pernambuco, Brazil, or Rio de Janeiro, Brazil, should reach this office not later than Saturday, April 26th, 1930.

# LUFTSCHIFFBAU ZEPPELIN G. m. b. H.

## F. W. von MEISTER, Special U. S. Representative

**578 MADISON AVENUE**                              **NEW YORK, N. Y.**

Advertisement from The Airpost Journal, May 1930, p. 14.[11]

top: The *Graf Zeppelin* at the anchor-mast in Recife.
bottom: The airship hangar at Campo de São José, Santa Cruz, near Rio de Janeiro, which opened in December 1936.[12]

Correio Aéreo: A History of the Development of Air Mail Service in Brazil

The original three stamps, issued 16 May 1930, were intended for the 1930 "triangle" flight only. A quantity of each value was overprinted in Brazil in black, "Graf Zeppelin/U.S.A.," for use on mail going to the U. S. However, demand for the lower two values of both of these sets was so great that the supply was exhausted the day after they were issued. This caused CONDOR to have a local printer typographically add reduced value surcharges to the high value stamp (see Appendix C).

By 22 May all of the Berlin-printed issue had been sold. Apparently panicked, CONDOR decided to have their own base 1,300rs stamp overprinted with the two low values intending to use them on mail to the U. S.. Ironically, there was no need for them and few were used outside of on cards between Rio de Janeiro and Recife.[13] The 10,000rs value was never officially issued (see Appendix C).

The Europe-Pan American Flight, with Dr. Hugo Eckener in command, departed Friedrichshafen on 18 May 1930.[14] The *Graf* landed at Seville the next day and took on more passengers and mail.[15] Although it had to endure its first tropical rainstorm over the Atlantic, the ship landed at Recife on 22 May. After a two-day lay over, refueling and exchanging mail, the *Graf* continued to Rio de Janeiro and then returned to Recife the next day.

Mail was transported between Rio and Recife from and to other cities by planes of the CONDOR company (see cover next page).[16]

After two more days it left, on 28 May, on a course to Havana, Cuba. A tropical storm canceled those plans and the ship continued on to Lakehurst. A storm off Cape Hatteras was the worst that the *Graf* experienced, but the ship came through undamaged and landed at Lakehurst on 31 May. It returned to Friedrichshafen on 3 June, traveling via Seville, and arrived there on 6 June.[17] The following year a spectacular flight to the Arctic preceded the commencement of three more flights to Brazil.[18]

Although the airship facilities at Recife were excellent, Eckener wanted the Brazilian government to build an airship hangar at Rio de Janeiro. The government, in turn, looked for more assurances that a steady, reliable service—including passengers—would be provided. Studies for an appropriate location near Rio de Janeiro, other than the military airfield *Campo dos Afonsos*, were started in 1932. On his part, Eckener realized that the *Graf*'s accommodations were also limited and, if passenger service was to become a reality, a bigger airship would be necessary. Plans for such a ship were started.[19] Both of these projects would be realized by the end of 1936.

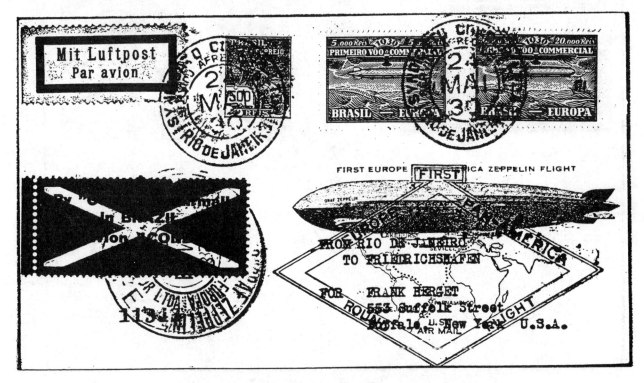

24 May 1930: Rio de Janeiro (by CONDOR) - Recife (by ZEPPELIN) - Friedrichshafen (by boat) - New York
500 rs. postage + 25,000 rs. Condor-Zeppelin air service

**24 May 1930: First Flight *Graf Zeppelin*: Rio de Janeiro - Recife - Lakehurst - New York**
**200 rs. postage + 5,000 rs. air mail on U.S. 1¢ postal card**

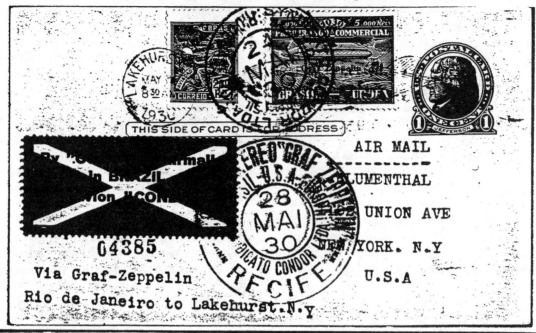

19 May 1930: On Board Posting - Rio de Janeiro - Curityba
4 mark Zeppelin rate + 2,000 rs. airs + 400 rs. registration = Correct rate for 680 km.
CONDOR stamps, for postings other than to Rio or Recife, were sold abroad, but only in Berlin. Few covers survive.

The original German-printed "Zepps" were intended only for the first "triangle" flight. In order to pay the airship fees, the Brazilian government needed new stamps. These came easily—by way of an overprinted surcharge—from the air mail issue of 1929, which contained two stamps with a lighter-than-air theme (see Appendix). These stamps were "2$500" for cards and "5$000" for letters and also bore the inscription "ZEPPELIN" above the new values. These stamps paid the fee both for the Zeppelin Company from Recife and for the services in Brazil of SYNDICATO CONDOR whose stamps were not used after 30 November 1930. It is not clear to this writer exactly how the financial arrangements between the Brazilian government (or, more directly, the Post Office Department) were arranged. In any event, the services using government printed or overprinted stamps continued for both companies (as well as for LUFT HANSA) until they no longer operated.

In 1931 the *Graf* made three flights to Recife. The Brazilian government, having already overprinted two stamps, chose to overprint (surcharge) another earlier stamp—that issued for the first NYRBA flight—as a so-called "emergency issue" for the second zeppelin flight of 1931. Curiously the stamp has only the reduced value "2.500 REIS" and no mention of "ZEPPELIN" (see cover, below). At least 80,000 copies were surcharged and some were still available when the stamp was withdrawn from sale in early 1933. "It is hard to see what the 'emergency'—so far as zeppelin mail was concerned—could have been."[20] The parentage, need for, and use of this issue has been a matter of some curiosity and a source of disagreement with stamp cataloguers. Variations exist.

Zeppelin flight covers were marked by cachet, usually different for each flight, in different color inks.

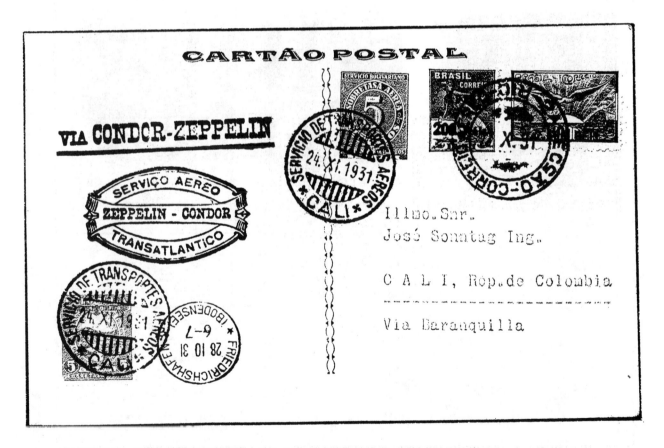

22 October 1931: Third Flight of 1931: Rio de Janeiro - Recife - Friedrichshafen - Cali, Colombia
200 rs. postage (incorrect) + 2,500 rs. air mail + 10 centavos Colombian postage
The *Graf* did not fly to Colombia; the card was returned to South America by boat one month later.

8 April 1932: Second Flight of 1932: Recife - Friedrichshafen
400 rs. postage + 3$500 rs. air mail

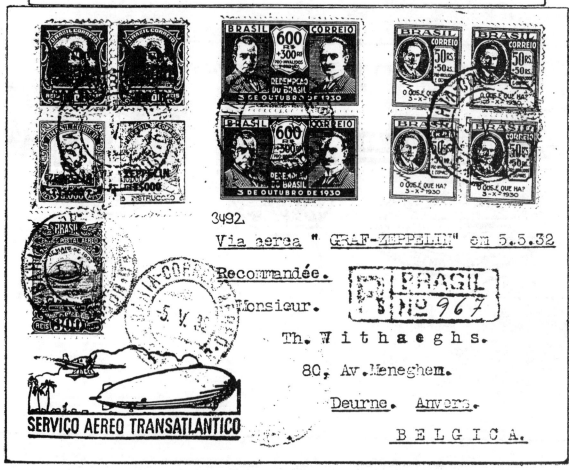

5 May 1932: Fourth Flight of 1932: Bahia - Recife - Friedrichshafen - Anvers, Belgium
2,200 rs. postage (registered) + 11,200 rs. air mail (registered)

(The Sieger *Zeppelin Post Katalog* lists a cachet, similar to that for the first flight of 1931 with the word "second," "SEGUNDO," replacing the word "first," "PRIMEIRO," which was apparently prepared in Parahyba, a town 70 miles north of Recife.)

On the second flight of 1931 a red advertisement was applied to some mail from Europe to Brazil: "The airship Graf Zeppelin waits four days in Pernambuco for your reply."

Luftschiff Graf Zeppelin wartet in Pernambuco vier Tage auf Ihre Antwort

Avião Graf Zeppelin espere em Pernambuco quatro dias sua resposta!

Another red cachet advertisement was applied to mail departing Europe on 17 October 1931, the third and final flight of the year, which advised: "Attention! Take advantage of the Zeppelin's return flight. Give your return mail to the Condor Air Service."

Achtung! Benutzen Sie Zeppelin-Rückfahrt. Übergeben Sie Ihre Antwort dem Flugdienst Condor.

Attençao. Approveite O Regresso Do „Zeppelin". Entregue sua resposta ao Serviço Aereo Condor.

The next year (1932) the number of flights increased to nine with three of the flights also continuing on to Rio de Janeiro—Eckener's aim: "...to whet the interest of the Brazilian government in a regular service to the capital. We just had to have an airship shed in Rio de Janeiro."[21]

On 18 April the Brazilian government overprinted two definitive stamps: "ZEPPELIN 3$500" on the 5$000 "Ruy Barbosa" for post cards and "ZEPPELIN 7$000" on the 10$000 "Education" for letters for this flight. For some unknown reason, the "Education" stamp was not used until two weeks later on the Fourth Flight. The rate for a card to Germany had been (1931) 400 rs. + 2$500 rs.; it was now 700 rs. + 3$500rs., and letters which were 400 rs. + 5$000 rs. now were 700 rs. + 7$000 rs.—more service, but higher fees![22]

**First flight of 1931**
**29 August - 7 September**

Departed Recife: 4 September
violet - black - green

Supplementary cachet
violet - red - black

**Second flight of 1931**
**18 September - 28 September**

Departed Recife: 25 September
violet - black - green

**Third flight of 1931**
**17 October - 28 October**

[Same cachet as the second flight of 1931.]

Departed Recife: 24 October
red - violet - black - green

**First flight of 1932**
**21 March - 29 March**

Departed Recife: 26 March 1932
violet - green - red - blue - yellow

**Second flight of 1932**
**5 April - 13 April**

[Same cachet as first flight of 1932.]

Departed Recife: 9 April 1932
violet - green - red - blue

**Third flight of 1932**
**18 April - 27 April**

[Same cachet as first flight of 1932.]

Departed Recife: 23 April 1932
violet - blue - red

**Fourth flight of 1932**
**2 May - 10 May**

[Same cachet as first flight of 1932.]

Departed Recife: 7 May 1932
black - violet

**Fifth flight of 1932**
**(1st flight of September 1932)**
**29 August - 7 September**

Departed Recife: 3 September 1932
blue - black - violet - green

**Sixth flight of 1932**
**(2nd flight of September 1932)**
**12 September - 21 September**

Departed Recife for Rio de Janeiro: 16 September
Departed Rio de Janeiro for Recife: 17 September
black - violet - blue-green - red

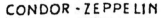

Departed Recife: 18 September 1932
black - violet - blue-green - red

**Seventh flight of 1932**
**(3rd flight of September 1932)**
**26 September - 4 October**

[see cachet on cover, top, opposite page]

Departed Recife: 1 October 1932
black - violet - blue - green

**Eighth flight of 1932**
**(1st flight of October 1932)**
**9 October - 19 October**

[Same cachet as on sixth flight of 1932.]

Departed Recife for Rio de Janeiro: 13 October
Departed Rio de Janeiro for Recife: 14 October
black

Departed Recife: 16 October 1932
blue - violet - red

**Ninth flight of 1932**
**(2nd flight of October 1932)**
**24 October - 3 November**

[Same cachet as on sixth flight of 1932.]

Departed Recife for Rio de Janeiro: 28 October
Departed Rio de Janeiro for Recife: 29 October
black

**22 September 1932: Seventh Flight of 1932: Rio de Janeiro - Recife - Friedrichshafen - Berlin**
**700 rs. postage + 3,500 rs. air mail (card rate, no letter enclosed)**

CONDOR SYNDIKAT
Lindenstrasse 35

Berlin SW 68.

- - - - - - - - - - - -

Allemanha

---

Departed Recife: 31 October 1932
black - violet - blue

On this ninth flight a stop was made at Seville, Spain, on the return trip. Nine flights were made again in 1933 now with regular stops at Rio de Janeiro—with the company pushing for facilities there—and intermittent return stops at Seville. The attempt was to broaden the base for the receipt and dispatch of mail from as many points as possible and to expose the services of the company's airship.

---

**First flight of 1933**
**6 May - 17 May**

Departed Recife for Rio de Janeiro: 10 May
Departed Rio de Janeiro for Recife: 11 May
Departed Recife: 14 May 1933
blue - black - violet

**Second flight of 1933**
**3 June - 13 June**

Departed Recife for Rio de Janeiro: 7 June
red

---

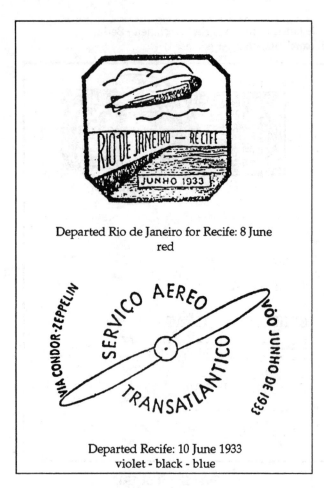

Departed Rio de Janeiro for Recife: 8 June
red

Departed Recife: 10 June 1933
violet - black - blue

### Third flight of 1933
### 1 July - 12 July

[Same cachet as second flight, with
"JULHO" in place of "JUNHO."]

Departed Recife for Rio de Janeiro: 5 July
green

[Same return cachet as second flight with
"JULHO" in place of "JUNHO."]

Departed Rio de Janeiro for Recife: 6 July
green

Departed Recife: 9 July 1933
violet - blue - black - green

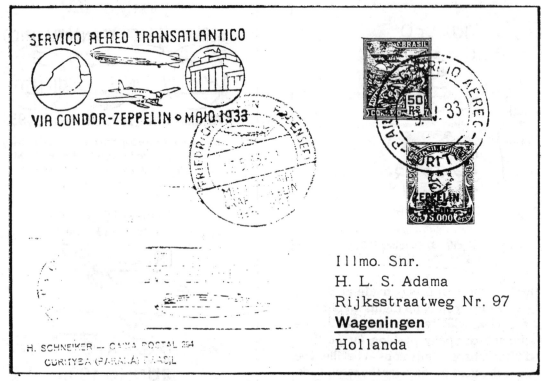

9 May 1933: First Flight of 1933: Curitiba - Recife - Friedrichshafen - Wageningen, The Netherlands
150 rs. postage + 3,500 rs. air mail (post card)

## Fourth flight of 1933
### 5 August - 15 August

[Same cachet as second flight, with "10-8-1933" in place of "JUNHO."]

Departed Recife for Rio de Janeiro: 9 August

[Same return cachet as second flight with "10-8-1933" in place of "JUNHO."]

Departed Rio de Janeiro for Recife: 10 August
blue

Departed Recife: 12 August 1933
violet - black - blue

## Fifth flight of 1933
### 19 August - 29 August

[Same cachet as second flight, with "23-8-1933" in place of "JUNHO."]

Departed Recife for Rio de Janeiro: 23 August
violet

[Same return cachet as second flight with "24-8-1933" in place of "JUNHO."]

Departed Rio de Janeiro for Recife: 24 August
violet

Departed Recife: 26 August 1933
violet - black - blue

## Sixth flight of 1933
### 2 September - 12 September

[Same cachet as second flight, with "6-9-1933" in place of "JUNHO."]

Departed Recife for Rio de Janeiro: 6 September
violet

[Same return cachet as second flight with "7-9-1933" in place of "JUNHO."]

Departed Rio de Janeiro for Recife: 7 September
violet

Departed Recife: 9 September 1933
green - blue - violet

## Seventh flight of 1933
### 16 September - 26 September

[Same cachet as second flight, with "20-9-1933" in place of "JUNHO."]

Departed Recife for Rio de Janeiro: 20 September
red

[Same return cachet as second flight with "21-9-1933" in place of "JUNHO."]

Departed Rio de Janeiro for Recife: 21 September
red

Departed Recife: 23 September 1933
red - blue - violet - green

# AIR MAIL INFORMATION
## In Connection with the Voyage of the Airship
# "GRAF ZEPPELIN"
### From GERMANY via BRAZIL to "A CENTURY of PROGRESS" Exposition in CHICAGO, ILL., U. S. A. and return to EUROPE

## SCHEDULE OF VOYAGE

| | | | |
|---|---|---|---|
| Depart: | Friedrichshafen, Germany | October 14th | 10 P. M. |
| Arrive: | Pernambuco, Brazil | " 17th | evening |
| Arrive: | Rio de Janeiro, Brazil | " 19th | 6 A. M. |
| Depart: | Rio de Janeiro, Brazil | " 19th | 6:30 A. M. |
| Depart: | Pernambuco, Brazil | " 20th | 11 P. M. |
| Arrive: | Miami, Florida, U. S. A. | " 23rd | morning |
| Depart: | Miami, Florida | " 23rd | |
| Arrive: | Akron, Ohio | " 24th | |

**20-24 Hour Flight**
to Chicago and return to Akron
between the 25th and 27th of October.

| | | | |
|---|---|---|---|
| Depart: | Akron, Ohio | " 28th | |
| Arrive: | Sevilla, Spain | " 30th | |
| Arrive: | Friedrichshafen, Germany | " 31st | |

These dates are only approximate due to technical reasons of refueling at Akron, Ohio.

### SPECIAL U. S. STAMP

In commemoration of the visit of the GRAF ZEPPELIN to "A Century of Progress" Exposition at Chicago, Illinois, U. S. A., the U. S. Postmaster General has announced the issue of a special 50 cent stamp. Non-registered postal cards and letters specially marked via Graf Zeppelin bearing U. S. Stamps will be carried on this voyage. The letters may carry a mailing address within the United States or abroad. The rates are as follows:

| | Cards and letters per ½ oz. |
|---|---|
| From U. S. A. by steamer to Friedrichshafen, Germany then by Graf Zeppelin to | Rio de Janeiro or Pernambuco, Brazil and for mail addressed to U. S. A. return by steamer $.50 |
| From U. S. A. by steamer to Friedrichshafen, Germany then by Graf Zeppelin to | Miami, Florida, U. S. A. 1.00 |
| From U. S. A. by steamer to Friedrichshafen, Germany then by Graf Zeppelin to | Chicago, Ill. or Akron, Ohio 1.50 |
| From U. S. A. by steamer to Friedrichshafen, Germany then by Graf Zeppelin | via Brazil, to United States and back to Sevilla, Spain or Friedrichshafen, Germany and for mail addressed to U. S. A. return by steamer 2.00 |

Mail with U. S. stamps to be sent to Germany by steamer for dispatch by GRAF ZEPPELIN must be sent in outer prepaid envelope to the Postmaster in New York, N. Y. in time to reach him by noon on October 4th, 1933.

### MAIL WITHIN THE U. S. A. AND FOR THE RETURN TRIP TO EUROPE

U. S. Mail specially addressed via GRAF ZEPPELIN will be carried as follows:

| Within the U. S. A.: | | Cards and letters per ½ oz. |
|---|---|---|
| From Miami, Florida | to Akron, Ohio, or Chicago, Ill. | $ .50 |
| From Akron, Ohio | to Chicago, Ill. World Fair | .50 |
| From Akron, Ohio | to Akron, Ohio Roundtrip | .50 |
| From Chicago, Ill. | to Akron, Ohio | .50 |
| Return Trip: | | |
| From U. S. A.: (Chicago or Akron) | to Sevilla, Spain, or Friedrichshafen, Germany | .50 |

Mail to be dispatched by airship must be sent in outer prepaid envelope to the Postmaster at Miami, Fla., Chicago, Ill. or Akron, Ohio in time to reach him on the dates shown in the schedule printed above.

### METHOD OF DISPATCH

All mail with U. S. stamps (using either the special stamp or regular U. S. stamps) carrying an address within the U. S. A. or abroad must be marked "Via GRAF ZEPPELIN" from.......... (Port of Departure) to....... (Port of Arrival). The mail must be sent in outer prepaid envelopes to the Postmaster at the port of call of the airship.

Mail carrying addresses within the United States to be dispatched by airship to a port of call outside the United States will be returned to the addressee by ordinary delivery.

### GERMAN STAMPS

The rates for airmail to be dispatched on the GRAF ZEPPELIN from Germany to the various ports of call on this flight with German stamps are: Rm. 0.15 for each postal card, and Rm. 0.25 for each letter, plus the airmail surcharge of Rm. 1.25 per each 5 grammes (about 1/6 oz.) of weight. These rates apply to each of the following three sections of the flight, namely from Germany to Brazil, from Brazil to U. S. A. and from U. S. A. to Europe.

### BRAZILIAN STAMPS

The rates for airmail to be dispatched from Brazil with Brazilian stamps to the various ports of call on this flight are for each postal card, Milreis 0$400, and for each letter, Milreis 0$700, plus the airmail surcharge of Milreis 3$500 for each 5 grammes (1/6 oz.) of weight. These rates apply for mail from Brazil to the U. S. A. and from Brazil via the U. S. A. to Europe.

### METHOD OF DISPATCHING MAIL

As a matter of convenience to philatelists in the U. S. A., this office has, with the consent of the U. S. Post Office Department, made arrangements to accept orders for letters and postal cards to be forwarded via the GRAF ZEPPELIN from ports of call outside the U. S. A., and which are to carry foreign stamps. Collectors, who wish to send covers and/or postal cards prepared by themselves for dispatch via the GRAF ZEPPELIN, and which are to receive German or Brazilian stamps, may send these covers and postal cards to this office. Such covers and postal cards must reach this office by noon on September 29th, if they are to be dispatched from Rio de Janeiro, Brazil. For dispatch from Friedrichshafen with German stamps, they must reach this office not later than noon, October 4th. Covers and cards so received will be listed and forwarded to the offices of Luftschiffbau Zeppelin in Germany or Rio de Janeiro, Brazil where the proper foreign postage stamps will be affixed, and the mail delivered for dispatch via airship. Mail sent in this manner will reach the addressee in the United States or abroad by regular postal service. Covers and/or postal cards prepared for dispatch from Pernambuco cannot be accepted, as there is no suitable steamer connection to connect with the GRAF ZEPPELIN'S sailing from that port.

### LATE ORDERS

Information on LATE ORDERS will be found on page 412. Rates follow:

| | | Postal Cards 5 gram. (1/6 oz.) | Letters 5 gram. (1/6 oz.) | Letters 10 gram. (1/3 oz.) |
|---|---|---|---|---|
| From Friedrichshafen, Germany | to Pernambuco or Rio de Janeiro | $ .60 | $ .60 | $1.00 |
| From Friedrichshafen, Germany, via Brazil | to U. S. A. | 1.05 | 1.10 | 1.90 |
| From Friedrichshafen, Germany, via Brazil and U. S. A. | to Sevilla, Spain or Friedrichshafen, Germany | 1.50 | 1.60 | 2.80 |
| From Rio de Janeiro, or Pernambuco, Brazil | to U. S. A. | .50 | .50 | .75 |
| From Rio de Janeiro, or Pernambuco, Brazil via U. S. A. | to Sevilla, Spain or Friedrichshafen, Germany | .50 | .50 | .75 |

All orders for letters and postal cards to be mailed with foreign stamps at foreign ports of call, and also all letters and postal cards sent to this office for dispatch with foreign stamps from foreign ports of call, must be accompanied by certified check or money order, covering the rate applicable as shown in the table above.

It is expressly understood that these arrangements are made as a matter of convenience to philatelists in the United States and that the dispatch by airship is not guaranteed.

*All Mail Carried Aboard the "Graf Zeppelin" Will Receive a Special Cachet and the Proper Cancellation.*

# LUFTSCHIFFBAU ZEPPELIN G. m. b. H.
### F. W. von MEISTER, Special U. S. Representative

**354 FOURTH AVENUE**     TELEPHONE: CAledonia 5-6483     **NEW YORK, N. Y.**

Advertisement from STAMPS Magazine, 16 November 1933, p. 400.

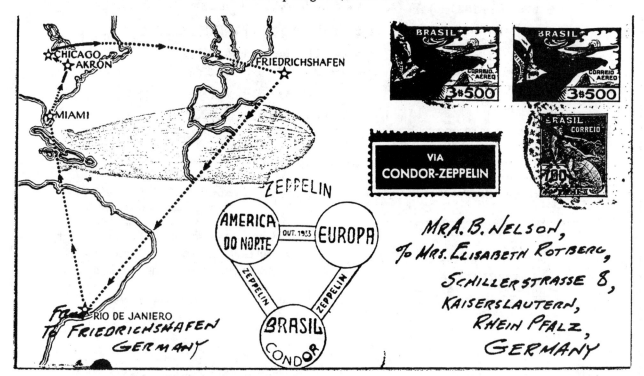

In 1933-34 "A Century of Progress" International Exposition was held in Chicago, IL. Eckener saw a great opportunity and arranged to have the *Graf* visit the Fair in a second "triangle" flight via Brazil. This was also an excuse to celebrate the 50th crossing of the Atlantic. The U. S. honored the event with a 50¢ stamp, but Brazil made no special overtures. The rates from Brazil were the same (400 rs. + 3,500 rs. per card and 700 rs. + 3,500 rs. per 5 gr. for letters) whether they went to the U.S.A. or to Europe. An advertisement for the flight appeared, appropriately enough, in *Stamps* magazine (opposite) in 1933. This was the last flight of 1933.

Another cachet (below) was reproduced in an article in *Brasil Filatelico* which apparently was to be used in lieu of the "triangle" cachet. No recorded use is known; however, a similar design with Spanish text was used on Paraguayan postings.[23]

There were 12 flights in 1934 which saw the use of a "standard" circular design. This cachet was also used on the LUFTHANSA catapult flights, so that the differences must be reconciled by dates relative to departure and/or backstamps (see page 36).

ZEPPELIN mail was backstamped (or sometimes, facestamped) at Friedrichshafen or Frankfurt, which became the center of zeppelin operations in 1936. Frankfurt cancels, utilizing a railway post office, read "Bahnpost." LUFTHANSA mail was backstamped at Stuttgart.

On the third flight of 1934 the *Graf* continued on to Buenos Aires, Argentina, after flying from Recife to Rio de Janeiro. This was the only other city that the airship landed at in South America other than Recife and Rio de Janeiro.

## Eighth flight of 1933
### 30 September - 10 October

[Same cachet as second flight, with "4-10-1933" in place of "JUNHO."]

Departed Recife for Rio de Janeiro: 4 October
green

[Same return cachet as second flight with "5-10-1933" in place of "JUNHO."]

Departed Rio de Janeiro for Recife: 5 October
dark green

Departed Recife: 7 October 1933
violet - green - blue - red

## Ninth flight of 1933
### 14 October - 2 November

[Same cachet as second flight, with "18-10-1933" in place of "JUNHO."]

Departed Recife for Rio de Janeiro: 18 October
black

[Same return cachet as second flight with "19-10-1933" in place of "JUNHO."]

Departed Rio de Janeiro for Recife: 19 October
blue

Mail posted at the International Samples Fair in Rio de Janeiro received this cachet.

Departed Rio de Janeiro: 19 October 1933
violet

Departed Recife: 21 October 1933
blue - green - violet - red

This was another so-called "triangular flight" taking the *Graf* to Chicago's Century of Progress Exposition before returning to Germany.

## First flight of 1934
### 26 May - 5 June

Departed Recife for Rio de Janeiro: 30 May
Departed Rio de Janeiro for Recife: 31 May
Departed Recife: 1 June 1934
violet - red - black

## Second flight of 1934
### 9 June - 19 June

[Same cachet as first flight of 1934.]

Departed Recife for Rio de Janeiro: 13 June
Departed Rio de Janeiro for Recife: 14 June
Departed Recife: 16 June 1934

## Third flight of 1934
### 23 June - 6 July

[Same cachet as first flight of 1934.]

Departed Recife for Rio de Janeiro: 27 June
Departed Rio de Janeiro for Buenos Aires: 29 June
Departed Buenos Aires for Rio de Janeiro: 30 June
Departed Rio de Janeiro for Recife: 1 July
Departed Recife: 3 July 1934

"TO SOUTH AMERICA IN 3 DAYS!"

An advertising poster from 1933. The Hamburg-Amerika (steamship) Line was the agent for the Zeppelin Company in Europe and North America. [from *Poster Art of the Airlines*, Don Thomas, 1989. Courtesy of the author.]

### Fourth flight of 1934
### 21 July - 31 July

[Same cachet as first flight of 1934.]

Departed Recife for Rio de Janeiro: 25 July
Departed Rio de Janeiro for Recife: 26 July
Departed Recife: 27 July 1934

### Fifth flight of 1934
### 5 August - 14 August

[Same cachet as first flight of 1934.]

Departed Recife for Rio de Janeiro: 8 August
Departed Rio de Janeiro for Recife: 9 August
Departed Recife: 11 August 1934

On the fourth and fifth flights a purple cachet was substituted on mail flown from Recife to Rio.

### Sixth flight of 1934
### 18 August - 28 August

[Same cachet as first flight of 1934.]

Departed Recife for Rio de Janeiro: 22 August
Departed Rio de Janeiro for Recife: 23 August
Departed Recife: 25 August 1934

On this flight another purple cachet was substituted on mail between Recife and Rio de Janeiro. This cachet was also used on the seventh flight, with the words "VIA ZEPPELIN" above and "RECIFE-FRIEDRICHSHAFEN" below, on mail leaving Recife for Europe.

### Seventh flight of 1934
### 1 September - 11 September

[Same cachet as first flight of 1934.]

Departed Recife for Rio de Janeiro: 5 September
Departed Rio de Janeiro for Recife: 6 September
Departed Recife: 7 September 1934

### Eighth flight of 1934
### 15 September - 25 September

[Same cachet as first flight of 1934.]

Departed Recife for Rio de Janeiro: 19 September
Departed Rio de Janeiro for Recife: 20 September
Departed Recife: 21 September 1934

### Ninth flight of 1934
### 29 September - 9 October

[Same cachet as first flight of 1934.]

Departed Recife for Rio de Janeiro: 3 October
Departed Rio de Janeiro for Recife: 4 October
Departed Recife: 6 October 1934

### Tenth flight of 1934
### 13 October - 23 October

[Same cachet as first flight of 1934.]

Departed Recife for Rio de Janeiro: 17 October
Departed Rio de Janeiro for Recife: 18 October
Departed Recife: 20 October 1934

### Eleventh flight of 1934
### 27 October - 6 November
[Same cachet as first flight of 1934.]

Departed Recife for Rio de Janeiro: 31 October
Departed Rio de Janeiro for Recife: 1 November
Departed Recife: 2 November 1934

On mail posted at the International Sample Fair in Rio de Janeiro, an additional cachet was provided. It was used on the 6th through 11th flights with a change in color and the flight ("VIAGEM") number changed. The colors were: blue, "6a"; carmine, "7a"; green, "8a"; violet, "9a"; red, "10a"; and black, "11a".

### Twelfth flight of 1934
### 8 December - 19 December

[Same cachet as first flight of 1934.]

Departed Recife for Rio de Janeiro: 12 December
Departed Rio de Janeiro for Recife: 13 December
Departed Recife: 14 December 1934

[The use of the round cachet from the first flight of 1934 continued throughout 1935.]

### First flight of 1935
### 6 April - 16 April

Departed Recife for Rio de Janeiro: 10 April
Departed Rio de Janeiro for Recife: 11 April
Departed Recife: 13 April 1935

### Second flight of 1935
### 20 April - 1 May

Departed Recife for Rio de Janeiro: 24 April
Departed Rio de Janeiro for Recife: 25 April
Departed Recife: 26 April 1935

On the second flight a red cachet was applied to mail that was posted at the Tourism Fair at Rio.

### Third flight of 1935
### 4 May - 14 May

Departed Recife for Rio de Janeiro: 8 May
Departed Rio de Janeiro for Recife: 9 May
Departed Recife: 10 May 1935

### Fourth flight of 1935
### 19 May - 28 May

Departed Recife for Rio de Janeiro: 22 May
Departed Rio de Janeiro for Recife: 23 May
Departed Recife: 24 May 1935

### Fifth flight of 1935
### 1 June - 11 June

Departed Recife for Rio de Janeiro: 5 June
Departed Rio de Janeiro for Recife: 6 June
Departed Recife: 8 June 1935

### Sixth flight of 1935
### 15 June - 25 June

Departed Recife for Rio de Janeiro: 19 June
Departed Rio de Janeiro for Recife: 20 June
Departed Recife: 21 June 1935

### Seventh flight of 1935
### 29 June - 29 July

Departed Recife for Rio de Janeiro: 3 July
Departed Rio de Janeiro for Recife: 4 July
Departed Recife: 5 July 1935

### Eighth flight of 1935
### 15 July - 25 July

Departed Recife for Rio de Janeiro: 19 July
Departed Rio de Janeiro for Recife: 20 July
Departed Recife: 21 July 1935

### Ninth flight of 1935
### 29 July - 7 August

Departed Recife for Rio de Janeiro: 2 August
Departed Rio de Janeiro for Recife: 2 August
Departed Recife: 4 August 1935

### Tenth flight of 1935
### 13 August - 22 August

Departed Recife for Rio de Janeiro: 16 August
Departed Rio de Janeiro for Recife: 17 August
Departed Recife: 18 August 1935

### Eleventh flight of 1935
### 27 August - 5 September

Departed Recife for Rio de Janeiro: 30 August
Departed Rio de Janeiro for Recife: 31 August
Departed Recife: 1 September 1935

### Twelfth flight of 1935
### 9 September - 18 September

Departed Recife for Rio de Janeiro: 13 September
Departed Rio de Janeiro for Recife: 13 September
Departed Recife: 15 September 1935

### Thirteenth flight of 1935
### 23 September - 2 October

Departed Recife for Rio de Janeiro: 27 September
Departed Rio de Janeiro for Recife: 27 September
Departed Recife: 29 September 1935

### Fourteenth flight of 1935
### 7 October - 16 October

Departed Recife for Rio de Janeiro: 11 October
Departed Rio de Janeiro for Recife: 11 October
Departed Recife: 13 October 1935

## Fifteenth flight of 1935
### 23 October - 4 November

Departed Recife for Rio de Janeiro: 27 October
Departed Rio de Janeiro for Recife: 27 October
Departed Recife for Rio de Janeiro: 30 October
Departed Rio de Janeiro for Recife: 30 October
Departed Recife: 1 November 1935

## Sixteenth flight of 1935
### 7 November - 10 December

Departed Recife for Rio de Janeiro: 10 November
Departed Rio de Janeiro for Recife: 11 November
Departed Recife to Gambia to Recife: 15 November
Departed Recife to Gambia to Recife: 22 November
Departed Recife to Gambia to Recife: 29 November
Departed Recife for Rio de Janeiro: 3 December
Departed Rio de Janeiro for Recife: 4 December
Departed Recife: 6 December 1935

## First flight of 1936
### 31 March - 10 April

Departed Rio de Janeiro: 6 April 1936

## Second Flight of 1936
### 13 April - 24 April

Departed Recife for Rio de Janeiro: 17 April
Departed Rio de Janeiro for Recife: 18 April
Departed Recife: 19 April 1936

## Third flight of 1936
### 27 April - 8 May

Departed Recife for Rio de Janeiro: 30 April
Departed Rio de Janeiro for Recife: 2 May
Departed Recife: 4 May 1936

## Fourth flight of 1936
### 11 May - 21 May

Departed Recife for Rio de Janeiro: 14 May
Departed Rio de Janeiro for Recife: 16 May
Departed Recife: 17 May 1936

## Fifth flight of 1936
### 25 May - 3 June

Departed Rio de Janeiro: 30 May 1936

## Sixth flight of 1936
### 8 June - 18 June

Departed Recife for Rio de Janeiro: 11 June
Departed Rio de Janeiro for Recife: 13 June
Departed Recife: 14 June 1936

## Seventh flight of 1936
### 24 June - 7 July

Departed Recife for Rio de Janeiro: 28 June
Departed Rio de Janeiro for Recife: 1 July
Departed Recife: 3 July 1936

## Eighth flight of 1936
### 9 July - 20 July

Departed Recife for Rio de Janeiro: 12 July
Departed Rio de Janeiro for Recife: 15 July
Departed Recife: 17 July 1936

## Ninth flight of 1936
### 20 July - 29 July

Departed Rio de Janeiro: 25 July 1936

## Tenth flight of 1936
### 30 July - 10 August

Departed Recife for Rio de Janeiro: 2 August
Departed Rio de Janeiro for Recife: 5 August
Departed Recife: 7 August 1936

## Eleventh flight of 1936
### 13 August - 24 August

Departed Recife for Rio de Janeiro: 16 August
Departed Rio de Janeiro for Recife: 19 August
Departed Recife: 21 August 1936

## Twelfth flight of 1936
### 27 August - 8 September

Departed Rio de Janeiro: 4 September 1936

## Thirteenth flight of 1936
### 9 September-21 September

Departed Recife for Rio de Janeiro: 13 September
Departed Rio de Janeiro for Recife: 16 September
Departed Recife: 18 September 1936

## Fourteenth flight of 1936
### 23 September - 5 October

Departed Recife for Rio de Janeiro: 27 September
Departed Rio de Janeiro for Recife: 30 September
Departed Recife: 2 October 1936

## Fifteenth flight of 1936
### 8 October - 19 October

Departed Recife for Rio de Janeiro: 11 October
Departed Rio de Janeiro for Recife: 14 October
Departed Recife: 16 October 1936

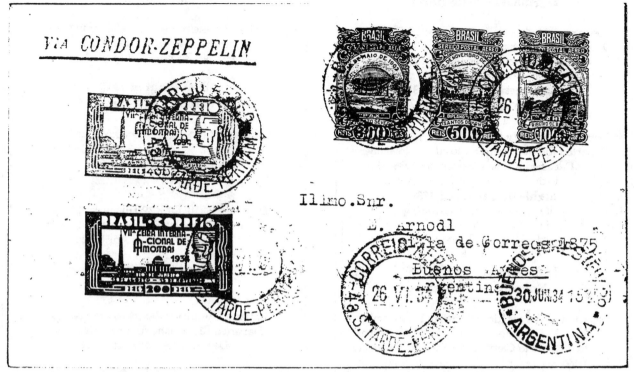

It is interesting to note that in 1935 the announced policy of the Brazilian government was that it had "never granted privileges or monopolies of any kind to aviation companies, and Brazilian aeronautical legislation prohibits concessions of this character."[24] However, the government had, in fact, constructed, at its own expense, a dirigible airport at *Campo de San José*, at Santa Cruz, about 35 miles southwest of Rio de Janeiro. This facility, which included a hangar and related services, was completed in December 1936 (see p. 42) in an effort to secure regular dirigible service to Brazil.[25] The Zeppelin Company, in turn, obligated itself to maintain a transatlantic service of a minimum of twenty round trips annually and to pay a fee for the use of a mooring mast and/or hangar facilities. There was, however, a proviso that dirigibles of other companies and/or countries could also use the facility. Zeppelin service to Brazil was authorized by decree dated 31 March 1934.

On 22 March 1935 LUFTHANSA and LUFTSCHIF-BAU ZEPPELIN formed the German Zeppelin Airline, DEUTSCHE ZEPPELIN REEDEREI, which was officially inaugurated by Herman Goring—the company now "enjoyed" full state support *and* control.[26] The *Graf* made 16 flights that year, carrying 720 passengers and 31,000 pounds (900,000 pieces) of mail. The use of the round cachet continued.

On the 15th flight of 1935 the *Graf* made two shuttle trips between Recife and Rio de Janeiro. On the next flight the *Graf Zeppelin* substituted for the depot ships in November 1935, while they were undergoing maintenance and repair, making shuttle flights to Bathurst, Gambia, and exchanging mail ("drop mail") via long ropes. LUFTHANSA planes brought the mail from Germany (and other points) to Bathurst—no mail originated there—and returned the mail destined for European points to Germany. No landings were made at Bathurst.

Twenty flights were made in 1936. The new, larger zeppelin, *Hindenburg* (LZ.129), under the operational control of Captain Ernst Lehmann, joined the *Graf Zeppelin* (LZ.127) in service and was used on the 1st, 5th, 9th, 12th, 16th, 18th, and 20th flights of that year. LZ.129 went to Recife only twice (16th and 20th) the other flights all went only to Rio de Janeiro. On the 19th flight the *Graf* flew twice to Rio de Janeiro and once to Bathurst. Again, there was no landing at Bathurst.

In Germany both airships were still housed at Friedrichshafen, as the new facility at Frankfurt-am-Main was still under construction. The new facility, at 300 feet above sea level, would facilitate take offs as it was 1,000 feet lower than that at Friedrichshafen.

## Sixteenth flight of 1936
### 21 October - 2 November

Departed Rio de Janeiro for Recife: 29 October
Departed Recife for Rio de Janeiro: 30 October
Departed Rio de Janeiro: 30 October 1936

## Seventeenth flight of 1936
### 29 October - 9 November

Departed Recife for Rio de Janeiro: 1 November
Departed Rio de Janeiro for Recife: 4 November
Departed Recife: 6 November 1936

## Eighteenth flight of 1936
### 5 November - 16 November

Departed Rio de Janeiro: 12 November 1936

## Nineteenth flight of 1936
### 11 November - 1 December

Departed Recife for Rio de Janeiro: 14 November
Departed Rio de Janeiro for Recife: 18 November
Departed Recife to Gambia to Recife: 20 November
Departed Recife for Rio de Janeiro: 23 November
Departed Rio de Janeiro for Recife: 25 November
Departed Recife: 27 November 1936

## Twentieth flight of 1936
### 25 November - 7 December

Departed Rio de Janeiro for Rio de Janeiro: 30 November
Departed Rio de Janeiro for Recife:3 December
Departed Recife: 4 December 1936

## First flight of 1937
### 16 March - 27 March

Departed Rio de Janeiro: 23 March 1937

## Second flight of 1937
### 13 April - 24 April

Departed Recife for Rio de Janeiro: 16 April
Departed Rio de Janeiro for Recife: 19 April
Departed Recife: 20 April 1936

## Third flight of 1937
### 27 April - 8 May

Departed Recife for Rio de Janeiro: 30 April
Departed Rio de Janeiro for Recife: 3 May
Departed Recife: 4 May 1936

This was the last flight from South America. The *Hindenburg* crashed on 6 May 1937 at Lakehurst.

4 April 1936: First Flight of 1936, First Flight of the *Hindenburg*. Rio de Janeiro - Friedrichshafen
5,500 rs. = 2,000 rs. postage (registered) + 3,500 rs. air mail

An advertising insert that is sometimes found in (unsealed) covers or with batches of mail.

There were three flights made to Brazil in 1937. The initial, now routine, flight of 1937 was made by the *Hindenburg* in March; the next two by the *Graf Zeppelin* which was over the South Atlantic returning from its second flight when word of the disaster at Lakehurst on 6 May 1937 was received. Commander von Schiller waited until the *Graf Zeppelin* reached Friedrichshafen—safe on the ground—before he advised his passengers of the fate of the *Hindenburg*. In all, 73 round-trips had been made to Brazil: 65 by the *Graf Zeppelin* and 8 by the *Hindenburg*. No more commercial flights were made and, although a new ship, *Graf Zeppelin II* (LZ.130), had been built, it was never put into regular service. The airship era was over.

In 1980 Brazil commemorated the 50th anniversary of the first flight to South America by the *Graf Zeppelin* with a postage stamp (below) picturing a profile drawing of the great airship.

In 1986 another stamp commemorated the 50th anniversary of the Bartholomeu de Gusmão Airport, formerly *Campo de San José*. The soil conditions of several sites for the zeppelin facilities, which would include a hangar for the airship, were evaluated. President Vargas favored the site of Santos Dumont airport, but Eckener convinced him that the Santa Cruz site was best. On 12 February 1942, five years after the *Hindenburg* disaster, the Bartholomeu de Gusmão Airport became the present Air Force Base at Santa Cruz.[27] The airship hangar is "still standing an exact duplicate, erected in 1936, of the last and most modern hangar originally built for the Zeppelin Company in Löwenthal, near Friedrichshafen, in 1932."[28]

The *Graf Zeppelin* made one more flight—a short trip back to Frankfurt on 18 May 1937. Three years later the *Graf Zeppelin* (LZ.127) and the newer *Graf Zeppelin II* (LZ.130) were reduced to scrap metal. The "magic" lives on, but only in the minds of dreamers and collectors.[29]

◊

**CORRESPONDENCIA**

**TAXA AEREA** (em sellos da Empreza além dos sellos do Correio Geral)
300 Rs. por 5 grammas ou fracção

**A DOMICILIO** (MÃO PROPRIA) depois de fechada a malá no Correio
2$500 Rs. por carta até 250 grammas

**PEQUENAS CARGAS**

**TAXA AEREA** 1$000 por 100 grammas ou fracção

**A DOMICILIO** 4$000 por volume até 10 kilos
Seguro de carga 2 o|o sobre o valor

**HORARIOS** (PROVISORIOS)

As malas fecham no Correio Geral ás 11 horas

PARTIDAS DO RIO                     PARTIDAS DE S. PAULO

Todas ás 2.ª e 5.ª feiras uteis ás 12 horas    Todas ás 3.ª e 6.ª feiras uteis ás 12 horas

---

CORRESPONDENCE

AIR RATES   (Company stamps plus the stamps of the Post Office)
300rs. for 5 grams or fraction.

TO DOMICILE   (BY PRIVATE HAND) after the Post closes
2$500rs. for letters up to 250 grams.

SMALL CARGO

AIR RATES        1$000 for 100 grams or fraction.
TO DOMICILE      4$000 for a volume up to 10 kilos.
                 Insure cargo at 2% of value.

HOURS (PROVISIONAL)
Mail pouch closed at 1100.

| Departs Rio | Departs São Paulo |
|---|---|
| Every Monday and Thursday | Every Tuesday and Friday |
| except holidays at noon. | except holidays at noon. |

An advertising rate schedule card for the EMPRESA DE TRANSPORTES AÉREOS LTDA. (ETA) airline company.

# EMPRESA DE TRANSPORTES AÉREOS LIMITADA

EMPRESA DE TRANSPORTES AÉREOS LTDA (ETA) was founded on 10 August 1928 by Ruy Vacani and two brothers, Benjamin and Alexandre Braga. They had neither the equipment nor financial backing of the two German-supported "domestic" lines, SYNDICATO CONDOR and VARIG, or the French line, AÉROPOSTALE. ETA did not, therefore, have the same ambitions of these three and was apparently content to plan only a mail service between Rio de Janeiro - São Paulo - Campos - Belo Horizonte. Accordingly, ETA acquired three Klemm open-cockpit monoplanes which were duly registered in December 1928.[1]

ETA authorized to operate on 1 March 1929 and to carry mail on 12 June 1929, began flying test flights between Rio de Janeiro and Campos on 19 June 1929, returning the next day.[2] Flight service from Rio de Janeiro to São Paulo was inaugurated on 29 July 1929 and the return flight was on 2 August 1929. Most, if not all, of the mail to São Paulo is backstamped "29 JUN 29."

As a domestic line ETA, like CONDOR and VARIG, was required to print and issue stamps for its services. The stamps utilized a design with a stylized airplane formed from its initials.

Basic stamp design (enlarged 150%)

The cancellation that it produced was a simple double circle containing the letters "ETA" behind a single date line.

In July 1928, while still in the forming stages, ETA attempted to force a merger with the NEW YORK, RIO & BUENOS AIRES Line (NYRBA), which had been founded by Ralph O'Neill in an attempt to establish an east coast route between New York and Buenos Aires (see NEW YORK, RIO & BUENOS AIRES LINE). ETA was rebuffed by O'Neill but later, while O'Neill was in South America, ETA representatives went north to New York and successfully approached some of NYRBA's sponsors with a claim of having an "exclusive contract" for operating rights within and from Brazil and secured $10,000, as a "partner," and a further commitment of $250,000 more in financial and/or equipment support. ETA would operate within Brazil; NYRBA would operate internationally.

Back in Brazil, on 28 December 1928, ETA's claim was successfully challenged by O'Neill.[3] ETA had no such "exclusive contract" and was, in fact, not even authorized to operate until 1 March 1929—and only in Brazil. ETA was down, but not quite out.

It should be noted that although ETA was much smaller than NYRBA in both finances and equipment, its authorization from the Brazil government did precede NYRBA's, but, as O'Neill well knew, it did not exclude it.

29 July 1929: First flight: Rio de Janeiro - São Paulo
400 rs. postage + 8,200 rs. air mail

29 July 1929: First flight: Rio de Janeiro - São Paulo
400 rs. postage + 2,000 rs. air mail

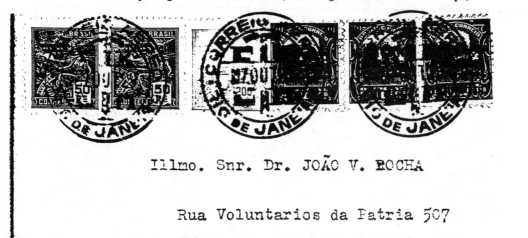

Illmo. Snr. Dr. JOÃO V. ROCHA

Rua Voluntarios da Patria 507

S Ã O   P A U L O

PELO CORREIO AEREO
DA
ETA

By February 1929 O'Neill had secured a contract from Argentina to carry mail. NYRBA's first survey flight from New York City to Buenos Aires was 11 June to 13 July 1929. Support bases had been located along the route. O'Neill formed a subsidiary, NYRBA DO BRASIL (authorized 24 January 1930), to comply with Brazilian laws.

O'Neill was attempting to prove his ability to carry the mail in a timely and safe fashion. However, he had to start from Buenos Aires and work his way north. On 19 February 1930 the first mail carrying service destined for the U. S. was begun up the east coast of South America. Three planes had to be abandoned before the mail reached Rio de Janeiro, the last leg by ground transport. There, ETA made one last effort to assert itself and, claiming a "breach of contract," attempted to have the waiting NYRBA plane impounded. ETA had obtained a court order in Rio de Janeiro and claimed "approximately $175,000 due under the contract, which provided for advancing $750,000, one third of which was to be the capital of 'Eta International,' the same amount for the 'Eta Brasilien,' and the last third to acquire the property of the Eta."[4]

O'Neill escaped in another plane and continued on to Miami arriving 26 February 1930. Eight different aircraft, and some other vehicles, had been utilized in the seven-day venture. But, O'Neill had no contract to transport the mail in the U.S., nor even to bring it there. U. S. postal officials wanted the lucrative contract to go to PAN AMERICAN (see PAN AMERICAN AIRWAYS).

In addition, NYRBA was feeling the effects of the stock market crash of October 1929, both in its capital and the reduced amount of business on the line, as the shock wave spread from Wall Street. By April 1930, NYRBA officials were negotiating with PAN AMERICAN.

Little ETA was also in trouble. Its limited twice-a-week service, with no round-trip the same day (see p. 62), could not be maintained. By the end of 1930 ETA had sold its "routes" to NYRBA and its aircraft to VARIG. ETA was no more.

◊

**1940 / LINHAS AEREAS ITALIANAS / 1940**

| JANEIRO | FEVEREIRO | MARÇO | ABRIL |
|---|---|---|---|
| D — 7 14 21 28 | D — 4 11 18 25 | D — 3 10 17 24 31 | D — 7 14 21 28 |
| S 1 8 15 22 29 | S — 5 12 19 26 | S — 4 11 18 25 — | S 1 8 15 22 29 |
| T 2 9 16 23 30 | T — 6 13 20 27 | T — 5 12 19 26 — | T 2 9 16 23 30 |
| Q 3 10 17 24 31 | Q — 7 14 21 28 | Q — 6 13 20 27 — | Q 3 10 17 24 — |
| Q 4 11 18 25 — | Q 1 8 15 22 29 | Q — 7 14 21 28 — | Q 4 11 18 25 — |
| S 5 12 19 26 | S 2 9 16 23 | S 1 8 15 22 29 | S 5 12 19 26 |
| S 6 13 20 27 — | S 3 10 17 24 — | S 2 9 16 23 30 | S 6 13 20 27 — |

| MAIO | JUNHO | JULHO | AGOSTO |
|---|---|---|---|
| D — 5 12 19 26 | D — 2 9 16 23 30 | D — 7 14 21 28 | D — 4 11 18 25 |
| S — 6 13 20 27 | S — 3 10 17 24 — | S 1 8 15 22 29 | S — 5 12 19 26 |
| T — 7 14 21 28 | T — 4 11 18 25 — | T 2 9 16 23 30 | T — 6 13 20 27 |
| Q 1 8 15 22 29 | Q — 5 12 19 26 — | Q 3 10 17 24 31 | Q — 7 14 21 28 |
| Q 2 9 16 23 30 | Q — 6 13 20 27 — | Q 4 11 18 25 — | Q 1 8 15 22 29 |
| S 3 10 17 24 31 | S — 7 14 21 28 | S 5 12 19 26 | S 2 9 16 23 30 |
| S 4 11 18 25 — | S 1 8 15 22 29 | S 6 13 20 27 — | S 3 10 17 24 31 |

| SETEMBRO | OUTUBRO | NOVEMBRO | DEZEMBRO |
|---|---|---|---|
| D 1 8 15 22 29 | D — 6 13 20 27 | D — 3 10 17 24 | D 1 8 15 22 29 |
| S 2 9 16 23 30 | S — 7 14 21 28 | S — 4 11 18 25 | S 2 9 16 23 30 |
| T 3 10 17 24 — | T 1 8 15 22 29 | T — 5 12 19 26 | T 3 10 17 24 31 |
| Q 4 11 18 25 — | Q 2 9 16 23 30 | Q — 6 13 20 27 | Q 4 11 18 25 — |
| Q 5 12 19 26 — | Q 3 10 17 24 31 | Q — 7 14 21 28 | Q 5 12 19 26 — |
| S 6 13 20 27 | S 4 11 18 25 | S 1 8 15 22 29 | S 6 13 20 27 |
| S 7 14 21 28 — | S 5 12 19 26 — | S 2 9 16 23 30 | S 7 14 21 28 — |

**Sahidas do Rio de Janeiro para a Europa e demais continentes todas as Sextas-feiras**

*Fechamento das malas aereas no Rio de Janeiro, ás quintas-feiras, ás 18 horas*

**SERVIÇO COMBINADO COM A VASP, CONDOR E PANAIR PARA TRANSPORTE DA CORRESPONDENCIA PARA O RIO DE JANEIRO.**

AVENIDA RIO BRANCO, 104
RIO DE JANEIRO **L. A. T. I.** TELS. Escrip.: 42-9572 / 22-9312 Agencia: 22-9320

LINHAS AEREAS TRANSCONTINENTAES ITALIANAS S.A.

"Leaving Rio de Janeiro for Europe and other continents on Fridays. Air mail pouch closes on Thursdays at 6 pm in Rio de Janeiro. Service combined with VASP, CONDOR, and PANAIR for transport to Rio de Janeiro." (A 1940 LATI advertising card/calendar, original in multi-color.)

# LINEE AEREE TRANSCONTINENTALI ITALIANE S.A.

The Second World War had a marked and far-reaching effect on air transportation services in Latin America. Services between Europe and South America which were on the verge of being extensively improved were, instead, severely curtailed.

LUFTHANSA had increased mail service frequency from once- to twice-a-week in July 1939, and was planning to commence passenger service in four-engine Dornier DO-26 flying boats, when it was forced to stop operations at the outbreak of the war. AIR FRANCE had been testing passenger service possibilities and, although it continued operating after a two-week hiatus in September 1939, service was ended with the collapse of France in June 1940. Under the pressure of the war English plans for a London - Rio de Janeiro - Buenos Aires route, via Lisbon and British West Africa, were scrapped. Any Dutch plans were abandoned with the fall of Holland in May 1940.

One country which did not enter the hostilities (openly) until June 1940, Italy, attempted to fill the widening gap between the continents.

In March 1938 a survey flight by ALA LITTORIA, the Italian national airline, was made between Rome and Buenos Aires. Umberto Klinger, the president of its Atlantic division, ALA LITTORIA LINEE ATLANTICHE, took the necessary precautions to negotiate operating rights which Brazil provisionally granted on 23 December 1938. A coastal route from Natal south was granted on 3 July 1939. Additional survey flights ensued.

In September 1939 ALA LITTORIA reformed its Atlantic division and established LINEE AEREE TRANSCONTINENTALI ITALIANE S.A. (LATI).[1]

LATI established an Italian mail and official passenger service from Rome, avoiding British and French territories by flying via Seville, Villa Cisneros (Spanish Morocco), Sal Island (Cape Verde Islands), and on to Natal, Recife, Bahia, Rio de Janeiro, São Paulo, and Porto Alegre. Although flying boats were planned, the initial planes were land-based: Savoia-Marchetti Models SM-75, SM-82 and SM-83.

The ill-fated inaugural flight left Rio de Janeiro on 21 December 1939; simultaneously, a similar plane left Rome's Guidonia airport for Brazil. The eastbound aircraft crashed in Mauritania, killing the crew and the passengers, including two Brazilian journalists. Some crash covers survive. The cachet used from Brazil used LATI's "winged gull" design which some thought was an "M" for Mussolini.[2]

Rio de Janeiro - Bahia - Recife
violet - black blue

Recovering from the initial tragedy, the line operated regular bi-monthly service—the only service across the South Atlantic and the first regular passenger service since the Zeppelin era. Primarily a mail and express service (outside the reach of Allied censorship) between Axis powers and South America, LATI carried a few passengers, usually Axis officials. Flights left Rome on Thursdays and reached Rio de Janeiro the following Sunday. On 5 June 1940 service was reduced to once a month. Five days later Italy declared war on the Allies.

In September LATI and it parent were militarized, but the transatlantic service resumed operation by the end of the month. LATI had originally used weather ships to help pilots navigate across the seas between the Cape Verde Islands and Fernando de Noronha, but these were recalled and radio silence was the rule. Another fatal accident occurred in January 1941.

Mail from other South American countries was brought to Brazil, primarily by CONDOR (see cover below), but other airlines were also utilized including LLOYD AÉREO BOLIVIANO (LAB), another German supported airline founded in Bolivia in 1925, and VIAÇÃO AÉREA SÃO PAULO (VASP) founded in São Paulo in 1933. The postage rates for the LATI service were 5,400 rs. for postage per 5 gm. and 1,300 rs. for registration.

In April 1941 the Brazilian government imposed a fine for an "extended flight" which was deemed to be other than a purely "civil diversion." LATI had

...made a nuisance of itself to the allies even before Italy became an enemy. Italian planes provided the Germans with a safe means of transportation for fifth-column agents to and from Latin America. On several occasions Italian airmen were known to have reported to submarine commanders the positions of allied convoys.[3]

By summer, service had become weekly and, in a demonstration of the "friendship" between Italy and Argentina, the line was extended to Buenos Aires on 25 July 1941.

Recife - Rio de Janeiro - São Paulo
yellow - blue violet - black violet - black

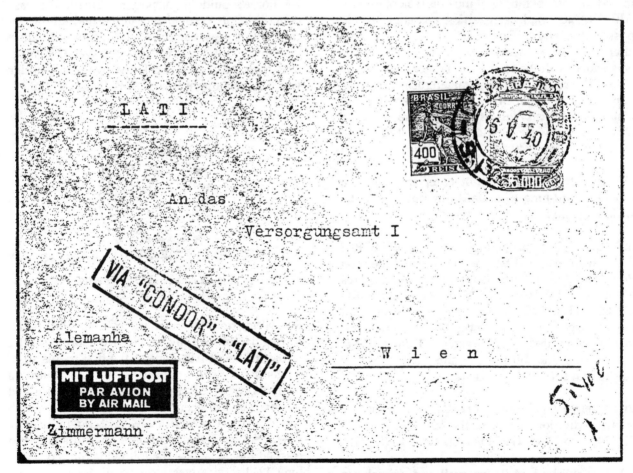

16 May 1940: Combined CONDOR-LATI flight: São Paulo - Vienna, Austria
5,400 rs. postage

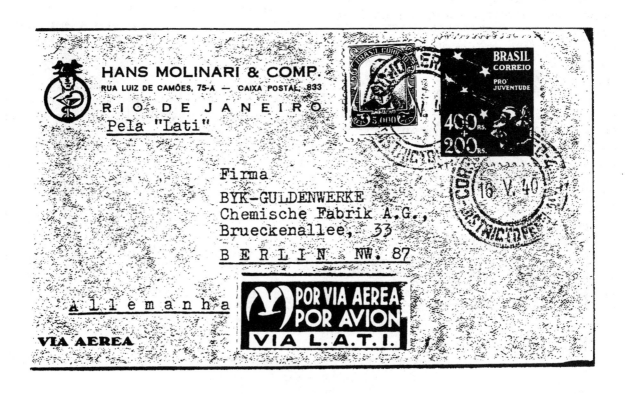

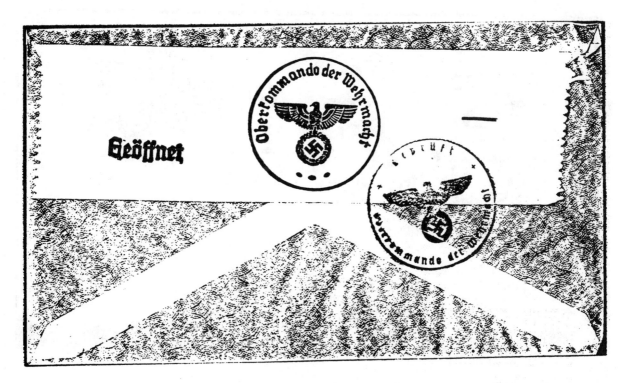

16 May 1940: Rio de Janeiro - Berlin, Germany
5,400 rs. postage (The 200 rs. semi-postal tax for child welfare was required only until 26 February 1940.)
LATI etiquette applied and German censor tape on reverse.

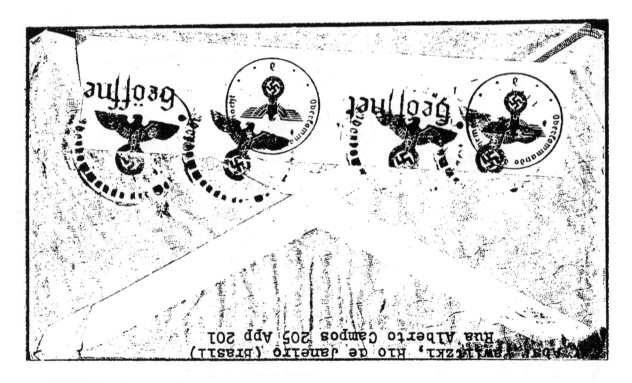

19 June 1941: Rio de Janeiro - Hanover, Germany
2,800 rs. postage + 8,000 rs. air mail
LATI etiquette applied and with a different version of the censor tape and cachet on the reverse.

Airplane drawings all to the same scale ~ 1 inch = 30 feet

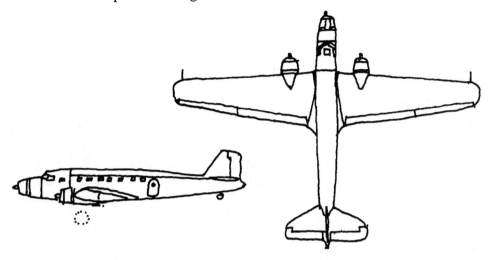

SIAI MARCHETTI SM-75

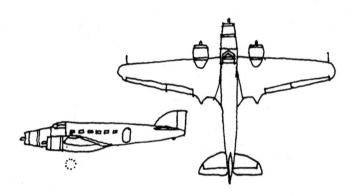

SIAI MARCHETTI SM-83

On 11 December 1941 LATI experienced problems relating to fuel supplies for its aircraft—the U.S. government cut off its supplies. Eleven days later operations ceased and some of the services were assumed by PAN AMERICAN.

With the demise of LATI, other attempts were made to reestablish the "connection." The German Armistice Commission had given AIR FRANCE an "ok" to resume transatlantic operations and, although acceptable to both Argentina and Chile, Brazil rejected the idea. The United States put the Axis-controlled company on the Proclaimed List ("blacklist") in September 1941. Spain's COMPANIA MERCANTIL ANONIMA IBERIA (IBERIA), founded in 1940 with heavy backing from LUFTHANSA, attempted to rebuild its air services which had been virtually destroyed in three years of civil war, but could not obtain the gasoline and equipment for transatlantic operations.

The end of LATI also marked the end of Axis-controlled lines operating in Brazil and became a constructive factor in the development of nationally owned and operated services. National lines had been the Brazilian government's goal for some time.

◊

Airplane drawings all to the same scale ~ 1 inch = 30 feet

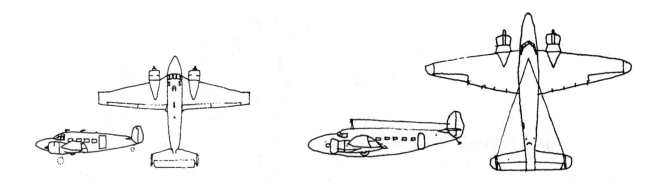

BEECH 18                    LOCKHEED 18 Lodestar

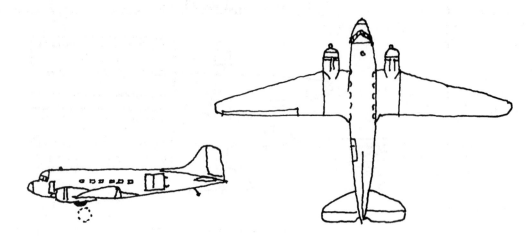

DOUGLAS DC-3

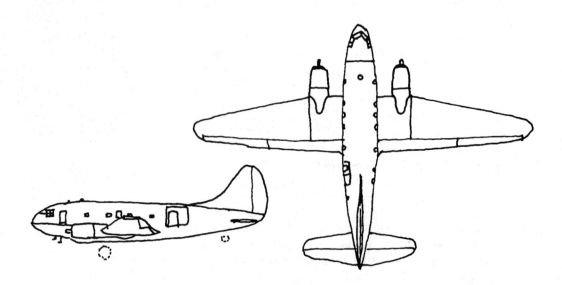

CURTISS C-46

# NAVEGAÇÃO AÉREA BRASILEIRA S/A.

In the late thirties government plans were under way for the establishment of a purely-Brazilian, civilian airline. Major Orsini de Araujo Coriolano was released from the Brazilian Air Corps to become technical director of NAVEGAÇÃO AÉREA BRASILEIRA S/A., which was incorporated on 28 February 1940.

NAB, as it was more popularly referred, utilized American equipment and technical assistance from AMERICAN AIRLINES, but the capital came from Brazilian investors. NAB's first aircraft were received at the beginning of January 1941 and on 28 March it started trial service, not over the established coastal "highway" but north to Recife via Belo Horizonte. NAB received formal authority to operate on 5 May 1941.

The route from Rio de Janeiro was opened, on 6 September 1941, north via Belo Horizonte, Bom Jesus da Lapa, Petrolina to Fortaleza on the northeast coast. The return flight was made the next day, the 120th Anniversary of Brazil's independence.

Rio de Janeiro
vermillion - black

6 September 1941: First flight: Fortaleza - Rio de Janeiro
1,200 rs. postage

NAVEGAÇÃO AÉREA BRASILEIRA S/A
**N. A. B.**
*VIAGEM INAUGURAL*
**P E T R O L I N A**

7 September 1941
Petrolina
vermillion - black

NAVEGAÇÃO AÉREA BRASILEIRA S/A
**N. A. B.**
*VIAGEM INAUGURAL*
**RIO  —  RECIFE**

26 March 1942
São Paulo
red

NAVEGAÇÃO AÉREA BRASILEIRA S/A.
**N. A. B.**
*VIAGEM INAUGURAL*
**RIO  —  RECIFE**

28 March 1942
Rio de Janeiro
vermillion - black

NAVEGAÇÃO AÉREA BRASILEIRA S/A.
**N. A. B.**
*VIAGEM INAUGURAL*
**RIO — RECIFE**
VIA
Belo Horizonte - Lapa - Petrolina

28 March 1942
Rio de Janeiro
vermillion

31 March 1942
Recife
vermillion

The original aircraft proved inadequate and, following additional government subsidies, new planes were obtained. On 28 March 1942 service was inaugurated from Rio de Janeiro to Recife over the same route . Mail from São Paulo is dated 26 March. The return flight was 31 March 1942.

On 26 April 1942 service along the line was extended to João Pessoa, with the return flight the following day (flight covers, opposite page). During October 1942 the line was extended to Teresina and Belém.

NAB made it through World War II and at war's end its small fleet included Lockheed and Douglas aircraft—including the last production model of the famous "workhorse," the DC 3.

Although it continued to appear to operate successfully—having added a link to São Paulo—it went through a series of serious financial difficulties. By March 1948 all service was suspended and the company was declared bankrupt on 17 August 1948.

To protect the creditors the Brazilian government took over the line and it continued to function on a much reduced scale, eventually trying to stay alive by offering discount fares and cargo fees.

It has been said that NAB's acronym allegedly meant *"Não Anda Bem"* (It doesn't go well) and finally that proved true.[1]  On 24 October 1961 N.A.B. was purchased by LÓIDE AÉREO NACIONAL. LÓIDE was founded on 24 August 1949 from the reorganization of TRANSPORTES CARGA AÉREA, S.A. (T.C.A.) which had been founded on 22 December 1947 by Ruy Vacani, one of the founders of ETA.

[These last two airlines, as well as a myriad of others formed after World War II, are not included in this current work.]

◊

27 April 1942: First Flight: João Pessoa - Rio de Janeiro
1,200 rs. postage (two special covers prepared by NAB)

Airplane drawings all to the same scale ~ 1 inch = 30 feet

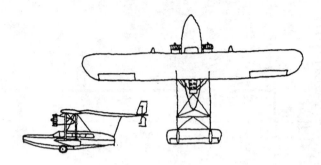

SIKORSKY S 38A

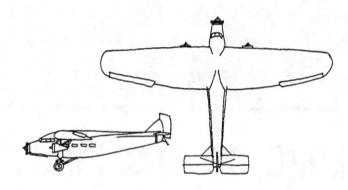

FORD 4AT TRIMOTOR

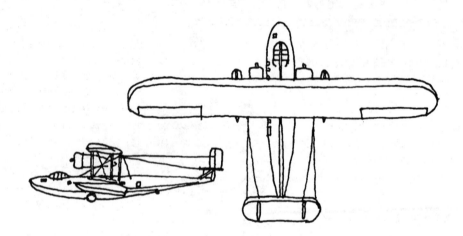

CONSOLIDATED COMMODORE 16

# NEW YORK, RIO & BUENOS AIRES LINE INC.

In 1920 a 23-year old ex-Air Force ace was traveling in the U. S. Southwest, Mexico and other Central American republics as a field engineer (mining) for the Hercules Powder Company. He was approached by the new president of Mexico, Adolfo de la Huerta, to help form a national air force for Mexico. Starting from scratch it was not easy, considering the difficulties involved in both manpower and equipment, but, over the next five years some progress was made. The Air Force helped put down a major rebellion in 1924 which, ironically helped lead to its own demise. A succeeding government apparently decided that such a weapon could be turned against those in power and drastically reduced air activities. The young man, Ralph A. O'Neill, returned to New York.[1]

American aviation was in its infancy in 1926. The Kelly Act (Contract Air Mail Act) of February 1925 had opened the doors to private commercial operators to bid on portions of the potentially lucrative post office-operated mail routes, but, although there were many bidders, few were in operational shape to successfully fly the routes. The first five contracts were awarded on 7 October 1925 and the first actual service, CAM 6 and CAM 7, were flown on 15 February 1926 by the Ford Motor Company.[2] Ford started carrying passengers in August 1926.

The Air Commerce Act, which followed in May 1926, directed the Secretary of Commerce to establish airways for mail and passengers, organize air navigation, and license aircraft and pilots. It became effective 31 December 1926.[3]

Military operations were minimal and gypsy "barnstormers" plied the country selling "joy-rides" and performing stunts at air shows.[4] The general attitude in financial circles was that airplanes and flying were only for daredevils or fools!

The following year another young man changed that attitude and gave aviation progress a sorely needed and popular boost. For the first time the public seemed willing to accept the idea that air travel could be dependable and safe, this in spite of the pilot's reported comment on landing in Paris— 33 1/2 hours after leaving on a solo-flight from New York—that it "felt like a reprieve from the Governor."[5] Investors, although not universally, were now willing to explore the future possibilities of aviation. Charles Lindbergh had made it happen, almost overnight!

Ralph O'Neill had maintained a dream of the potential future of commercial aviation and, perhaps, partly from his travels in Central America and his time spent in Mexico, earnestly believed that a route could (should) be developed linking the Americas. He was especially interested in the east coast, including South America, as the mountains to the west appeared formidable. By 1927 in an attempt to explore this idea, after failing with several other companies, he had convinced the Boeing Airplane Company to back a plan to modernize the military and civilian aircraft of Argentina, Brazil, and Chile. He became their sole sales representative for everything south of the Rio Grande. The following March (1928) he sailed for Rio de Janeiro.[6] It didn't hurt that a fellow passenger on the long voyage was the Ambassador of Brazil, a contact that was to prove useful.

O'Neill's major promotional efforts were to be the F2B, a military pursuit plane; the 40A, a passenger-mail aircraft; and a small flying boat. The 40A was never shipped, the flying boat couldn't fly, and the F2B was demolished in Minas, Uruguay (northeast of Montevideo) in O'Neill's attempt to impress the military with a Rio de Janeiro - Buenos Aires speed flight.[7] The demolition of the F2B, which almost cost him his life, did cost him his job and Boeing's withdrawal (July 1928) opened the way for the young man to pursue his original dream, now with the encouragement of local government officials.

The basic idea was for relatively fast, inexpensive transport between New York and Buenos Aires—to be provided by a new airline, utilizing seaplanes (flying boats) and a new circuit of air service facilities. If air traffic rights could be obtained along the 7,800 mile route—which would involve some 30 cities in 16 countries—the airplanes would run from dawn-to-dusk making 1,000 miles in four stops to pick up passengers and mail—a complete round-trip requiring about two weeks. In addition to the aircraft for the long over-water portions, the project would need operating funds. O'Neill left for New York, the "financial capital."

After six months of effort, often frustrated by the intervention of the only other airline interested in Latin America—PAN AMERICAN—he finally obtained backing of James Rand (Remington-Rand) and Major Reuben Fleet (Consolidated Aircraft). The new company assumed the name of another—TRIMOTOR SAFETY AIRWAYS—a company incorporated by Rand based on his own, and only, Ford Trimotor aircraft. O'Neill didn't care much for the name since it conveyed, albeit indirectly, a sense of insecurity about the idea of flying. A new name, modeled on the New York, New Haven & Hartford Railroad line of the time—"linking the great cities of the Atlantic"—was devised. The new company was called the NEW YORK, RIO & BUENOS AIRES LINE.

The NEW YORK, RIO & BUENOS AIRES LINE, or as it was more commonly known, NYRBA or the "near beer" line, was incorporated on 17 March 1929 after securing a mail transport contract from Argentina (February 1929) which was shortly followed by an agreement with Uruguay.[8] Shares were sold and, in the course of the next year, some $6 million had been provided by investors.

Possibly as a result of O'Neill's long-standing friendship with Rear Admiral William A. Moffett, Chief of the U. S. Navy's Bureau of Aeronautics, the first production model of the Sikorsky S-38 amphibian, now dubbed the S-38A, was diverted to NYRBA.[9] On 11 June 1929 O'Neill left New York to survey the route, arriving in Buenos Aires on 13 July, a month later after a rather eventful (and sometimes harrowing) flight—hops, really—down the undeveloped coastline.

O'Neill ordered 14 Consolidated Commodores, flying boats of much greater capacity than the Sikorsky, and acquired some Ford Trimotors which were put to immediate use. On 21 August 1929 the 142-mile trip from Buenos Aires to Montevideo was inaugurated. On 15 October NYRBA received its Brazilian authorization and four days later the route Buenos Aires - Santiago was opened.[10] This was followed on 15 November by a survey flight to La Paz, Bolivia.

(Don Thomas, *Nostalgia Panamericana*, 1987, Courtesy of the author.)

In order to comply with the restrictions imposed by the Brazilian government, a subsidiary, NYRBA DO BRASIL, S.A., was founded on 22 October 1929. The decree (No. 19,079) of 24 January 1930 authorized its functions, however, a survey flight had been made between Buenos Aires and Rio de Janeiro 12 days before. The first return flight occurred on 7 February 1930 and was, to my knowledge, the first time a cachet and the distinctive cancellation were used (opposite page, above).[11]

Because NYRBA was an international carrier it, like AÉROPOSTALE, had to use the government's stamps, i.e., it could not issue its own stamps. Additional survey flights were made, one stage at a time, in preparation for the first through-service northbound. By the end of 1929 NYRBA had four Sikorsky's, three Fords and one Commodore in service, and mail contracts with the Brazil and Argentine governments. O'Neill was anxiously awaiting the opportunity to bid on the lucrative Foreign Air Mail (FAM) contracts being awarded by the U.S. Post Office. It would be the basis for the entire line, but it would not be his. O'Neill had underestimated the competition.

Correio Aéreo: A History of the Development of Air Mail Service in Brazil

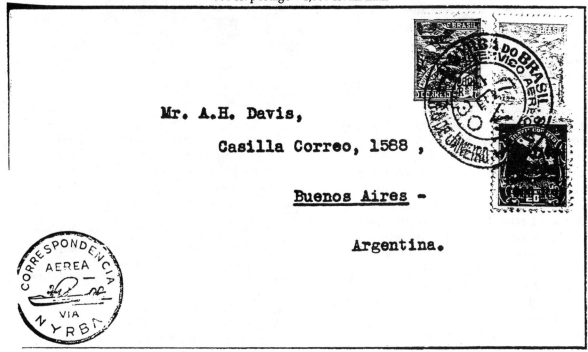

Mr. A.H. Davis,

Casilla Correo, 1588 ,

Buenos Aires -

Argentina.

In his original planning O'Neill counted on securing—or at least being allowed through competitive bidding to try to secure—U. S. governmental mail contracts which would help subsidize operations. After some personal difficulties with Assistant Postmaster General Glover, but with the intervention of Rand's senatorial friend, O'Neill was granted an appointment with President Calvin Coolidge. "Silent Cal" assured O'Neill that the Foreign Air Mail Act of the previous year required competitive bidding and no favoritism would be shown.

Times change, so do Presidents. Herbert Hoover took office in 1929 and with him came the Republican Party Chairman, Walter F. Brown, in the role of Postmaster General. There was no love lost between Brown and O'Neill. Accounts differ, but, suffice to say, FAM 5, 6, 7, and 8 routes went to PAN AMERICAN in the first three months of the year. (PAN AMERICAN had been awarded FAM 4, Key West, Florida - Havana, Cuba, in October 1927 as the low—and apparently only—bidder.) FAM 9, the west coast of South America, was awarded to PANAGRA in May.[12] PAN AMERICAN, therefore, covered all of the Caribbean, Mexico and Central America, and all of South America, except the portion between Dutch Guiana and Buenos Aires. Accusations and scandal regarding the awards followed. Nevertheless, O'Neill felt that he had not only the right, but the advantage, in bidding on

FAM 10, the east coast route he was in the process of developing. Logical, idealistic, but, overly naive.

Anticipating the announcement of the bidding period O'Neill pressed on and early the next year he thought the time ripe to prove his efforts. The second and third Commodores were damaged on their flights down, so the route north would be flown with available equipment—all of it! On 18 February 1930 the first plane left Santiago and did an overnight stop in Buenos Aires. The next morning O'Neill, himself, took over—for this was to be an enormous publicity venture and the "establishment" of NYRBA! Mail bags were stuffed—with what was mostly souvenir covers.

There are a variety of accounts of the actual flight, the events that took place, and the equipment used. The trip was filled with accidents and other mishaps.[13]

A Consolidated Commodore 16, *Rio de Janeiro*, and a Sikorsky S-38B, *Tampa*, left Buenos Aires loaded with mail. The *Rio* was forced down at Florianópolis with a broken oil line and the *Tampa* damaged a pontoon landing at Santos. Mail was then transported by auto over 400 miles of dirt roads to Rio de Janeiro where it was to be put aboard another Sikorsky, *Porto Alegre*. It was this plane that the fledgling ETA (see EMPRESA DE

TRANSPORTES AÉREOS LIMITADA) officials "libeled" with a $175,000 damage suit, claiming that NYRBA had "violated their contract." Postal officials apparently tried to intervene on the basis that such an impoundment of the plane was interrupting the conveyance of the mail.

Not to be outdone, O'Neill had ordered another Sikorsky, *Bahia*, to position itself in Nictheroy (now Niteroi, upper right in map, right), a "small town across the bay,"—and out of the jurisdiction of the Rio courts.[14] A motor launch provided the escape and O'Neill and the mails were soon on their way northward bound for Fortaleza where the mails would be transferred to yet another aircraft. Apparently, at least seven planes were used during the trip. Finally, on 26 February, Miami was reached. Much to his chagrin, O'Neill was forced to turn over the mail, that he had carried from Buenos Aires and points along the route, to the U.S. postal authorities—he had no contract with the U.S. and, accordingly, could not complete the transport to his final destination, New York.

NYRBA had developed several different cachets proclaiming: "First Brazilian - U.S.A. Air Mail," or "Primeira Mala Aérea Brasileira - Americana," in a variety of type faces, sizes, and colors (right).

Map of the Bay of Rio de Janeiro
(Funk & Wagnals Comp[any's] *1924 Atlas of the World and Gazetteer*).

## NYRBA DO BRAZIL

### VÔO INAUGURAL
### Porto Alegre - New York

First Brazilian U.S.Airmail

First Brazilian USA Air Mail

19 February 1930: First Flight: Rio de Janeiro - U. S. A. (by air only to Miami, FL)
700rs. postage + 3,000 rs. air mail

NYRBA produced a rather colorful label (below) picturing a gull bearing a "letter" across the waters between New York (Statue of Liberty) and Rio de Janeiro (Sugar Loaf mountain). The Brazilian government apparently used this as a basis for a 3,000rs. stamp (150% enlarged, right) that was issued for this inaugural flight on 19 February 1930, patterning the design on the NYRBA etiquette, but substituting the words "Aérea" for "NYRBA."

The philatelic value of this first flight was not lost on any of the "players" of the day. A. H. Davis sends a souvenir to none other than the infamous stamp dealer A. C. Roessler (opposite, below). Fritz Hammer (see SYNDICATO CONDOR) obliged two of his cohorts via SCADTA's New York office with special NYRBA envelopes and the first day of issue of the new stamp (below).

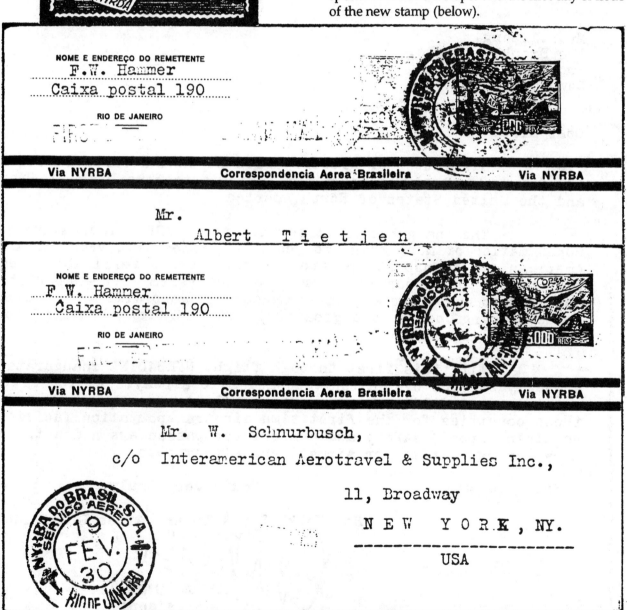

19 February 1930: First Flight: Rio de Janeiro - U. S. A. (by air only to Miami, FL)
300 rs. postage + 3,000 rs. air mail.

# LINEAS AEREAS NYRBA

### "NEW YORK, RIO & BUENOS AIRES LINE INC."
### DE LA "TRIMOTOR SAFETY AIRWAYS Inc."
### BUENOS AIRES

DIRECTORIO LOCAL:
Av. R. SAENZ PEÑA 637
U. T. 38. MAYO 2824

DIRECTORIO CENTRAL:
929, GRAYBAR BUILDING
LEXINGTON AVE. & 43 ST.
NEW YORK

Dirección Telegráfica: "NYRBALYNE"

ADMINISTRACION:
Av. R. SAENZ PEÑA 910
U. T. 35, LIBERTAD 1800

Feb. 19 1930.

Mr.F.J.Lang,
The Brooklyn Eagle,
Broklyn,
New York, U.S.A.

Dear Sirs:

This letter of greeting from NYRBALINE comes to you on the first direct airmail service linking Argentina, Uruguay, Brazil, and the United States of North America.

The inauguration of service over NYRBA lines signalizes consummation of more than two years of pioneering; years in which American air transport operators working under formidable handicaps have laid foundations for a modern system of transportation designed to encourage a greater measure of good will and to assist in developing better and greater trade relations between the peoples of the Americas.

With this first through flight NYRBALINE inaugurates a weekly service over a ten thousand mile airway, spanning sixteen countries and colonies, and makes available for the people of those countries for the first time air transportation facilities combining speed, safety and comfort for passengers and a tremendous saving of time for airmail and air-express.

Yours very truly,

New York, Rio & Buenos Aires Line, Inc.,

R. A. O'Neill
President.

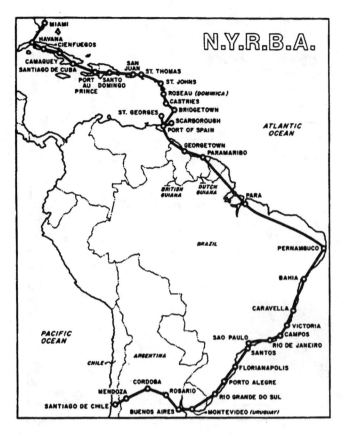

Miami to Santiago Route[15]

After a management hassle in Miami, O'Neill continued on to New York. There he found that Jim Rand had lost his money in the stock market crash, and the company had a somewhat different "administration." Undeterred, O'Neill returned to South America to develop his "railroad."

Regular eight-day service ensued between Miami and Buenos Aires. O'Neill had divided the route into eight divisions: each about 1,000 miles; each with its own shops, equipment and personnel; and each a costly operation.[16] O'Neill felt that the "rest" between divisions would mean that the equipment would last longer. PAN AMERICAN, on the other hand, believed that the planes would become—as they did—obsolete so fast that there was no reason to "save" them.

Planned docks and floats along the route were slow in coming and the small boat (or dugout canoe) transfers were somewhat hazardous. Gasoline was added from five-gallon cans, manually poured into the top wing through a chamois-covered funnel! Most of the repairs had to be made to the Commodores while they were still in the water, as only Buenos Aires had facilities to haul the craft out. Part problems usually resulted in the cannibalization of other planes. PAN AMERICAN publicly offered its facilities to NYRBA, but, it appears, at the same time they were attempting to sabotage it.

The Argentina Post Office suddenly ordered NYRBA to comply with the contract requirement that their mail be delivered to the U.S. in seven days rather than eight. O'Neill was forced to use chaser planes (faster single-engine models) to catch up to a plane further along the route. An effective solution, but an expensive one. PAN AMERICAN's initial survey flights down the east coast were permitted to use NYRBA's facilities—until PAN AMERICAN announced a weekly service to Rio de Janeiro.

The Consolidated Commodore *Havana* in service for NYRBA.[17]

20 February 1930: Recife - U. S. A. (by air only to Miami, FL)
300 rs. postage (meter dated 13 February 1930) + 3,000 rs. air mail

? February 1930: Pará - U. S. A. (by air only to Miami, FL)
500 rs. postage + 6,000 rs. air mail
The unusual and undecipherable cancel and the excessive postage make the parentage of this cover questionable.
The particular two-line text cachet is known only on similar covers.

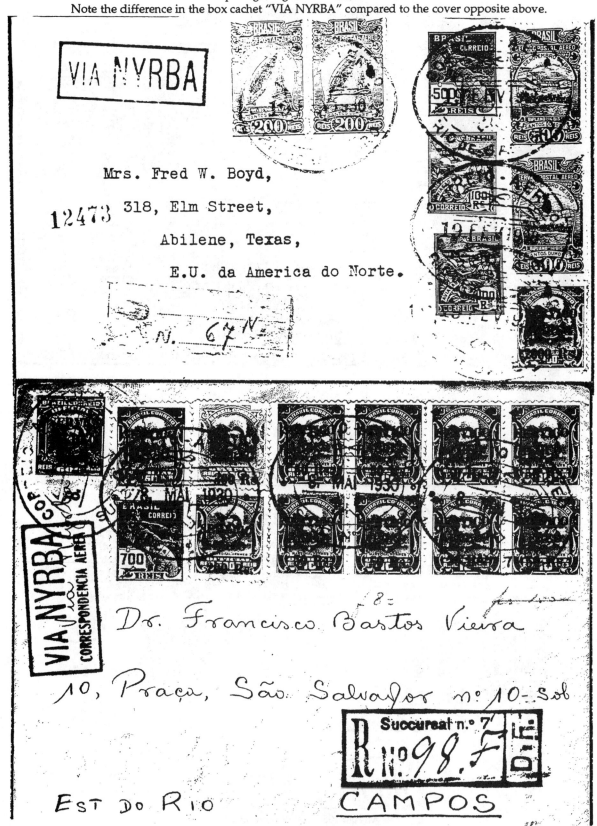

19 February 1930: Rio de Janeiro - U. S. A. (by air only to Miami, FL)
700 rs. postage/registration + 3,400 rs. air mail
Note the difference in the box cachet "VIA NYRBA" compared to the cover opposite above.

VIA NYRBA

Mrs. Fred W. Boyd,

12473   318, Elm Street,

Abilene, Texas,

E.U. da America do Norte.

N. 67 N.

VIA NYRBA
CORRESPONDENCIA AEREA

Dr. Francisco Bastos Vieira

10, Praça, São Salvador nº 10-sob

Succursal nº 7
R Nº 98.F   D.F.

Est do Rio   CAMPOS

8 May 1930: Rio de Janeiro (?) - Campos
700 rs. postage /registration + 1,700 rs. air mail

28 August 1930: Pará - U. S. A. (by air only to Miami, FL)
300 rs. postage + 3,200 rs. air mail
Contrast between cancels on this cover and that at the bottom of page 84.
Circular NYRBA cachet applied in very light red ink.

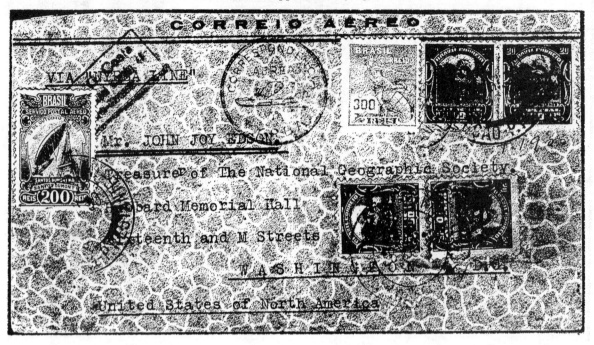

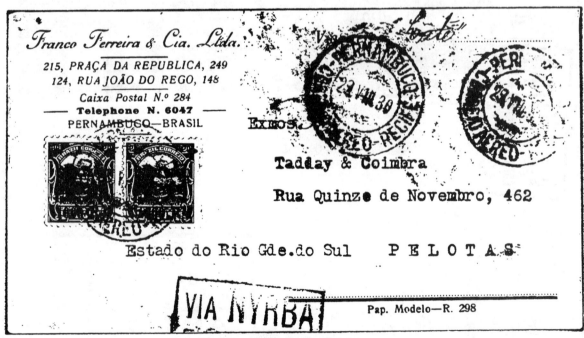

29 August 1930: Recife - Pelotas
300 rs. postage + 2,000 rs. air mail
Both of these covers testify that NYRBA was still flying while in the death throes with PAN AMERICAN.

## For Speed — Comfort — Safety
### Travel by Nyrbaline
Use Nyrbaline Airmail and Express Facilities

NEW YORK, RIO & BUENOS AIRES LINE, INC.
420 Lexington Avenue, New York City.

NYRBA DO BRAZIL, S. A.
Edificio Guinle, Rio de Janeiro.

LINEAS AEREAS NYRBA.
Avenida Saenz Peña 910, Buenos Aires.

**NYRBA LINES**

**LINKING THE AMERICAS**

### Weeks Faster to SOUTH AMERICA
### BRAZIL — URUGUAY — ARGENTINA

BY THE ROUTE of the GIANT FLYING YACHTS

# NYRBA
## NEW YORK RIO & BUENOS AIRES LINE Inc.

Advertising for a service ahead of its time. (Courtesy of Don Thomas.)

O'Neill continued to spend his time and money developing the route in Argentina and Brazil—NYRBA may have bought out ETA's limited routes—ignoring his New York office, where the funds came from, and Washington officials, where the mail contracts came from. The new Postmaster General did not favor competitive bidding. PAN AMERICAN already had the Miami - Dutch Guiana Contract, so the choice for the Dutch Guiana - Buenos Aires Contract seemed obvious. Additionally, O'Neill had air mail contracts with the South American governments at very low rates. His contracts with Argentina and Uruguay, for example, were for $6.50 per pound, whereas, PANAGRA's FAM 9 (west coast) was $22.50.[18]

NYRBA was now losing money at the rate of almost half-a-million dollars a month. PAN AMERICAN started pressuring the New York investors to dispose of their operations. Postmaster General Brown would not advertise the east coast contract until the competition was eliminated.[19] Brown did not concern himself with questions of anti-trust violation.[20]

With the continually mounting financial losses, NYRBA's net worth (stock) dwindled. On 19 August 1930 (officially, 15 September) NYRBA surrendered and sold out to PAN AMERICAN. U. S. contract route FAM 10 was advertised the next day and awarded to PAN AMERICAN. On 17 October 1930 NYRBA DO BRASIL became PANAIR DO BRASIL.

◊

A PAN AMERICAN Sikorsky S-42 flying boat over Sugar Loaf mountain and the harbor with the huge statue of Christ the Redeemer on Corcovado overlooking Botafogo Bay in an artist's concept for a 1938 poster advertisement (from Don Thomas, *Poster Art of the Airlines*, 1989, courtesy of the author.).

# PAN AMERICAN WORLD AIRWAYS, INC.

In the early years of this century land routes in many parts of Latin America were poorly developed—a result of terrain and economic conditions. In some places, the airplane was found to be not only the most efficient and safest means of transport but, often, the only means. Latin American governments were therefore willing to grant favorable franchises to those promoters who wished to—and financially could afford to—develop air services in their respective regions.

One of the earliest successful promoters was a World War I Austrian "warbird," Doctor Peter Paul von Bauer, who, in December 1919, established the first successful airline in South America.[1] The SOCIEDAD COLOMBO-ALEMANA DE TRANSPORTES AÉREOS (SCADTA) was incorporated in Colombia, began survey flights in 1920 and started regular service the following year. The line connected the isolated mountain capital, Bogotá, via rail from Girardot, with the seaport, Barranquilla, some 650 miles away.[2] The airplane covered the distance in about seven hours, whereas the surface route—rail and steamer down the Magdalena River—took a week in the wet season and almost a month in the dry. Time saved combined with a good safety record produced heavy traffic in spite of relatively high fares. SCADTA was also allowed, but not required, to establish its own postal system—offices, rates, and stamps—and to retain all the revenue from such operations. It received no direct subsidy from the Colombian government.

Dr. von Bauer had envisioned a major expansion of services to Central America, the Caribbean, and, eventually, the United States. On the other hand, the U. S. expansion interests were limited to a few pioneers who, without any real government or aircraft industry support, developed some routes to Mexico and the Caribbean. The first (1920), AERO-MARINE AIRWAYS, operated a winter (mostly tourist) service between Key West and Havana until the short season and high operating costs caught up to it after two years.

In 1925 and 1926 Dr. von Bauer visited Washington with the aim of obtaining landing rights. Apparently fearful of a foreign airline operating close to the Panama Canal, the U. S. government refused. By then, the government had begun to realize the value of such a line connecting the countries of the Western Hemisphere and was eager, therefore, to help any American interested in Latin America.[2] In 1927, there were three possibilities.

First, there was FLORIDA AIRWAYS, organized by Captain Eddie Rickenbacker, who would eventually build EASTERN AIR LINES, but who, in this case, would run into financial setbacks. Second, PAN AMERICAN, INCORPORATED, had secured a mail contract with the Cuban government.[3] But, it was the third, the AVIATION CORPORATION OF AMERICA, under the control of Juan Terry Trippe, which secured exclusive landing rights in Cuba. Thus, PAN AMERICAN's mail contract was virtually useless and the company sold out to Trippe, who renamed it PAN AMERICAN AIRWAYS, INC., absorbing FLORIDA in the process.

On 8 March 1927 PAN AMERICAN AIRWAYS, INC. was formed with the financial support of East Coast shipping and railroad interests. Headquartered in Miami, the southern terminus of those transportation companies, it was in a good position to deal with the inevitable expansion to the south. PAN AMERICAN was awarded the Key West - Havana (FAM 4) contract and, with a borrowed airplane, hastily started operations on 19 October 1927 to comply with the terms.[4] Regular service was to follow within ten days and passenger service started the following September. By the end of 1928 seven planes were operating.

It should be noted that President Coolidge's message to Congress on 6 December 1927 called for an overall, planned, system of air mail services for South America. On 8 March of the following year Congress voted the Foreign Air Mail Act (FAM) and by the end of the month, bids were advertised. Needless to say, PAN AMERICAN was awarded FAM 4 officially, since it had been already in operation.

The company was under the almost absolute control of Juan Trippe, whose ambitious appetite soon consumed other operational airlines. WEST INDIAN AIR EXPRESS (Cuba-Dominican Republic-Puerto Rico) and COMPANIA MEXICANA DE AVIACION, S.A. (Texas-Mexico) were absorbed in January 1929, the latter providing the basis for the lucrative FAM 8, as the company had exclusive landing rights in Mexico.

Government mail contracts, far more profitable on international lines than on domestic, were obtained through a combination of advanced planning and a favorable attitude of the Postmaster General Harry S. New and his successor (1928) Walter F. Brown.[5]

American operators in foreign lands were expected to need maximum government support against foreign competition (supported by their respective governments), and, therefore, dividing up the routes to various low bidders would, eventually, lead to their individual financial starvation. Consolidating the work and, hence, the support was deemed to be the answer. It was also a way to build a strong airline. Brown demanded a company of substance with sound financial support and a determination to succeed—a "chosen instrument."[6]

These criteria were tailor-made for Juan Trippe, who had one other guarantee of success—an uncanny ability to be one step ahead of the opposition, especially in the area of acquiring foreign concessions. Stymied by the fact that mail and small packages could be shipped faster from Rio de Janeiro and Buenos Aires to Europe than to the United States—over a longer distance and with a South Atlantic crossing—Brown looked to Trippe to provide reliable, efficient service rather than concern himself with the free enterprise system. PAN AMERICAN would be awarded successive FAM contracts, each at the highest subsidy rate allowed.

Transportation services down the west coast of South America were under the domination of W. R.

Grace and Company—importer/exporter, bank, and steamship line. Grace had an entrenched position with the political and economic powers in the area. Trippe's only chance of penetrating this field was to form an equal partnership with Grace in February 1929: PAN AMERICAN-GRACE AIRWAYS, INC. (PANAGRA).

A month later FAM 9 was awarded and service was started as far as Peru by May, extended to Santiago (July) and, finally, to Buenos Aires (October). This was not a happy "marriage" for Grace. A year and one half later, when it swallowed NYRBA (see NEW YORK, RIO & BUENOS AIRES LINE), PAN AMERICAN would have an alternate route to Argentina and PANAGRA would be neglected. As an equal partner, PAN AMERICAN could block expansion of the west coast services and it would look on PANAGRA as a branch or subsidiary line.

PAN AMERICAN was authorized to operate in Brazil on 25 June 1930 and immediately started some survey flights along the coast sharing some facilities with NYRBA, just as NYRBA had done with PAN AMERICAN north of Brazil. As the pressure was applied to end the competition, open hostilities developed between the two companies. On 30 June 1930 PAN AMERICAN "inaugurated" service northbound, perhaps in reply to NYRBA's February flight. Covers exist from both São Paulo and Rio de Janeiro on that date.

On 7 July 1930 NYRBA made a flight from Recife to Rio de Janeiro which was provided with a cachet (top right) about a month before the company surrendered to PAN AMERICAN. Financially and politically squeezed, NYRBA sold out 19 August 1930. FAM 10, the entire east coast of South America, was awarded to PAN AMERICAN, "the chosen instrument," the next day. Formal transfer of NYRBA was accomplished on 15 September.

Shown (right) is a cachet for a NYRBA DO BRASIL flight—Manaus - Belém - Rio de Janeiro—and a PAN AMERICAN propaganda cachet (below right) for the route—Ceara - Rio de Janeiro—dated the following day. NYRBA was still flying, but no longer under the auspices of Ralph O'Neill.

On 17 October 1930, NYRBA DO BRASIL became PANAIR DO BRASIL, S.A. It was authorized by the Ministry of Transportation on 22 November and by the postal authorities on 8 December, although it actually initiated its first international flight—Rio de Janeiro - New York on 1 December. (The post office approval was possibly delayed by the October 1930 revolution which brought a new administration to power under Getúlio Vargas.) Several stops were made along the route in Brazil, but apparently only Rio was provided with a cachet (at right, reduced). PANAIR was headquartered in Rio, but its main facilities were at Belem—some 2,500 miles and, initially, 5 days away—the northern terminus and connecting point for PAN AMERICAN services. The first passenger service was provided on 2 March 1931.

By early 1931 identity symbols (labels at right) were developed which linked the "parent" and "child."

On 11 October 1931 PANAIR marked the opening of service from Bahia to Rio de Janeiro with a blue cachet (below right).

Between 1 and 3 November 1931, PANAIR extended its service from Rio de Janeiro through to Buenos Aires, with overnight stops at Florianópolis, Porto Alegre, Rio Grande do Sul, and Montevideo (AAMS F6-100). At this time there was no night flying on the route. The return flight from Buenos Aires to Miami started out on 7 November 1931. (Shown, next page, are two covers, each carried on a leg of one of these flights: AAMS Nos. F6-100a and F6-107b/t. The idea of airmail souvenirs complete with cachets and carefully placed stamps was not a new one, but a well used one.)

NYRBA
JUL-7'04
RECIFE (PERNAMBUCO)

NYRBA, 7 July 1930

MANÃOS-AMAZONAS E ACRE
**VIA NYRBA**
Corresp. aerea REGISTRADA

NYRBA, 4 September 1930

CORRESPONDENCIA AEREA
**PAA**

PAN AMERICAN, 5 September 1930

FIRST FLIGHT
AIR MAIL
UNDER
F. A. M. 10
BRAZIL–UNITED STATES

PANAIR DO BRASIL, 1 December 1930

VIA
PAA

Via PANAIR        Correspondencia Aerea

PAN AMERICAN AIRWAYS label
PANAIR label

PANAIR DO BRASIL
OCT 11 '31
BAHIA

PANAIR, 11 October 1931

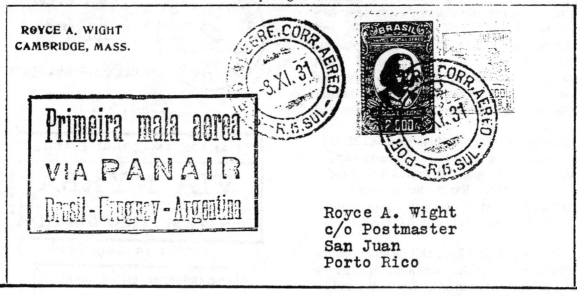

First Return Flight: 1 November 1931: Porto Alegre - Florianópolis
200 rs. postage (the additional surtax on the commemoratives was not collected) + 500 rs. air.

With the absorption of NYRBA in 1930 and the withdrawal of the French AÉROPOSTALE the following year, PAN AMERICAN/PAN AIR had only one serious competitor for services within Brazil: the German supported, SYNDICATO CONDOR, whose lines mostly paralleled PAN AIR. The feud would last almost 12 years with PAN AMERICAN developing long distance routes linking the capitals of Argentina and Brazil with the United States,

while CONDOR worked on domestic routes within the countries and developed service facilities, leaving long distance service to its associate, LUFT HANSA. This competition had the net effect of making Brazil into a viable airline nation, with routes and service facilities linking the important coastal points and extensions into the interior, which had little—in some cases, no—surface ties. Airplanes became a "normal" means of travel and, as a result, for some time after the Second World War, Brazil's passenger traffic volume was second only to that of the United States.[7]

On 24 February 1932 service between Bahia and Rio de Janeiro saw the first use of a new propaganda cachet applied in purple. The cachet pictures the Commodore 16, one of the fleet that PANAIR acquired from the NYRBA transaction. On 14 February 1933 the same route found the first use of a new purple propaganda cachet used in conjunction with the blue Bahia cachet/date stamp.

PANAIR opened up an Amazon service to connect Belem with Manaus, a city still of some importance but no longer the expanding capital of the rubber boom years. With an eye to its public image, PANAIR produced stationery and envelopes which suggested a measure of the formal, quality service it offered. Pictured (below) is a Commodore 16. These envelopes, modified over time, showed the ever changing aircraft in the PANAIR system providing a mini-history of the aircraft used (see p. 99).

PANAIR, 24 February 1932

PANAIR, 14 February 1933

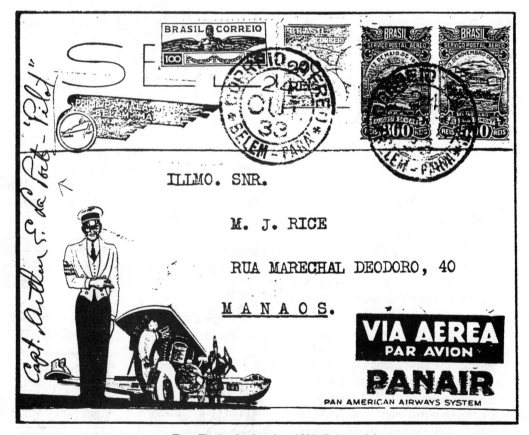

First Flight: 24 October 1933: Belém - Manaus
300 rs. postage + 800 rs. air + 100 rs. airport facilities tax

PAN AMERICAN pushed the development of long range flying boats by aircraft manufacturers and, in 1934, had the four-engine Sikorsky S-42 in operation in South America (see illustration, page 88).

In February 1934, amidst a government scandal, President Roosevelt had all domestic air mail contracts canceled. (FAMs were not affected.) For a brief period of time the U. S. Army would fly the mail in the United States, until the obvious results of their inexperience, including many fatalities, caused the general public to demand a return to the contract system. Under the new contracts, domestic carriers suffered heavy losses for at least the first two years and, in general until 1939, in spite of increased passenger and mail traffic. Some consideration had been made to terminate PAN AMERICAN's contracts, as it was felt that they had been awarded without competitive bidding, and, in fact, public hearings were held in January 1935. It was eventually decided that continuation of the contracts was in the best interests of the United States and in protection of U. S. interests in Latin America. It was also determined that no other airline—apparently including the U. S. Navy—could perform the services provided by PAN AMERICAN.

In May 1934 PANAIR commenced service between Manaus and Rio de Janeiro. Letters received a special postmark cachet.

In November 1935 PAN AMERICAN took over the main routes from PANAIR, leaving it to develop local services. It should be remembered that while PANAIR and the Latin American arm of PAN AMERICAN were developing routes in the Americas, other divisions of PAN AM—as it came to be called—were extending the lines of the company around the world. The first *China Clipper* took off from San Francisco bound for Manila, on 22 November 1935, loaded with mail. PAN AM was rapidly becoming a major world airline "system," a word that had already been added to the parent company name.

The Douglas DC-3 was introduced into Latin America in 1937. Lockheed Electras were also introduced and both would become the workhorses for those areas where the flying boats were of little use—the interior expansion. On 21 March 1937 PANAIR inaugurated service between Rio de Janeiro and Belo Horizonte, the first use of the Electras in Brazil.

This service was followed, eight days later, with a Manaus - Rio Branco route, with return the following day. (The aircraft in the cachet, below, may be an attempt at a rendering of a Sikorsky S 43, Baby Clipper, but it appears to have only one engine.)

Meanwhile PAN AMERICAN developed international ties with a diagonal route line opened between Rio de Janeiro, Brazil - Asunción, Paraguay - Buenos Aires, Argentina (1,600 miles) and marked by a cachet on 28 December 1937.

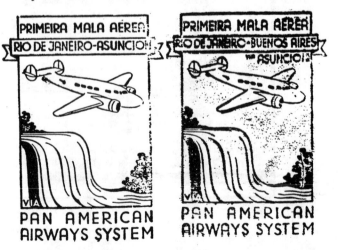

Consolidated Commodores were replaced by Sikorsky S 43's—"Baby Clippers"—and, as a result of a 1936 governmental decree, by September 1938 the American pilots and staff of PANAIR were replaced by Brazilian nationals. This was the first step on the part of the government to decrease or eliminate "foreign" influence and control of airlines operating within Brazil. By 1942 PAN AM would reduce its 100% ownership of PANAIR by selling off its stock to Brazilian investors, so that by 1945 it would have less than 50% of the shares. As we shall see, the Brazilian government's response to CONDOR would be much more drastic. The spirit of nationalism would prevail.

When the U. S. Foreign Air Mail Act was drafted (1928), the maximum rates—which PAN AM had received at the outset—were presumably fixed to allow reasonable profits from the low volume traffic and expenses resulting from the inefficient equipment of the time. However, the ten-year contracts of 1929-1930 obviously assured very satisfactory returns with the higher volume and improved equipment of the late 1930s—so much so that routes, especially PAN AM's, might be the subject of competitive bidding when up for renewal.

However, in July 1938 the U. S. Civil Aeronautics Act came into effect, and the Authority (later, Board) was established to regulate technical and economic aspects of the American air transportation industry. Airlines, which previously held title to their respective routes only by virtue of the mail contracts that had been won, were now to be granted certificates of public convenience and necessity (similar to utilities).

Competitive bidding was abandoned. The Authority would grant franchises on competition "necessary to assure sound development" of air transport systems "properly adapted to the present and future needs of the foreign and domestic commerce of the U. S., the postal service and the national defense." The Authority would also set the rates.

PAN AM and PANAGRA received the necessary certificates in August 1940 and continued to operate under rates originally established in their post office contracts until the middle of 1942. Net payments to PAN AM/PANAGRA for the period 1 July 1929-30 June 1940 totaled $47.2 million, while during the same period all the U.S. domestic lines received $59.8 million—while flying almost eight

A 1939 stationery folder given to passengers (Don Thomas, *Nostalgia Panamericana*, 1987, courtesy of the author).

times the passenger mileage of PAN AM. The PAN AM mail rates—which in 1940 were three times those of U. S. domestic lines—were drastically reduced in July 1942. The rates were now more comparable.

In January 1939 PANAIR inaugurated the lines Rio de Janeiro - Belo Horizonte - Araxa - Uberaba and Rio de Janeiro - Belo Horizonte - Pocos de Caldas.

The advent of World War II, the rise of the Axis powers, and the potential threat to the stability of the "Free World," or more specifically the Western Hemisphere, was evident. However, the attitude of the American republics—including the U. S.—was far from clear; most South American nations were psychologically and/or technically unable to take any single-handed action against the potential "menace" of what were nothing more than public utilities, however important.

Additionally, the individual Axis-sponsored airlines were not unpopular: some had rendered satisfactory service for 10 years or more; all employed large segments of the local populations. Moreover, many of the countries were wholly dependent on the Axis lines for air transportation services.

It became evident that only the United States could offer an alternative—the capability of supplying the airplanes, the technicians and, most importantly, the financial help—for substitutive services. As we shall see, the United States was instrumental in the removal of the Axis influence from air transportation in the Western Hemisphere.

It is interesting to note here that SCADTA, founded in Colombia by Germans in 1919 and primarily run by Germans, operated to within 300 miles of the Panama Canal. When the American Congress began to investigate this "threat," it was surprised—as was the Colombian government—to learn that this "national" airline had been almost wholly owned by PAN AM since 1931. The "threat" was easily and swiftly eliminated by the wholesale replacement of the German personnel in June 1940.

Sometimes PAN AM's dealings back-fired. In mid-1940 PAN AM secured the rights to a shorter route from Belem to Rio de Janeiro by way of the Barreiras Cutoff—cutting directly across the "shoulder" from the mouth of the Amazon to the (then) national capital. The government was to later take the position that this route freed the coastal operations for domestic lines and, because the government-protected lines had given up the internal route (which, in fact, they never had), the national lines would be given exclusive rights along the coast in "compensation."

On 6 November 1940 PANAIR opened the line, Rio de Janeiro - Governador Valadores. The return flight was 14 November to Rio and Belo Horizonte and from Belo Horizonte back on 21 November.

In May 1939 PAN AM had initiated a "mid-Atlantic route" New York - Bermuda - Lisbon - Marseilles, the first flight of the *Yankee Clipper*, the last of the big flying boats, a Boeing B-314. This was followed by the "North-Atlantic route" to England, via Newfoundland and Ireland. The security of these routes was brought to question with the clouds of war on the horizon and President Roosevelt pushed PAN AM and Brazil into the mutual development of weather/radio stations, service and docking facilities, and passenger/crew accommodations for an alternative route along Brazil's northern coast to Natal and across to Africa.[8] On 8 December 1941 PAN AM christened the route: Belem - Natal - Bathurst - Lagos - Leopoldville.[9]

Airplane drawings all to the same scale ~ 1 inch = 30 feet

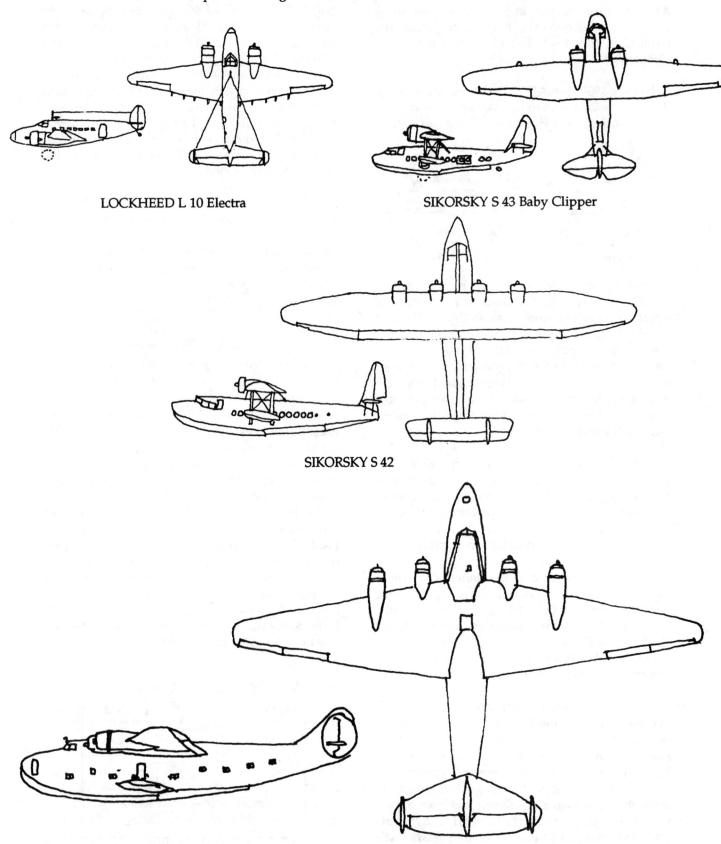

LOCKHEED L 10 Electra

SIKORSKY S 43 Baby Clipper

SIKORSKY S 42

BOEING B 314 Yankee Clipper

Europe (29 March) and the openings of direct service between Rio de Janeiro and Madrid (22 May) and Zurich (5 September). The following year the 1,000th transatlantic crossing was honored.

Specially prepared covers honored the Silver Anniversary of PANAIR with printed cachets, but eleven years later, PANAIR went bankrupt and its services were taken over by the national line, CRUZEIRO.[11] In March 1963 PAN AM took occupancy of its world headquarters sitting on top of Grand Central Railroad Station in New York. Juan Trippe handed the reins over to Harold Gray, a former Chief Pilot, in 1964, the same year that the company's Latin American Division closed down.

PAN AMERICAN AIRWAYS continued to operate worldwide. Its fleet enjoyed the top-of-the-line jets that poured from designers' drafting boards at a seemingly awesome rate.

After many years of in-fighting and court litigation, PAN AM's relationship with Grace ended when PANAGRA merged with BRANIFF (1967). After additional legal battles were ended in 1980, PAN AM acquired a domestic airline, NATIONAL AIRLINES, in competition with EASTERN AIR LINES. Some have questioned whether this was an advisable move.[12]

After the death of Juan Trippe, on 3 April 1981, the company continued on a somewhat unsteady course under the Airline Deregulation Act passed the year before.[13] The advent of terrorist attacks on the most visible image of the U. S. did not help ridership on its international routes and culminated in the disaster over Lockerbie, Scotland, in December 1988.

The 1940 printed envelope (see page 93).[10]

During the war PAN AM's facilities, planes and experience were directed to the war effort—training of military pilots, ferrying supplies and aircraft across the Atlantic, and building new airbases in Africa and elsewhere. PAN AM was also very active in the Pacific.

PAN AM had already started selling its assets—the routes it pioneered in the Pacific went to UNITED. Finally, it too succumbed to the pressures of finances and competition. PAN AMERICAN AIRWAYS was at last a victim to the same kind of treatment it had used on others. The company filed for bankruptcy on 8 January 1991. In 1993 the name and logo were sold to a communications company. PAN AM, which held a virtual monopoly on international travel until World War II, with management skilled at lobbying in Washington and conducting diplomacy abroad, had become the United States' "almost official" airline.[14] Now it is no more.

Nighttime service was inaugurated—Rio de Janeiro - São Paulo—on 1 May 1944 and was marked with a green cachet (above, reduced). Following the war, service was inaugurated between Brazil and Europe via Africa, from Rio de Janeiro (29-31 March 1946) and São Paulo (1 April 1946).

In 1947 service was opened between Brazil and Egypt (Cairo) and Turkey (Istanbul). In 1948 direct lines were opened between Rio de Janeiro and Buenos Aires (26 March) and Frankfurt, Germany (30 March). Also in 1948 cachets marked the second anniversary of PAN AM's transatlantic service to

◊

A VARIG Junkers F 13 (possibly *Livramento*) aircraft over the state of Rio Grande do Sul, with VARIG's route lines indicated and the *Lagôa dos Patos* (Duck's Lake) and the Atlantic Ocean in the foreground, in a c.1932 advertisement (enlarged from Don Thomas, *Nostalgia Artistica*, 1993, courtesy of the author).

# S.A. EMPRESA DE VIAÇÃO AÉREA RIO GRANDENSE

Ernst Otto Meyer Labastille was born in Nieder-Marschhacht in the Prussian Province of Hanover on 25 November 1897, the son of Sidney Carl Heinrich Meyer, born in the same province and living in Haiti as an import-exporter, and Marie Aline Mariette Labastille, a Haitian. Ernst passed his childhood years in Haiti and was schooled (1904-1914) in Hamburg and Ratzeburg. In September 1914 he volunteered for the war, was assigned into the infantry and, in 1917, transferred to the Prussian Aviation Force. He received many decorations for his service in the War. After the war he found work in Hamburg.[1]

Otto Ernst Meyer (1897-1966)

On 27 January 1921 he emigrated to Brazil under an employment contract to the textile firm of Lundgren Brothers in Recife, then he moved to Rio de Janeiro and the office of Theodor Wille & Co. The climate and malaria problems did not suit him, so he moved further south, and by 13 January 1923 he was in Porto Alegre—where he finally settled—working in the import-export business, eventually establishing his own company.

Sometime after his arrival in Brazil, Ernst Otto Meyer Labastille officially changed his name to Otto Ernst Meyer (he became a Brazilian citizen on 2 February 1934).

Meyer, as well as most of his contemporaries, was frustrated in attempting to travel within Brazil—roads were bad at best, the railroads were neither connected nor coordinated—it was faster and safer to travel by ship along the coast than by land. Settling in the state of Rio Grande do Sul—which had a large German population—Meyer endeavored to create a commercial airline within the state, hopefully with financial backing from the local German community, but his first efforts were not immediately successful.

> ...we strove to bring the aeronautical experience we had acquired in Europe to Brazil, a country which was already becoming aware of the necessity—due to its geographical problems—of assuring for itself a prominent place in the still early days of commercial air transport. Nevertheless, because public and business mentality was still immature, between the beginning of 1921 and the end of 1924, two attempts made by me and my old comrades in arms (Hans Joesting and Hans Cronau), failed to create an air transport company in the country.[2]

Undaunted, his efforts continued, and he began to stir some interest in political and financial circles. Meyer gained the support of the President of the local Chamber of Commerce, Major Alberto Bins (future Mayor of Porto Alegre), who arranged a meeting with the Governor of the State, Dr. Antonio Borges de Medeiros. The Governor supported Meyer with a proposed 15-year tax abatement for the future company which was initiated on 30 October 1926.[3] A new airline was born: SOCIEDADE ANONIMA EMPRESA DE VIAÇÃO AÉREA RIO GRANDENSE (VARIG).

Meyer now had political and financial support—ten local businessman, including Major Bins, formed the nucleus of the proposed company and prepared to sell stock shares to the general public.[4]

With recognition achieved and financial support seemingly assured, Meyer returned to Germany in November 1926, seeking the other necessary ingredients: equipment, technical support and, of course, trained pilots. The German airlines had already been reformed under the DEUTSCHE LUFT HANSA banner in January of that year.

Meyer proceeded to contact DEUTSCHE LUFT HANSA and CONDOR SYNDIKAT representatives in Hamburg.[5] They entered into negotiations which lead to an exchange of 21% of VARIG stock for the future "lease" of the Dornier Wal, *Atlântico*, then undergoing overhaul and engine modifications in Germany; technical support; and the services of three top men: pilot, Commander Rudolf Cramer von Clausbruch (LUFT HANSA); pilot, Franz Nuelle (SCADTA); and flight engineer, Max Sauer (CONDOR SYNDIKAT).[6] The "technical support" obviously included the expertise of the CONDOR SYNDIKAT in Brazil, especially that of chief pilot and technical expert, Fritz W. Hammer.

The men and equipment from the CONDOR SYNDIKAT arrived in South America before Meyer— the *Atlântico* flew from its arrival port, Montevideo, to Buenos Aires. On 17 November 1926, with Fritz Hammer, Max Sauer and Herman Teegan as crew, the aircraft flew from Buenos Aires, carrying Dr. Hans Luther, former Chancellor of Germany, to Rio Grande, where it arrived two days later. The "Luther flight" reinforced the idea of the "safety" of air transport. The *Atlântico* (now in Portuguese) still bearing its German markings "D-1012," continued, via Florianópolis, São Francisco and Santos, to Rio de Janeiro, touching down in Guanabara Bay on 27 November 1926.

On New Year's Day, 1927, the *Atlântico*, with Captain von Clausbruch at the controls (assisted by Franz Nuelle), transported Brazil's Minister of Transportation and Public Works, Doctor Victor Konder, a Brazilian of German descent, on a demonstration flight from Rio de Janeiro to Florianópolis.[7] The passenger list also included two Brazilian journalists, Raul Portugal and Machado Florence; filmmaker Alberto Botelho; and Fritz Hammer, who provided on-the-spot details of the features of the aircraft.

Meyer arrived back in Rio de Janeiro on 25 January 1927. The next day, Victor Konder temporarily authorized the CONDOR SYNDIKAT to transport passengers and mail "for ordinary and extraordinary flights" within Brazil.[8] Two days later, Meyer boarded the *Atlântico*, and from the early morning mists on the bay at Rio the craft departed for Porto Alegre, arriving there on the 29th after joyous receptions at Santos, São Francisco and Florianópolis. The stage was set for an important event in VARIG's and Brazil's aviation history.

On 2 February 1927 the SYNDIKAT using the *Atlântico* inaugurated the "Linha da Lagôa" (Lake Line) by flying the route—Porto Alegre - Pelotas - Rio Grande—over and down the *Lagôa dos Patos* (Duck's Lake/Lagoon) with the first three paying passengers: Miss Maria Echenique, an official representative conveying greetings between the Mayors of the "joined" cities, Otavio Rocha (Porto Alegre) and João Fernandes Moreira (Rio Grande); Guilherme Gastal; and João Oliveira Goulart. This flight is commemorated as the "start of commercial aviation in Brazil," although it was not the start of regular scheduled service—the *Atlântico* was laid up for servicing at Rio Grande—which had to wait until 22 February. [9] The publicity was successful, however, and new potential shareholders emerged throughout the state of Rio Grande do Sul.

In early 1927 Meyer sought a "Secretary" to help with the increasing administrative responsibilities. A minimal salary offer produced minimal response:

> One candidate, however, an energetic young man of 19 who attached little importance to the salary I could afford to pay him, interested me greatly and I invited him at once to hang up his hat and coat and get the typewriter going, so that we could attack the avalanche of work that was threatening to drown our business.[10]

It was a wise choice. The man was Ruben Martin Berta who eventually would succeed Meyer as President of VARIG (1941) and whose tireless efforts supported the fledgling company.[11]

Following the Decree of 17 March, the first regularly scheduled flight carrying mail was run by the CONDOR SYNDIKAT on 27-28 March with von Clausbruch and Nuelle in the *Atlântico*.[12] Within two months the 50th flight had been recorded.

After a preparatory meeting on 1 April, a general meeting was held on 7 May.[13] VARIG added more

shareholders—now 550—70% of whom came from within the state. Meyer was elected Managing Director, Captain von Clausbruch and Franz Nuelle were made Technical Directors and Captain Fritz Hammer became Deputy Director. On 10 June 1927 the new company received permission to operate, under Decree No. 17832, within the state of Rio Grande do Sul, along the coast of Santa Catarina, and, with Uruguay's permission, to Montevideo.

On 15 June 1927 the *Atlântico* was transferred to VARIG in exchange for about 1,000 shares of stock (US $50,000). It was then registered, the first under new Brazilian rules, as "P-BAAA." VARIG also "inherited" the *Linha da Lagôa.* Meyer asserted:

> Thus, all the commitments that I had assumed six months ago in Berlin—leasing of the airplane, contracting its crew, services of technical assistance, maintenance, procurement of 'know-how'—were liquidated...there remains now the counterpart of our commitments: the commitment of that company (CONDOR SYNDIKAT) to establish, as soon as possible, a regular service between Rio de Janeiro and Porto Alegre.[14]

Fritz Hammer was attempting to do just that. The CONDOR SYNDIKAT would "cease operations"

on 1 July 1927, but its "offspring," SYNDICATO CONDOR, was allowed to start flying a scheduled route—Rio de Janeiro to Porto Alegre—on 9 November.[15] The four-day round trip, allowing for an extension to Rio Grande, resulted in 22 flights—with 160 passengers—by year's end.

To meet the requirements of the Decree of 17 March, VARIG and CONDOR prepared triangular "pre-stamps" with similar inscriptions. VARIG's triangle was elongated and inverted, point down. The first known use is VARIG's first scheduled flight, on the former CONDOR route—Porto Alegre - Pelotas - Rio Grande—on 22 June 1927.[16]

VARIG pre-stamp

On 13 July 1927 *Atlântico* was out-of-service for repairs, and VARIG leased the Junkers G-24 *Ypiranga* from SYNDICATO CONDOR until 24 September. An experimental flight was made by Heintz Puetz who flew the plane from Porto Alegre to Tapes and return on 17 July. Some mail was carried. A *Ypiranga* cover of 29 July with pre-stamp is shown below and another, from Pelotas to Arroio do Meio via Porto Alegre, 12 August 1927, using a handwritten unusual rate for 300 km. in the blank pre-stamp, is shown (opposite page, above). The latter cover bears the wording "Por via aérea até PORTO ALEGRE" ("By air until Porto Alegre"). The cover was carried over land to Arroio do Meio, its destination.

The *Atlântico*, back in service, flew a survey flight, Pelotas - Buenos Aires on 24 September and then Porto Alegre - Rio Grande on 7 October. Some mail was carried on both trips. A joint flight with CONDOR was made on 9-12 November using another Dornier Wal, *Santos Dumont*. A cover from this flight (opposite, below) also marks the first use of a VARIG stamp—the green 1$300 reis value of the CONDOR set without the "Syndicato Condor" overprinted "VARIG" in red (see Appendix C). This cover also bears the first of only two circular cancellations VARIG used: a double circle reading: "SERVIÇO AEREO - V.A.Ri.G." with the date in the center in three lines.[18] A clearer, later example of this cancel is shown below.

An example of the first circular cancel design

29 July 1927: Pelotas - Porto Alegre
1,000rs. postage including 700rs. special delivery + 1,300rs. air = Correct rate for 225 km.
"EXPRESSO"= Mandatory special delivery has been paid.[17] Note pen notations (at top): "6gr" denotes weight of cover and "pela aérea Ypiranga" = "by air *Ypiranga*," a Junkers G 24 leased from CONDOR between July and September 1927.

Correio Aéreo: A History of the Development of Air Mail Service in Brazil

2 July 1928: Rio Grande (do Sul) - Porto Alegre
300 rs. postage + 1,300 rs. air = Correct 20 gr. rate for 250 km.

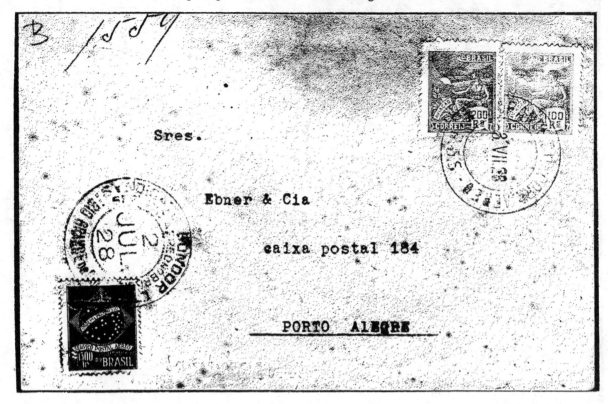

10 May 1929: Rio Grande - Porto Alegre
300 rs. postage + 1,300 rs. air mail = Correct rate for 300 km.

Correio Aéreo: A History of the Development of Air Mail Service in Brazil

VARIG got the Dornier Merkur *Gaúcho* as its second aircraft, which entered service on 24 November.[19] It was taken out of use within a week, because of structural problems, and overhauled. On 2 January 1928 von Clausbruch piloted the *Gaúcho* on an experimental flight—Porto Alegre - Torres and return and, a week later—Porto Alegre - Tramandahy. Small amounts of mail were carried.

Illustrated (opposite) are two covers bearing the second over-printing of "VARIG" on the basic stamp, but the letters are only 9.5 mm in overall width instead of the original 12.5 mm (see Appendix C). Since only 3,650 copies were printed in the smaller size, not many copies still exist on cover.

Captain Gerhard Kolhe inaugurated the route—Pelotas - Jaguaro and return—in the *Bandeirante*, a Junkers F 13 owned by CONDOR. Covers were specially printed and inscribed (and postmarked) with the date "17 August 1928."[20] Pilot Kolhe had flown the same plane on 2 August on a trial flight—Porto Alegre - Barra do Riberio and return—however, no mail was carried. Similarly, the *Gaúcho* carried pilot August Wilhelm Paschen—Porto Alegre - Santo Amaro and return—also without mail, on 23 September.

In 1929 the second of the circular cancellations was put into use. The lower part, separated on either side by six square dots, indicated the place of origin. According to Ahrens, this cancel was in use at Porto Alegre, Pelotas and Rio Grande; in 1931, at Santa Cruz and Santa Maria; from 1932, at Bagé, Cruz Alta, Livramento and Uruguayana; from 1933, Palmiera; and from 1934, Quarai.[21]

Second (and final) circular cancel design.

VARIG developed advertising cachets/slogans in consort with SYNDICATO CONDOR, including "Utilize the National Hydroplanes." VARIG also created others urging response by air mail.

"Utilize the National Hydroplanes"

"Não me faça esperar
responda via aérea
VARIG"
"Don't let me wait, reply by VARIG air mail"

It is not the place here to discuss the political history of Brazil. It is pertinent to our story however, to understand that the financial upheaval, which commenced in New York in October 1929 would soon make its violent rounds throughout the South American republics. Even Argentina, thought to be culturally safe from such activity, found itself unseating its government.

With the deepening financial crisis, the international market for coffee waned, directly effecting the political "muscle" of São Paulo, the largest coffee-producing state. São Paulo had shared the selection of candidates for the presidencies of Brazil with its neighbor, Minas Gerais, evidently as a carry-over of the semi-patriarchal system under the Empire, which had long irritated politicians in other states, especially third-ranked Rio Grande do Sul. Of the eight civilian presidencies, four had been "Paulistas" and three "Mineiros," and it was now Minas' turn. The incumbent "Paulista" President, Washington Luis Pereira de Sousa, made the erroneous decision to nominate as his successor another "Paulista," Julio Prestes, thereby negating the gentlemen's agreement with Minas. This resulted in

Minas joining with Paraiba in support of the opposition candidate, Getúlio Vargas of Rio Grande do Sul.

Getúlio Dornelles Vargas (1883-1954)

Now known as the "Liberal Alliance," the group attracted other support throughout the country. Prestes won the election in March 1930, but the battle was not over. In July, João Pessoa, the Alliance's vice-presidential candidate from Paraiba, was assassinated. Rebellious groups moved on the capital; the Army deserted; and the incumbent president, Washington Luis, was taken prisoner. On 3 November 1930 Vargas was installed in the Palace, the First Republic was ended, and a new administration was begun in Brazil. There is some indication that Rio Grande do Sul's "native airline" assisted in paramilitary operations in connection with and in support of the revolution. In any event, it is with this political/financial climate in mind that we resume our study.

VARIG and CONDOR continued their cooperative efforts during 1929. It is, of course, during this period that at least two other airlines were born, only to die the following year—ETA and NYRBA (discussed elsewhere in this book).

In March 1930 CONDOR commenced its ship-to-shore services with the *Cap Arcona*, and in May CAB made its one and only flight (see pp. 14-15). On 17 May VARIG, on a flight from Rio Grande to Porto Alegre, made first use of a new cachet (above right); CONDOR also used a very similar cachet.

"O HYDRO-AVIÃO VENCE
TEMPO E DISTANCIA!"
"The Hydroplane overcomes time and distance!"

Airline news for the remainder of May and June was dominated by the *Graf Zeppelin* and the first Europe - Pan-American round trip flight. In June 1930, Jean Mermoz attempted the Brazil - Europe return run for AÉROPOSTALE.

On 6 September 1930 the route—Porto Alegre - Passo Fundo and return—was opened with the *Gaúcho* piloted by Franz Nuelle. It was the first use of specially printed envelopes featuring Icarus in flight, previewing a design that would be adopted for future stamps. (It should be noted here that Otto Meyer was a stamp collector and apparently believed in the philatelic, as well as the publicity, value of flight souvenirs, as stamp and cancel placement would testify.)

6 September 1930: First Flight: Porto Alegre-Passo Fundo

VARIG continued its routine flights up to and during the Revolution of 1930, which obviously did not help promote air travel, and VARIG suffered.[22]

VARIG did not have the financial or aircraft resources of CONDOR. It required subsides from the state and had started operations with only one aircraft, the *Atlântico*; then leased the Junkers G 24

Correio Aéreo: A History of the Development of Air Mail Service in Brazil

*Ypiranga* while the Wal was overhauled; and subsequently bought the Dornier Merkur *Gaúcho*—all hydroplanes. However, Rio Grande do Sul's climate and inland terrain were not suitable to the continued use of the hydroplanes and VARIG shifted to land plane types for its further development. The *Gaúcho* and *Atlântico* were sold back to CONDOR. In November 1930 VARIG acquired two Klemm L 25s from the short-lived ETA, but one crashed, leaving the company at year's end, again,

with only one aircraft. With additional state support it purchased five new aircraft—all land-planes.

A new series of stamps followed a rate change and the basic green stamp was overprinted and surcharged (see Appendix C) in December 1930. On 23 February 1931 the route—Porto Alegre - Santa Cruz - Santa Maria and return—was opened. A new version (below) of the special commemorative cover was utilized.

23 February 1931: First Flight: Porto Alegre - Santa Cruz - Santa Maria and return

19 April 1932: First Flight: Porto Alegre - Bagé - Livramento

Correio Aéreo: A History of the Development of Air Mail Service in Brazil

VARIG's new fleet was reduced by one in April 1931 when one of the Junkers crashed after only three months in service, severely injuring and "side-lining" its pilot, former CONDOR pilot and VARIG technical director Franz Nuelle. By the end of the year VARIG, again in financial difficulties and having equipment problems, was reorganized, and in early 1932 the state government of Rio Grande do Sul provided loan funding for the acquisition of two Junkers F 13s: the *Livramento* and the *Santa Cruz*. On 19 April the *Livramento*, with pilots Max Frantz and Roberto Lau, inaugurated the route—Porto Alegre - Bage - Livramento—with the return trip the following day. At least two distinctly different pre-printed covers (opposite page) were used in both directions.

The route—Rio Grande - Bagé - Livramento—was opened on 15 July 1932, with the return trip on 17 July. Landing could not be made at Rio Grande, so Pelotas was used instead. On 25 July another first flight was made—Porto Alegre - Santa Cruz - Santa Maria - Uruguayana—with return the following day. Again a variety of pre-printed envelopes were used (below). The aircraft was the *Livramento*, with Harald Stunde and Sebastiao Eder at the controls.

The month-long revolution of October 1930, which brought Getúlio Vargas to power, was followed by a revolt in São Paulo state which broke out on 9 July 1932. This time the complaint was that Vargas had broken political promises and was slow in adopting a new constitution. São Paulo had expected moral support from the rest of the country and military support from Minas Gerais and Rio Grande do Sul. That would not be the case; in fact, it was just the opposite. Both states joined the federal government in its move against the Paulistas. Threatened with bombing from the air (possibly by VARIG's aircraft), its coastline blockaded by the navy, denied international recognition of a state of war requested by the Governor of the foreign consuls in his capital city and having lost public opinion throughout the country, the Paulistas surrendered on 29 September 1932. But, in spite of the military loss, the goal was won—a constitutional congress was formed. Mail of the period was subject to censure and was approiately marked ("Livre" means "free.").

## Livre de censura

## CENSURADO
### RIO GRANDE — R. G DO SUL

Revolutionary Censor markings

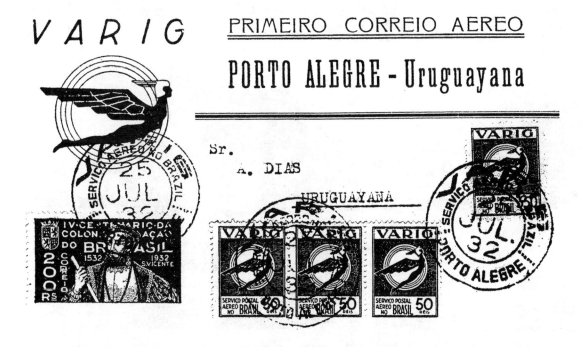

25 July 1932: First Flight: Porto Alegre - Uruguayana

Top to bottom: A Junkers A-50 Junior (VARIG 1931, unnamed and apparently not put into active service); *Livramento*, VARIG's first Junkers F 13 (1932); *Gaúcho*, a Dornier Merkur/Sea, VARIG's second (1927) aircraft. (VARIG photographs)

Correio Aéreo: A History of the Development of Air Mail Service in Brazil

em trafego mutuo com as congeneres.

# HORARIO DE INVERNO

# SEMANAL

### MANDE SUA CORRESPONDENCIA
## PARA EUROPA

### VIA
## CONDOR — LUFTHANSA
## ZEPPELIN

### O UNICO SERVIÇO AEREO REGULAR
### ENTRE
### BRASIL—EUROPA

### As malas fecham todas as Quartas-feiras
na

# VARIG

**TEL. 5616 — ANDRADAS, 1151**

---

## TARIFA DA LINHA SUL

| DE LOCALIDADE | PARA Espcie das Tarifas | PORTO ALEGRE | PELO-TAS | RIO GRANDE | BAGÉ | LIVRA-MENTO |
|---|---|---|---|---|---|---|
| P. Alegre | Passagens | — | 180$000 | 195$000 | 300$000 | 380$000 |
| | Cargas e excesso bagagens | — | 3$000 | 3$500 | 5$600 | 7$000 |
| Pelotas | Passagens | 180$000 | — | 35$000 | 155$000 | 250$000 |
| | Cargas e excesso bagagens | 3$000 | — | $700 | 2$800 | 4$900 |
| R. Grande | Passagens | 195$000 | 35$000 | — | 190$000 | 310$000 |
| | Cargas e excesso bagagens | 3$500 | $700 | — | 3$300 | 5$500 |
| Bagé | Passagens | 300$000 | 155$000 | 190$000 | — | 145$000 |
| | Cargas e excesso bagagens | 5$600 | 2$800 | 3$300 | — | 2$400 |
| Livramento | Passagens | 380$000 | 250$000 | 310$000 | 145$000 | — |
| | Cargas e excesso bagagens | 7$000 | 4$900 | 5$500 | 2$400 | — |

**PASSAGENS:** Por passageiro, até 100 kgs. de pêso pessoal. Excesso por kg. pela tarifa de Bagagens. CREANÇAS: até 3 anos, quando viajarem em companhia de adultos, pagarão sómente 10 % da passagem normal. Os menores de 3 a 12 anos pagarão meia passagem, desde que seu pêso, inclusive bagagem, não passe de 40 kgs. O excesso será cobrado por quilos, de acôrdo com a tarifa de cargas e bagagens.

**BAGAGENS:** Por quilo de pêso. Os primeiros 10 kgs. nada pagam.

**Cargas Aéreas** Por quilo de pêso. Frações de ½ kg. Taxa minima 1 kg.

### CORREIO AÉREO

**Serviço Estadoal:** Dentro do Estado do R. G. do Sul ...... $700

**Serviço Interestadoal** Dentro do Brasil, em tráfego mútuo com as congêneres ...... 1$000

**Serviço Transoceanico** Para a Europa e Africa, em tráfego mútuo com as congêneres ...... 4$200

Cartas ou cartões postais por 5 grs. ou fração. Impressos, amostras e encomendas por 25 grs. ou fração.

O serviço postal aéreo INTERESTADUAL é executado em TRAFEGO MÚTUO com o SINDICATO CONDOR LTDA., a AIR FRANCE e a PANAIR do BRASIL.

O serviço postal aéreo TRANSOCEANICO é feito em TRÁFEGO MÚTUO com o SINDICATO CONDOR LTDA., em combinação com a DEUTSCHE LUFT HANSA A. G. e o LUFTSCHIFFBAU ZEPPELIN G. m. b. H., e com a AIR FRANCE.

## LINHA SUL

| IDAS | VOLTAS |
|---|---|
| 3.ª e 6.ª-feiras | 4.ª-feiras e sabados |

Partidas de P. Alegre.. 10,00 hs.    Partidas de Livramento 12,00 hs.
Partidas de Pelotas .... 11,45 hs.    Partidas de Bagé .... 13,10 hs.
Partidas de Bagé .... 13,20 hs.    Partidas de Pelotas .... 14,45 hs.
Cheg.ª em Livramento 14,15 hs.    Chegadas em P. Alegre 16,15 hs.

**OBSERVAÇÕES** — Os aviões de quartas-feiras, de Livramento a Porto Alegre, têm combinação com o SERVIÇO TRANSOCEANICO CONDOR - LUFTHANSA - ZEPPELIN - para a EUROPA.

Os de sabados têm combinação com o serviço costeiro e europeu da AIR FRANCE.

| 4.ª-feiras | 5.ª-feiras |
|---|---|

Partidas de P. Alegre.. 15,00 hs.    Partidas de Pelotas .... 15,00 hs.
Chegadas em Pelotas .. 16,30 hs.    Chegadas em P. Alegre 16,30 hs.

(Estas viagens estão em combinação com o SERVIÇO TRANSOCEANICO ZEPPELIN - LUFTHANSA - CONDOR, da EUROPA).

(Estas viagens estão em combinação com o serviço nacional e internacional da PANAIR DO BRASIL).

### TRANSPORTE DE VALOR

| Sôbre o PESO | Sôbre o VALOR (não incluindo seguro) | | |
|---|---|---|---|
| ENVELOPES DE REMESSAS | De 50$ — 1:000$ | Por 100$ ou fração | 1,2 % |
| Por 5 grs. ou fração Taxa: $700 | De 1:001$ — 10:000$ | Por 1:000$ ou fração | 5 % |
| OUTROS ENVÓLU-CROS | De 10:001$ — 30:000$ | Por 1:000$ ou fração | 2 % |
| Por ½ kg. ou fração Taxa: 4$500 | De 30:001$ — 100:000$ | Por 1:000$ ou fração | 1 % |

Recomenda-se que os remetentes avisem os destinatários pelo mesmo avião. - A taxa do seguro, que é facultativo, importa em 3 por mil.

VARIG timetable and rate schedule (c. 1934)

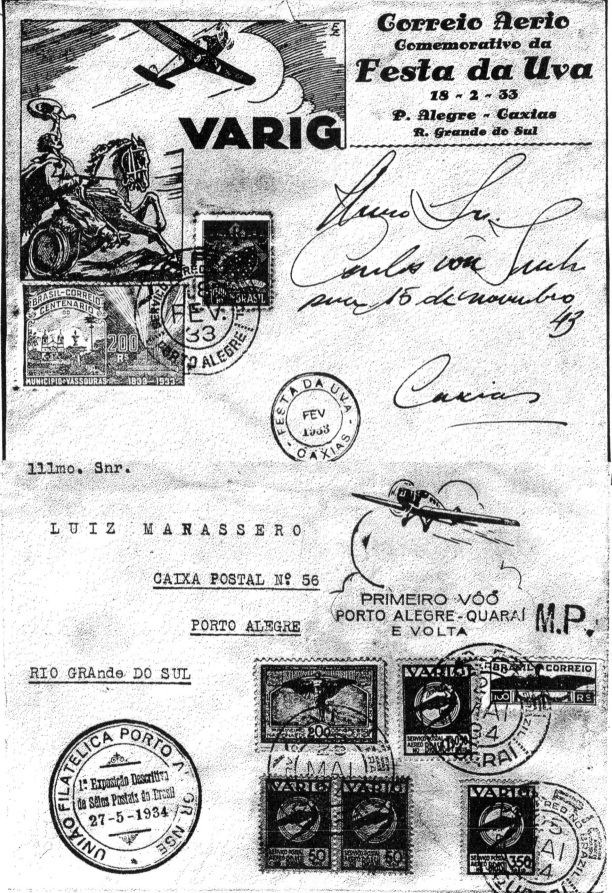

The last first flight of 1932—Porto Alegre - Cruz Alta, and return —was made, utilizing the aircraft *Santa Cruz*, piloted by Max Frantz and Roberto Lau, in October. In January 1933 Jean Mermoz and his crew flew the *Arc-en-Ciel* establishing a new time record across the South Atlantic for AÉROPOSTALE. On 18 February 1933 another VARIG first flight was recorded—Porto Alegre - Caxias—in consort with the grape festival, and another specially printed cover was used (top, opposite page). On 26 May the route—Porto Alegre - Dores de Camaquam and return—was flown in the *Livramento*, piloted by Harald Stunde and Karl Heinz Ruhl.

In October 1933 the *Graf Zeppelin* made its second "triangular flight" to the "Century of Progress" Exhibition in Chicago. In Brazil, VARIG opened the route—Porto Alegre - Jacui - Palmeira and return. One printed design (below) formed the base of a first flight cachet on the cover (opposite page, below) and of a handstamp "GAUCHO!–AUXILIA A VARIG, Que foi fundada para te servir" ("Gaúcho help VARIG, which was founded to serve you").

GAUCHO!-AUXILÍA A VARIG,
QUE FOI FUNDADA PARA TE SERVIR
Advertising cachet

A first flight in the *Livramento*, piloted by Harald Stunde and Hans Leo Kley, occurred on 25 May 1934—Porto Alegre - Pelotas - Quarai and return.

VARIG continued its route development and connected with PRIMERAS LINEAS URUGUAYAS DE NAVEGACIÓN AÉREA (PLUNA), a Uruguayan company formed around 1936 and operating from Montevideo to the border with Brazil.

17 October 1933: First Flight: Palmeira - Porto Alegre

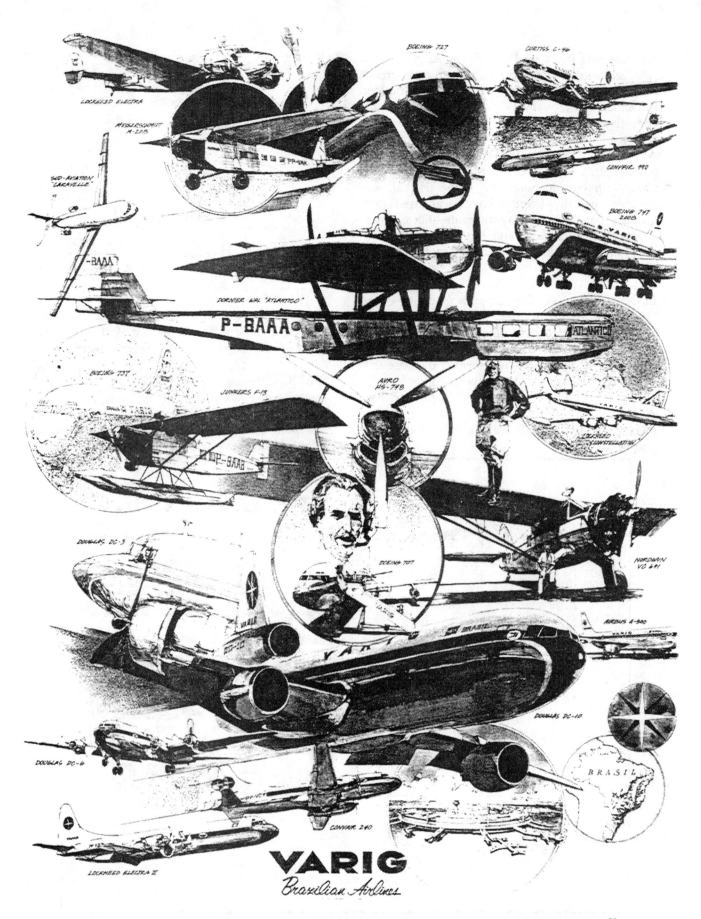

An artist's collage of the important aircraft in VARIG's history. (Illustration courtesy of VARIG airlines.)[23]

Correio Aéreo: A History of the Development of Air Mail Service in Brazil

Advertising art via baggage label.

With the advent of war, Otto Ernst Meyer turned the management of VARIG over to Ruben Martin Berta, the Brazilian national who would continue the operation. Direct flights to Montevideo were initiated the following year (1942). Starting in 1946, other lines were added to Florianópolis, São Paulo, Curitiba and Rio de Janeiro, linking the capitals of the southern states. The route—Porto Alegre - São Paulo - Rio de Janeiro—became the mainstay of the line and accounted for more traffic than all the other routes combined.

After the war, VARIG acquired a fleet of DC-3s. It was not until 1951, however, that VARIG ventured north—through the acquisition of AERO GERAL—and extended its lines to Natal, along a 1,572 mile coastal network north of Rio. The following year the line extended south from Porto Alegre to Buenos Aires. In 1955 VARIG was granted a foreign carrier permit by the U. S. Civil Aeronautics Board, which designated Washington, D.C., and New York as landing sites. Super-Constellation service was inaugurated on 29 July 1955. In 1957 Caravelle jets were added; three years later, Boeing 707's replaced them.

In 1961 VARIG became *the* major Brazilian airline with the absorption of REAL and the acquisition of routes to Los Angeles, Lima, Bogotá, Mexico City, Miami and Central America. With the demise of PANAIR operations in 1965, VARIG assumed the responsibility of services to Europe. Ruben Berta died in 1966. The company came under the control of Eric de Carvalho until 1979 and, then, Helio Smidt. The company remains today as one of the most important in South America, if not, the world.

◊

"The future of Brazil depends on its communications." An advertising poster, c.1932, picturing a Dornier Wal seaplane and the *Graf Zeppelin* in the skies over Rio de Janeiro with the slogan: "Save time and money utilize the 'CONDOR' air service" (from Don Thomas, *Poster Art of the Airlines*, 1989,. courtesy of the author).

# SYNDICATO CONDOR LIMITADA

At the start of World War I, Germany, like the other countries involved, had little regard for the military potential of the airplane, and its air force consisted mostly of unarmed aircraft designed to be used with observers in support of ground troops. The war would change all that.

German aircraft development changed rapidly over the years. Germany had built a total of 24 planes in 1911, 136 in 1912, 1,348 in 1914, 4,532 in 1915, 8,182 in 1916, 19,746 in 1917, and 14,123 up to November 1918. War production saw the completion of some 48,537 models.

The first all-metal (corrugated Duralumin—an early version of aluminum) airplane to fly was the Junkers-J 1 (12 December 1915). By the end of the war Junkers had produced ten more models. Hugo Junkers then transferred his staff's design efforts to commercial rather than military use and their first product, the J 12, was not built. It was superceded by the improved J 13 which was built as the F 13. The first of this model went into service on 18 July 1919. Junkers had a great product, but few buyers— most of the German airlines had already developed ties with other manufacturers such as Dornier and Fokker. Junkers looked abroad for sales.

In the meantime, several countries in South America were looking for a means to overcome the problems of transportation over difficult terrain. One of the first to attack the problem was Colombia.

Barranquilla, Colombia, 2,000 miles due south of New York City, had a strategic position near the mouth of the Magdalena River, which (until 1925) was denied ocean-going steamer traffic by sand bars. Some 650 miles up-river was Girardot, connected to the capital, Bogotá, 8,400 feet above, by mule or horse overland (or later, by a seven-hour rail-ride). The need for an easier link between the

Pacific and Caribbean seaports and the capital had convinced the Colombian government to support any attempt to bridge that gap by air. Bogotá was the political, social, cultural, artistic and economic center of life in Colombia. Connecting it with the outside world by a relatively rapid and safe means was the goal.

The first group to respond—several Colombian businessmen—formed the short-lived COMPAÑÍA COLOMBIANA DE NAVEGACIÓN AÉREA (C. C. N. A.) on 16 September 1919. Even utilizing the talents and experience of ex-war pilots like U. S. flyer William Knox-Martin, credited with flying the first air mail in Colombia in June of that year, the company could not overcome the continuous losses in men and machines—large, mostly French equipment not designed for the arduous terrain—and by 1922 was all but out of business. Perhaps its biggest contribution, to philately anyway, was the issuance of the Curtiss "labels" which are recognized as Colombia's first air mail stamps.

On 5 December 1919, two days after C. C. N. A. was authorized to carry mail, the SOCIDAD COLOMBO ALEMANA DE TRANSPORTES AÉREOS (SCADTA) was founded by a group of five Colombian businessmen including Ernesto Cortissoz, elected SCADTA's first President, and three German residents: importer Albert Tietjen (elected Chairman); Fritz Klein; and a German salesman-engineer, Werner Kämmerer, who had assembled the group.

While the others were establishing their infra-structure to operate in Colombia, Kämmerer went to Germany in search of a suitable aircraft for the planned use; met Fritz Hammer, a Junkers salesman, and ordered two Junkers F 13 float-planes.

When they finally arrived in Colombia in late July 1920, they came with two very important additions—Fritz Hammer, the sales agent for Junkers and a former naval pilot, and aircraft engineer Wilhelm (Guillermo) Schnurbusch, who would become SCADTA's technical director for the next two decades. They were soon joined by another German pilot, Hellmuth von Krohn, who would go on to become the airline's chief pilot, and together they conducted survey flights up the Magdalena River. The all-metal F 13s proved very reliable and better able to cope with the conditions of climate and terrain than the fabric and wood planes used by C. C. N. A.

The "instant airfields" of the river came in handy for the first successful flight—actually more a hop-skip-and-jump—with von Krohn at the controls and Schnurbusch along to make the necessary, and frequent, repairs on 19 October 1920.

Successful, yes, but only after the aircraft had been rebuilt—with an automobile radiator for additional cooling—for the abnormal conditions of climate and terrain. South America, it was soon learned, was not Europe. The craft finally reached Girardot, but Bogotá, the capital, would have to wait for more modifications and two more months. Hammer would fly the second plane, with a "new" undercarriage of used piping and automobile wheels, to a successful landing on the high plateau. Christened *Bogotá* on the spot, plane—and pilot—were famous.

Fame does not always spell fortune. In spite of the prize money awarded by the Bogotá newspapers and an exclusive government contract, insufficient funds were on hand for the equipment and material needed for expansion or, for that matter, even continuation of service.[1]

A German-Czech geographer-industrialist from Austria, Dr. Peter Paul Ritter von Bauer (1888-1965), became involved with SCADTA about the turn of the year 1920-21.[2] Dr. von Bauer had lived in South America from 1908 to 1916, had participated in a Amazonian expedition in 1911, and had returned to Colombia in 1920—depressed from the effects of the war on his native land. He took on the role of company representative; traveled to Germany, disposed of his investments in Europe; and plowed the money into SCADTA. With details supplied by Schnurbusch and Hammer, he ordered two more F 13s that were modified for the tropics. Before the end of 1921, twice-weekly flights, often with passengers seated atop the mailbags, were being run between Barranquilla and Girardot.

Having gained financial control and the directorship of SCADTA by 1922, Dr. von Bauer developed a scientific division which did aerial survey and mapping work for the Colombian government. He also established a SCADTA network in Berlin, Hamburg, Paris, other European capitals, and major cities, including New York, sprouting agencies with enough promotional material and special stamps (overprinted Colombian issues) there and in most Colombian consulates, that the world soon knew that SCADTA had arrived and was *the* airline in South America. By June 1922 SCADTA operated 15 airports in Colombia and over 50 agencies worldwide. By the end of that year, C. C. N. A. had abandoned its hopes and on 5 December 1922 SCADTA executed a contract with the Colombian government to carry the air mail but, unlike other airlines in Europe and the United States, received no government subsidy.

It may be argued that the government's allowing SCADTA to issue stamps for its services was a form of subsidy, albeit an indirect one. However, it should be noted that the government allowed the company to collect its fees via stamps, but it did not require them to do so, nor were the stamp designs subject to government approval. This was not the case later in Brazil, where the government required the domestic lines—ETA, VARIG and CONDOR—to issue stamps (with designs to meet the governments approval) for their fees.

SCADTA appeared to be successful but was not without its disappointments and mishaps, for example, the tragic loss of the F 13 *Tolima* and its four passengers and crew, which included the pilot Wilhelm Fischer, SCADTA's first President Cortissoz, and their chief pilot von Krohn, during a small Barranquilla air show on 8 June 1924.

The first night mail was flown across the continental United States in July 1924 and, in October, the LZ.126 arrived at Lakehurst, after an uneventful ocean crossing, to become the ZR-3, *Los Angeles*. Meanwhile in Colombia, the idea of "SCADTA INTERNATIONAL" was born in the minds of Dr. von Bauer and a young politician, Enrique Olaya-Herrera (1881-1937), and with it the need for more suitable aircraft and, of course, more financial support. Fritz Hammer and von Bauer went back to Germany in search of both, and a new company was born—the CONDOR SYNDIKAT. (It is not clear why the name "Condor," an Andean vulture, was chosen. It is not native to Germany.)

Three of SCADTA's Junkers F 13s lined up on the shore of the Magdalena River near Girardot, river port of the capital city, Bogotá. From the left: A-4, *Bogotá*—one of the first two delivered in 1920; A-8, *Magdalena*; and A-10, *Caldas*. The photograph had to have been taken between 1921, when the later two were delivered, and 3 September 1926 when *Caldas* crashed. *Bogotá* crashed in 1927, and *Magdalena* was returned to Junkers in 1929.

On 5 May 1924 DEUTSCHER AERO LLOYD A. G., one of LUFT HANSA's predecessors, in partnership with Schlubach, Theimer and Co. of Hamburg, a German trading company, formed the CONDOR SYNDIKAT in Berlin.[3] SCADTA took a 10% interest. The purpose of the new company was to study the viability of aircraft operations in South America, including the possibility of transatlantic flight, and to promote Junkers and other German aircraft exports now starting to recover from the devastating effects of the war. Fritz Hammer, who would become the catalyst for development of several airlines in South America, was named marketing director of the SYNDIKAT.

Who was Fritz Hammer? Fritz Wilhelm Hammer was born 6 December 1888 in Berlin. After studying at the Technischen Hochschule in Münich and Berlin (like the Massachusetts Institute of Technology) and the Höhere Maschinenbauschule (Machine Building School) at Hildburghausen, he went to flying school and became a pilot in 1913, the same year he was awarded a national prize for an eight-hour flight. During the war, Hammer worked

Fritz Wilhelm Hammer (1888-1938)

on the training of pilots and observers and participated in the development of land-based torpedo planes. He later moved to the "front lines" and by 1915 was in charge of four seaplanes or, more properly, float-planes—land planes equipped with pontoons instead of wheels or skids.

After the war, Hammer became a technical representative for the Junkers Flugzeugwerke at Dessau. It is believed he was instrumental in Junkers looking to Latin America as a source of sales. Commercial aviation was far more advanced in Europe than in the United States and the rest of the world. On the west side of the Atlantic no one, with a few minor exceptions, had seriously looked at the potential of the Caribbean and Latin America as an airline market.[4]

SCADTA, with an impetus from the SYNDIKAT, looked to expand beyond the boundaries of its own homeland and started some survey flights to Venezuela. To go beyond the limits of its tested Junkers—the F 13s were clearly not up to long, over-water flights—more potent equipment would be needed. Through Hammer's efforts the SYNDIKAT turned to Dornier, who because of the "Nine Rules" (see DEUTSCHE LUFTHANSA, p. 30) was then building aircraft in Italy through a subsidiary, Construzioni Meccaniche Aeronautiche (CMASA). The SYNDIKAT got two Dornier Wals.

The Wal (Whale), first flown in November 1922, was an evolution from earlier models and one of Claude Dornier's finest designs.[5] Capable of carrying up to ten cabin passengers, its crew of two was situated in an open cockpit below the wing's leading edge. Above the wing, two engines, mounted in tandem, operated pusher and puller (tractor) blades. The body was metal—Duralumin, the same material used in the F-13s and, later, the zeppelins. About 150 CMASA Wals were eventually built, the first six being acquired by Spain.[6] Other models were flown almost to the North Pole (Roald Amundsen) in 1925 and across the North Atlantic to the United States (Wolfgang von Gronau) in 1930. Various models and engines were produced during the Wal's lifetime.

In an arrangement with the SYNDIKAT, Hammer returned to Colombia with the two Wals in crates and with another pilot, old friend and former war ace, Freiherr von Buddenbrock. A suitable assembly site was found on an island off Curaçao (Dutch West Indies) and, after reconstruction, the planes were flown to the Barranquilla base under lease to SCADTA.

On or about 10 August 1925 these Wals, named *Atlántico* and *Pacífico*, and under Colombia's colors, commenced a counter-clockwise flight around the Caribbean, stopping in every country in Central America and finally arriving in Havana, Cuba, on

The Dornier Wal flying-boat *Pacífico* being christened at Barranquilla prior to her Central American flight.

The *Pacifico* landing on Lake Amatitlan in Guatemala during the Central American flight.

19 September. This was just four days after other agents from Junkers and a few local German residents had helped establish LLOYD AÉREO BOLIVIANO (LAB) in Bolivia. Junkers had also formed the short-lived LLOYD AÉREO CÓRDOBA in Argentina earlier that year, but it proved no match for AÉROPOSTALE and AEROPOSTA ARGENTINA and it survived less than two years.

Dr. von Bauer and Fritz Hammer were on board the flight as good will ambassadors and negotiators for SCADTA's planned expansion. The trip was not without incident and was a good test—in tropical conditions and varying terrain—of the aircraft and the pilots, who, for lack of the necessary radio and navigational equipment, relied on and flew by the order of the day—"'the seat of their pants, and communicated with each other by hand signs."[7] At each stop the planes and men were admired and von Bauer "secured" passenger and mail commitments from the local governments. The flight continued across British Honduras (Belize) and the Yucatan to Havana, Cuba.

In April 1925 von Bauer had made overtures to the U. S. Post Office Department and, seemingly, had been well received. However, the two aircraft were denied entry into the United States. After some delay in Havana waiting permission to cross, only the *Pacifico* was permitted to fly to West Palm Beach.

From there, the two negotiators traveled overland.

Hammer went to New York looking for potential commercial and travel customers and for investment support, and von Bauer went to Washington to discuss his plans with the Postmaster General. He even obtained a meeting with President Coolidge, but the response was anything but warm. Coolidge had already been advised of the fears of the military—German U-boats had plied the waters of the Caribbean within the previous decade and there was, of course, the Panama Canal, where over-flight restrictions were in effect—and the Postmaster General, and others apparently, already had dreams of an American airline accomplishing von Bauer's goals. SCADTA INTERNATIONAL was stillborn, but the "Inter-American SCADTA Flight" would have a catalytic effect on air transportation developments.

U. S. Air Force General H. H. ("Hap") Arnold was one of those who reacted to the "threat" and, as he recalled in his book, there was an implication that his zeal was, perhaps, not entirely patriotic:

In a sense, the formation of Pan American Airways turned out to be the first counter-measure the United States ever took against Nazi Germany, though Hitler was unknown in America then, and in jail at Landsberg-am-Lech as a mild punishment for his Beer Hall Putsch at Munich the previous November. (The airfield at Landsberg was to be a target for our Eighth Air Force bombers twenty years later.)

In my job as Information Officer, I saw reports from the military attaché in Colombia which gave repeated data about a German air line, Scadta, run by a Captain von Bauer, and operating between Barranquilla and Bogotá. All pilots, mechanics, and equipment of this line running up the Magdalena River, and far too close to the Panama Canal to be ignored, were German. Then I received information that Captain von Bauer wanted to expand his successful air line, pushing it up not only to Panama itself, but extending it through the Central Americas to Cuba and the United States to carry mail and passengers.

That was the last straw. I immediately went to see G-2 of the War Department, and after that I called on Postmaster General New. I asked the Postmaster General whether, if Captain von Bauer arrived in Washington and requested authority to carry U. S. mail from the United States to Barranquilla and Bogotá, under the law he would have to give him the contract. Mr. New thought it over for a while and said he thought he would, unless there was some other line, preferably an American line, that could perform the service. I asked him whether the American line must be "in being" or if it could be one in the process of organization. He said he would have to wait and see just what I meant by that.

I went back to my office, took a map, and drew a sketch of an air line operating from Key West to Havana, to the Western end of Cuba, to the northeast point of the Yucatan Peninsula, down through British Honduras, Guatemala, Nicaragua, and to Panama. I then called in Major Spaatz and Major Jack Jouett. We talked it over for hours, and finally we called in an ex-Navy man by the name of John Montgomery. Together, we drew up a prospectus of such an air line and how it might make money. Then we sent John Montgomery to New York. Montgomery interested some moneyed people and funds were set up for an air line operating between Florida and Cuba and Panama. We found out that the Standard Oil Company had to send supplies to Havana, Key West, and to the Central American ports, and the freight charges and the funds received for carrying the mail between Key West and Havana would pay for the operating expense of that part of the line. We also found out that most of the ports where we were going to land had ships arriving but once every thirty days. We figured that we would start out by giving these ports airplane service once a week, and later on, give them service twice a week, which would save from thirty to forty-five days in delivery of goods.

With that information, and knowing that the capital in New York was interested in the line, we went back to Postmaster General New and told him just what happened. When Captain von Bauer made his final appearance and applied for permission to run the Scadta Line from Barranquilla to Panama and to the United States, he was refused.

Very few people in the War Department, or in Panama, knew that at that moment, jobs had been offered to Spaatz, to be operating director of the new company; to Jouett, to handle all personnel; to Montgomery, to be field manager on the line when it was in operation; and to me, to be president and general manager of Pan American. Just what would have happened had my tour in Washington remained unbroken, I do not know.[8]

Juan Terry Trippe (of PAN AMERICAN) did.

The trip, a failure for von Bauer and the SYNDIKAT, ironically, stirred the sleeping giant to the north into a new interest in the Caribbean and South America and the development of both guideline controls and airline companies—the Air Mail and Air Commerce Acts were passed in 1926 and PAN AMERICAN AIRWAYS (PAN AM), founded in 1927, started service between Key West and Havana the following year.

While von Bauer accepted his defeat and became content to make SCADTA a successful domestic airline—all the while hoping that some other airline, even one from the U. S., would connect with SCADTA—Hammer was outraged and blamed U. S. military-political intrigue for their failure.

The *Pacifico* returned to Havana and the two Wals were boat-shipped back to Germany for maintenance and overhaul. The *Pacifico*, outfitted with new, more powerful engines, was returned in pieces to SCADTA and, after reassembly on the island, was destroyed on the return flight to Barranquilla. "Don Guillermo" Schnurbusch and co-pilot von Buddenbrock barely survived.

As 1926 arrived the German airline operations of the rivaling JUNKERS LUFTVERKEHR and DEUTSCHER AERO LLOYD were consolidated in the formation of DEUTSCHE LUFT HANSA A. G. (LUFT HANSA). The CONDOR SYNDIKAT apparently retained its identity and its mission. The interest in South American flight operations intensified, but this time on the east coast. LUFT HANSA management declared at a press conference at the time:

The quantity of mail which is transported across the Atlantic is so great that it would be a simple matter to pick out the urgent mail and fill a few planes with it every day...Here lies a chance to become self-supporting.[9]

Two Wals, the *Atlántico* and the *Hai* (Shark), were shipped to Montevideo and then flown to Buenos

Aires. The *Hai* was damaged on a pier in landing, but a new era was about to begin—again with the technical help and promotional support of Fritz Hammer.

Otto Ernst Meyer (see VARIG) was in the process of attempting to form a local airline in the southern state of Rio Grande do Sul. Looking to obtain the best in equipment and staff, he went to Germany and contacted the CONDOR SYNDIKAT in early

Dr. Hans Luther, while visiting SCADTA in 1926, standing (left) on the wing of *Bogotá*, one of the first of two F 13s delivered in 1920, which crashed in 1927.

November 1926. At his behest, and a 21% share of his future company, he was promised the Wal *Atlántico* and technical support, but he would not receive the plane or government authorization to operate his airline until seven months later.

Meanwhile, on 17 November 1926 with Fritz Hammer again at the controls, the *Atlántico* transported the former German Reich Chancellor, Dr. Hans Luther—an avid civil aviation supporter—northward from Buenos Aires to Rio Grande where it arrived two days later to a triumphant reception by the local Germans and the President of Brazil. Luther helped negotiate for permission to conduct scheduled airline services. Luther was not a "stranger" in South America and had already visited SCADTA earlier that year (see illustration, left). This famous "Luther flight" had demonstrated the reliability of the Wal and, of course, the capability of its pilot. "It was really much more of a 'Hammer Flight.'"[10] Eight days later the *Atlántico*, now with a Portuguese name, but still bearing German registration markings, made its landing on Guanabara Bay at Rio de Janeiro on 27 November 1926.

On New Year's Day 1927 the plane flew from Rio de Janeiro, via Santos, to Florianópolis. This time Hammer was not the pilot but the on-board, ardent salesman, demonstrating the features of the aircraft to its illustrious passengers, including Dr. Victor Konder, Brazil's Minister of Transport. Apparently impressed, Konder granted the CONDOR SYNDIKAT authorization (26 January) to operate air services for a one-year period. The flight is officially referred to as "the start of commercial aviation in Brazil."[11] The *Atlántico* was moved to Porto Alegre

The *Atlântico*, still with German markings, at Porto Alegre after a demonstration flight across the Lagôa dos Patos.

and on 3 February 1927 inaugurated the run from Porto Alegre - Pelotas - Rio Grande over the *Lagôa dos Patos* (Ducks' Lake), a lagoon which stretches along almost half of the length of the coastline of the state. After overhaul at Rio Grande, the *Atlântico* started scheduled passenger service on 27 February.

On 17 March Dr. Konder signed a document, which changed air—and philatelic—history in the country (see Appendix B); it specifically stated that the transporting agents must issue special stamps to collect the fees for services.[12] Government-issued postage stamps must also be used for the normal (surface) delivery portion. The regulations allowed the use of "cancellers or any other device convenient to the carriers" in lieu of stamps, during the first six months of the carrier's operation after government approval. All designs and rates to be charged were to be approved by the government.

Within ten days, CONDOR SYNDIKAT was the first to take advantage of these regulations in conjunction with its first scheduled flight on the *"Linha Lagôa dos Patos"* (Ducks' Lake Line), using the

*Atlântico* under the command of Captain Rudolf Cramer von Clausbruch. The SYNDIKAT utilized a triangular cachet "stamp" in black reading, "O futuro do Brasil depende das suas communicações" ("The future of Brazil depends upon its communications"). Rubber stamps were made in 700, 1,000, 1,300 and 1,500 reis values and, also, with a "blank" center in which the appropriate value was to be entered by hand. It should be noted that on some of the 1,300 reis stamps (see cover below) "communicações"is misspelled "com*u*mnicações"

1,000 rs. pre-stamp with correct spelling

As with VARIG, these triangles were actually "pre-stamps," with designs approved by the Brazilian government, and were required to be used until adhesive stamps were printed. It is believed that

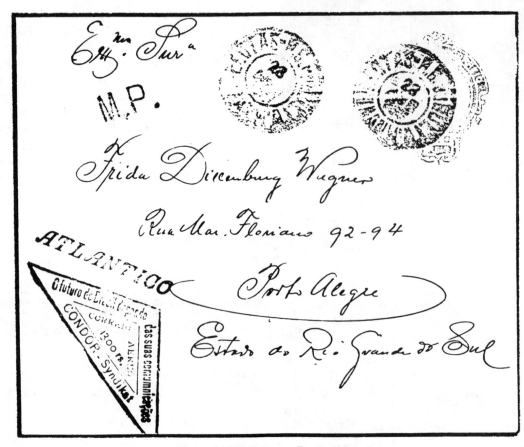

23 April 1927: Pelotas - Porto Alegre
200 rs. postage + 1,300 rs. air mail (20 gr. rate for 225 km.)
"M.P." = "Mão Propria" (by hand), i.e., carried outside of postal system (by airline) for part of its journey.

early collectors did not realize the conditions under which they were produced and they were, for the most part, looked upon as simply another cachet. Accordingly, not many survive.

The initial (1927) government-established rates are shown in the table (right). In addition, 200 rs. regular government postage was required, which was increased to 300 rs. by the end of the year, and Registration (400 rs.) and Special Delivery (700 rs.) fees were also specified.

| Distance (km) | First 20 gr. (50 gr. for printed matter) | Add 20 gr. |
|---|---|---|
| up to 500 | 1,300 rs. | 700 rs. |
| 500 to 1,000 | 2,000 rs. | 1,000 rs. |
| 1,500 to 3,000 | 3,000 rs. | 1,500 rs. |
| 3,000 to 4,500 | 4,000 rs. | 2,000 rs. |

# CONDOR-SYNDIKAT

Itinerario provisorio n.º 4 para o hydroavião „ATLANTICO" de 30 de Abril até 31 de Maio de 1927 na linha:

## RIO GRANDE — PELOTAS — PORTO ALEGRE — SANTA VICTORIA
e vice-versa

| | | | | | |
|---|---|---|---|---|---|
| 30/4 | Sabbado | Partida | Rio Grande | ás 10,— | horas |
| | | | Pelotas | 10,55 | |
| | | Chegada | Porto Alegre | 12,55 | |
| 3/5 | Terça-feira | Partida | Porto Alegre | 10,— | |
| | | | Pelotas | 12,30 | |
| | | Chegada | Rio Grande | 12,55 | |
| 4/5 | Quarta-feira | Partida | Rio Grande | 10. | |
| | | | Pelotas | 10,55 | |
| | | Chegada | Porto Alegre | 12,55 | |
| 5/5 | Quinta-feira | Partida | Porto Alegre | 10,— | |
| | | | Pelotas | 12,30 | |
| | | Chegada | Rio Grande | 12,55 | |
| 7/5 | Sabbado | Partida | Rio Grande | 10,— | |
| | | | Pelotas | 10,55 | |
| | | Chegada | Porto Alegre | 12,55 | |
| 9/5 | Seg.-feira | Partida | Porto Alegre | 10,— | |
| | | | Pelotas | 12,30 | |
| | | Chegada | Rio Grande | 12,55 | |
| 11/5 | Quarta-feira | Partida | Rio Grande | 10,— | |
| | | | Pelotas | 10,55 | |
| | | Chegada | Porto Alegre | 12,55 | |
| 12/5 | Quinta-feira | Partida | Porto Alegre | 8,— | |
| | | | Pelotas | 10,30 | |
| | | Chegada | Rio Grande | 10,55 | |
| 13/5 | Sexta-feira | Partida | Rio Grande | 14,— | |
| | | | Pelotas | 14,55 | |
| | | Chegada | Porto Alegre | 16,55 | |
| 14/5 | Sabbado | Partida | Porto Alegre | 10,— | |
| | | | Pelotas | 12,30 | |
| | | Chegada | Rio Grande | 12,55 | |
| 17/5 | Terça-feira | Partida | Rio Grande | 8,— | |
| | | | Pelotas | 8,55 | |
| | | Chegada | Porto Alegre | 10,55 | |
| | | Partida | Porto Alegre | 14,— | |
| | | | Pelotas | 16,30 | |
| | | Chegada | Rio Grande | 16,55 | |
| 19/5 | Quinta-feira | Partida | Rio Grande | 10, | |
| | | | Pelotas | 10,55 | |
| | | Chegada | Porto Alegre | 12,55 | |
| 20/5 | Sexta-feira | Partida | Porto Alegre | 10,— | |
| | | | Pelotas | 12,30 | |
| | | Chegada | Rio Grande | 12,55 | |
| 23/5 | Seg.-feira | Partida | Porto Alegre | 10,— | |
| | | | Pelotas | 10,55 | |
| | | Chegada | Porto Alegre | 12,55 | |
| 24/5 | Terça-feira | Partida | Porto Alegre | 8, | |
| | | | Pelotas | 10,30 | |
| | | Chegada | Rio Grande | 10,55 | |
| | | Partida | Rio Grande | 14,— | |
| | | Chegada | Sta. Victoria | 16. | |

Monte Sarmiento e D. Pedro

"Cap Norte" „Werra"

IDA e VOLTA „Weser"

Sta. Victoria

| | | | | | |
|---|---|---|---|---|---|
| 25/5 | Quarta-feira | Partida | Sta. Victoria | as 14.— | horas |
| | | Chegada | Rio Grande | 16.— | |
| 27/5 | Sexta-feira | Partida | Rio Grande | 10.— | |
| | | | Pelotas | 10.55 | |
| | | Chegada | Porto Alegre | 12.55 | |
| 28/5 | Sabbado | Partida | Porto Alegre | 8.— | |
| | | | Pelotas | 10.30 | |
| | | Chegada | Rio Grande | 10.55 | |
| | | Partida | Rio Grande | 10.— | |
| | | | Pelotas | 10.55 | |
| 31/5 | Terça-feira | Partida | Pelotas | 10.55 | |
| | | Chegada | Porto Alegre | 12.55 | |

Este horario está sujeito a modificações sem previo aviso.

## PREÇOS

| | |
|---|---|
| Rio Grande - Porto Alegre | Rs. 220$000 |
| ida e volta | Rs. 400$000 |
| Pelotas - Porto Alegre | Rs. 200$000 |
| ida e volta | Rs. 360$000 |
| Rio Grande — Pelotas | Rs. 50$000 |
| Rio Grande — Santa Victoria | Rs. 200$000 |
| ida e volta | Rs. 360$000 |

Voos circulares sobre as cidades de Porto Alegre, Pelotas e Rio Grande Rs. 80$000

Creanças até 2 annos não pagam passagem, de 2 a 10 annos a metade.

Bagagem: Cada passageiro adulto terá direito ao transporte livre de bagagens, até 10 kilos; qualquer quantidade que exceder, será cobrada na razão de 1$000 p. kg. e deve ser avisada em tempo pelo Sr. passageiro.

## Serviço Postal

Cartas até 20 gr. . . . . . . 1$000 | Amostras sem valor por
Mais de 20 gr. por fracção 0$700 | cada 50 gr. . . 1$000
Manuscriptos p. cada 50 gr. 1$000 | encommendas post. c. 50 g. 1$000

Endereços e agencias do

## CONDOR-SYNDIKAT

BERLIN W 66, Mohrenstrasse 11/12, Telegrammas „SINCONDOR"
PORTO ALEGRE, Rua das Flores 11, Teleph. 3616 „SINCONDOR"
RIO GRANDE, Rua Rheingantz 673, Telegrammas „SINCONDOR"

RIO DE JANEIRO: Hermann Stoltz & Cia., Avenida Rio Branco, Telegrammas „NORDLLOYD"
SANTOS: Zerrenner, Boslow & Cia. Lida., Rua do Commercio 55. Telegr. „NORDLLOYD"
FLORIANOPOLIS — SÃO FRANCISCO: Hoepke & Cia. Telegrammas „HOEPKE"
PORTO ALEGRE: Bromberg & Cia., Rua das Flores 11, Telephone 5616, Telegr. „OTERNO"
PELOTAS: A. Doormann, Rua G. Osorio 601, Teleph. 1279-Casa 83-M e R. Telegr. „DOORMANN"
RIO GRANDE: C. Albrecht Jr., Rua Marechal Floriano 437, Teleph. 162, Telegr. „NORDLLOYD"

Porto Alegre, em 25 de Abril de 1927.

CONDOR-SYNDIKAT.

Para não perder o avião os Srs. Passageiros devem apresentar-se no porto 30 min. antes da hora marcada para a partida.

Typographia Do Centro, Porto Alegre

Original CONDOR service schedule for Rio Grande - Pelotas - Porto Alegre - Santa Victoria route

On 20-21 May 1927 Charles A. Lindbergh, "Lucky Lindy," and the *Spirit of St. Louis* entered the history books and, ten days later, *Atlântico* opened the route Rio Grande - Rio de Janeiro, via Pelotas - Porto Alegre - São Paulo (or rather Santos—the port city—which afforded a landing place for seaplanes). The triangular "stamp" and a circular cachet (below) were used.

Oval government cachet

Circular airline cachet

On 2 June 1927 the SYNDIKAT marked the return flight, Rio de Janeiro - Porto Alegre, with the same circular cachet, the triangular "stamps," and an oval air mail postmark—presumably applied by postal authorities.

With postal service started on the "*Linha da Lagôa dos Patos*," the SYNDIKAT brought in another aircraft, a Junkers-G 24, the *Ypiranga*, for a proposed service from Porto Alegre to Rio de Janeiro and made a flight on 3 June returning on 9 June.[13]

Otto Meyer's company, S. A. EMPRESA VIAÇÃO AÉREA RIO GRANDENSE (VARIG), was officially registered on 1 May and received authorization to operate—within the state of Rio Grande do Sul—on 10 June, and legally became Brazil's first airline. On 15 June the *Atlântico* and the "*Linha*" were taken over by VARIG (with the SYNDIKAT receiving its sizable interest share and Hammer a place on its Board of Directors), and seven days later VARIG made its first scheduled flight replacing the SYNDIKAT service in Rio Grande do Sul.

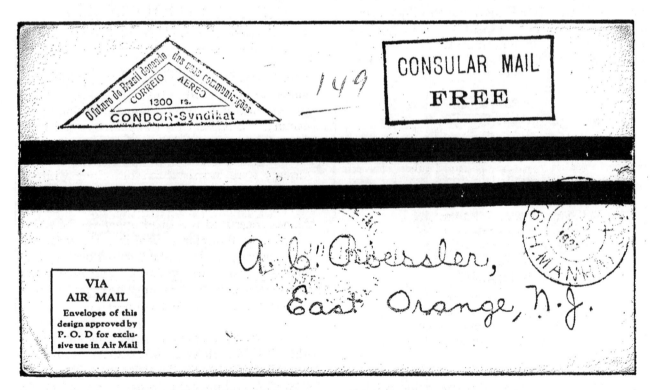

15 October 1927: Santos - Rio de Janeiro - East Orange, NJ
Consular mail + 1,300 rs. air mail = Correct 20 gr. rate for under 500 km.
Stamp dealer Roessler apparently had this cover sent via diplomatic pouch since there was no air service to the U. S.

The CONDOR SYNDIKAT ceased to operate, officially, on 1 July 1927, although it continued survey flights. Somewhat confusingly, and perhaps on purpose, a new Brazilian company of almost the same name, SYNDICATO CONDOR LTDA. (CONDOR) was formed with many of the SYNDIKAT personnel on its board and its capital provided by Fritz Hammer, Herm Stoltz (a company in Rio de Janeiro which represented the SYNDIKAT in Brazil) and a few others.

CONDOR, with Fritz Hammer as its Director General, operated somewhat "illegally" because it was not formally incorporated until 1 December and not officially authorized to operate until 20 January 1928. Official Brazil recognition often came several months after "unofficial" approval and/or actual operations. However, on 20 August 1927 CONDOR obtained provisional permission to fly the route between Rio de Janeiro and Natal and to operate its aircraft between the mainland and the island of Fernando de Noronha, off Natal—the first step into and, eventually, across the South Atlantic.[14]

On 9 November 1927 CONDOR carried the mail from Rio de Janeiro to Porto Alegre and, the next day, VARIG continued it on to Pelotas and Rio Grande. A large CONDOR cachet was used together with smaller date stamps. This was the first use of CONDOR's newly produced stamps, which were also adapted by VARIG through the use of overprints (see p. 105).

Rio de Janeiro: 9 November (violet)
Porto Alegre: 10 November (violet)
Pelotas: 10 November (violet)
Rio Grande: 12 November (violet)

CONDOR was the means for VARIG to extend beyond the borders of Rio Grande do Sul, as it had the equipment and the financial support necessary to provide such service.

Two more Wals, the *Santos Dumont* and the *Bartholomeu de Gusmão*, had been added by the company in 1927, but they were lost to accidents the following year. The Wals *Olinda* and *Jangadeiro* were also acquired. Other aircraft, Junkers F 13s and G 24s, were added in 1928. In the early weeks of June 1928 CONDOR, using a Junkers G 24, conducted an expedition to the far north of Brazil and reached most of the cities which would eventually become part of its network.

The following month the LUFT HANSA Dornier Wal *Lubeck* did some exploratory work on the eastern side of the system flying to the Canary Islands under a Spanish contract with a Spanish crew—one of the many ways around the limitations of the "Rules." It was later added to CONDOR's fleet as the *Gunabara*. In December a graphic cachet developed with VARIG, picturing a stylized Wal, was introduced: "Utilize the National Hydroplanes."

In the United States, the year 1928 saw a virtual revolution in the aircraft industry following the successes of men and women who had the ability (and stamina) to pioneer. New companies were formed with new capital and old companies were merged into bigger companies to develop new aircraft. Airports were increased ten-fold along with the number of applications for pilot licenses. Flying miles doubled, quantity of mail carried tripled, and the passenger load was quadrupled. By the end of the year, 4,500 airplanes were in commercial use. Public lethargy had vanished almost overnight. In June 29-year-old Amelia Earhart had become the first woman to fly the Atlantic (with two men). Four years later she would do it again—alone!

In the same year Brazil saw the establishment of AEROPOSTAL BRASILEIRA, C.G.A.'s subsidiary (see AÉROPOSTALE); the founding of the short-lived ETA; and the groundwork being laid for the ill-fated NYRBA line, much of which was done with the cooperation of CONDOR.

In early 1929 CONDOR developed a new cachet hand stamp (above) advising one and all: "Do not keep me waiting Reply by 'CONDOR AIR'."

CONDOR developed several flights with VARIG and another cachet (below) soon appeared commemorating these joint venture flights.

**VARIG-CONDOR**

In January 1929 Admiral Byrd made his first flight over "Little America"; in February Frank B. Kellogg, U. S. Secretary of State, sent a letter to Enrique Olaya Herrera,[15] Colombia's minister to Washington, agreeing to the Kellogg-Olaya Herrera Pact, the first U. S. reciprocal aviation agreement; in March the third non-stop crossing of the South Atlantic was made from Seville to Bahia; and, in August the *Graf Zeppelin* completed the first airship flight around the world.

In October the world's largest flying boat—the largest aircraft at that time—lifted off a lake between Germany and Switzerland on its first flight. Suffering from an overworked factory in Italy—CMASA was building aircraft for 21 different countries—Dornier had established a factory, A.G. fur Dornier Flugzeuge at Altenrhein, Switzerland, a spit of land projecting into the lake roughly due south of Friedrichshafen on the German side. The lake, of course, is Lake Constance (Konstanz), also known as Bodensee; the plane was the Dornier DO-X.[16]

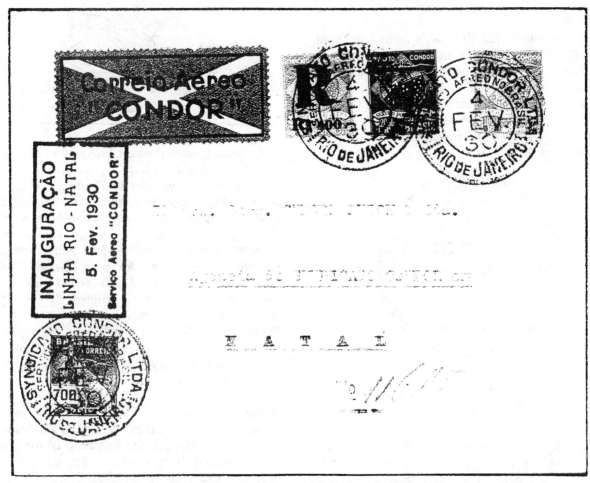

5 February 1930: First Flight: Rio de Janeiro - Natal
700 rs. postage + 3,000 rs. air + 400 rs. registration = Correct rate for 2,200 km.

Three days later, "Black Thursday" hit Wall Street in New York—the Great Depression was on its way. On 5 February 1930, in spite of the economic trauma starting to engulf the world, CONDOR tripled its network mileage by inaugurating service on the 1,400 mile line between Rio de Janeiro and Natal (opposite, below). The return was on 9 February.

The economic conditions in Germany following the First World War had prompted thousands to move elsewhere—to places like Brazil and Argentina. To accommodate the situation, the Hamburg-Amerika Line built several vessels for carrying only third-class and steerage passengers. But they also built a luxury, three-stacker, the *Cap Arcona*, "the most wonderful ship in the German merchant navy." It was commissioned in November 1927. Its 575 first-class staterooms were all outside and each had private bathroom facilities—a luxury for its time.[17] Its engines could push its 27,560 gross tons at 20 knots. It was an ideal vehicle for the rapid transfer of mail across the Atlantic.[18]

A new era opened on 21 March 1930 (below) when CONDOR flew its inaugural route from Brazil to Europe. Planes carried the mail from Rio de Janeiro - Bahia - Natal and on the 22nd the Dornier Wal *Jangadeiro* flew out to the *Cap Arcona* landing on the open sea. The pilot was Fritz Hammer. Two days were saved (19 vs. 21) in time, but subsequent transfers would be made in the sheltered bay of

Fernando de Noronha. The mail was ferried across to the Canary Islands for further air service by LUFT HANSA. There was still their desire to produce true through service—totally by air, using heavier-than-air equipment—but this was destined to wait for improvements in the basic aircraft designs.

CONDOR also served as the Brazilian agent for the interconnecting services (and sale of stamps) for the first Zeppelin flight to and from Brazil. On 18 May 1930 the *Graf Zeppelin* left Friedrichshafen on the first of many trips to Brazil. At the Guiquia field in Recife, the mail was taken over for further transmittal by CONDOR aircraft. The transfer time between Rio de Janeiro and Berlin was now reduced to five days. CONDOR would continue to service subsequent flights of the *Graf* and, later, the *Hindenburg*, but such service would be paid through government issued stamps (see DEUTSCHE LUFT-SCHIFFBAU ZEPPELIN and Appendix C).

The CONDOR/LUFT HANSA air-sea-air experiments continued, but the exchanges at Fernando de Noronha were far from successful. The service was dependent on the steamship schedules either north or southbound, consequently, scheduled mail service did not exist. Mail transfers were planned for 18 April and 3 May 1930 but were canceled. The fourth planned transfer took place successfully on 14 June (backstamped Berlin 23 June).

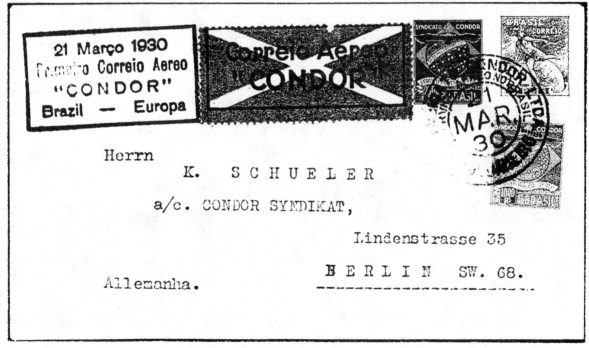

21 March 1930: First Flight: Rio de Janeiro - Natal - Berlin
500 rs. postage + 3,000 rs. air = Correct rate.

22 March 1930: First Flight: Rio de Janeiro - Natal - Berlin
The Dornier Wal *Jangadeiro* fighting heavy seas off the island of Fernando de Noronha.

22 March 1930: First Flight: Rio de Janeiro - Natal - Berlin
The Dornier Wal *Jangadeiro* approaching the steamship *Cap Arcona* for mail transfer by small boat.

Correio Aéreo: A History of the Development of Air Mail Service in Brazil

The fifth transfer was on 1 July. A sixth exchange was scheduled for 15 July, but no mail is known. The *Cap Polonio*, a smaller liner,[19] participated in the seventh venture, but the plane intending to meet it lost an engine on leaving Natal—the mail was forwarded to Europe via AÉROPOSTALE.

The eighth transfer took place on 16 August (the *Cap Arcona* had sailed from Rio on the 13th). As in all the transfers, shipboard passengers could also forward mail or send messages back to Brazil. The use of CONDOR stamps ended on 30 November 1930. Since almost all of this mail was commercial and the CONDOR stamps, which might have appealed to collectors, were no longer used, much of it has been lost over time. The last two at sea transfers were made in 1931. The ninth operation involved no transfer off Natal, but the *Cap Arcona*, which departed Rio on 13 August, transferred mail to LUFT HANSA aircraft at Las Palmas on the 20th.

The final service attempt was after the *Cap Arcona* left Hamburg on 1 September. The mail was transferred to the *Olinda* at Fernando de Noronha and flown to Natal. In attempting to lift off at Natal, the *Olinda* hit a submerged object and blew up. Two bags of mail were salvaged later, some of it being marked "CORRESPONDENCIA SALVA / DO ACCIDENTE / DO HYDROAVIÃO 'OLINDA'" ("Correspondence salvaged from accident of hydroplane 'Olinda'.")

Fritz W. Hammer (waving at camera) overseeing SYNDICATO CONDOR's first, rather hazardous, transfer of mail from the Dornier Wal flying-boat *Jangadeiro* to a small boat from the Hamburg-Südamerika Line steamship, *Cap Arcona*, off the coast of the island of Fernando de Noronha on 22 March 1930. Rio to Berlin in eight days, but not all air.

**HORARIO CONDOR**

| Terça Dienstag Tuesday | Quarta Mittwoch Wednesday | Quinta Donnerstag Thursday | Sexta Freitag Friday | Estações | Terça Dienstag Tuesday | Quarta Mittwoch Wednesday | Quinta Donnerstag Thursday | Sexta Freitag Friday |
|---|---|---|---|---|---|---|---|---|
| | 6:00 | | | Natal | | | 13:00 | |
| | 7:00 | | | Parahyba | | | 11:45 | |
| | 8:00 | | | Recife | | | 10:30 | |
| | 9:30 | | | Maceió | | | 9:15 | |
| | 11:00 | | | Aracajú | | | 7:45 | |
| | 13:00 | | | Bahia | | | 6:00 | |
| | | 6:00 | | Bahia | | 15:00 | | |
| | | 7:15 | | Ilhéos | | 13:00 | | |
| | | 8:15 | | Belmonte | | 12:00 | | |
| | | 9:45 | | Caravellas | | 10:30 | | |
| | | 11:30 | | Victoria | | 8:30 | | |
| | | 15:00 | | Rio de Janeiro | | 6:00 | | |
| 6:00 | | | 8:00 | Rio de Janeiro | 15:00 | | | 15:00 |
| 8:00 | | | 8:00 | Santos | 13:00 | | | 13:00 |
| 10:30 | | | 10:30 | Paranaguá | 10:30 | | | 10:30 |
| — | | | 11:00 | S. Francisco | 9:30 | | | 9:30 |
| 12:00 | | | 12:00 | Florianopolis | 8:30 | | | 8:30 |
| 15:00 | | | 15:00 | Porto Alegre | 6:00 | | | 6:00 |

IDA: Natal – Porto Alegre  VOLTA: Porto Alegre – Natal

**SYNDICATO CONDOR LTDA.**
RUA ALFANDEGA 5  RIO DE JANEIRO  TEL. 4:6241

(top) CONDOR's *Atlântico*, with the Brazilian registration number "P-BAAA," forms the cover of a timetable and rate schedule. The graphic design conveys a sense of passenger sophistication and service luxury offered, which was common in advertisements of the period (c.1930).
(bottom) The schedule lists the days of the week in Portuguese, German and English.

(top) The timetable and rate schedule's back cover features the CONDOR logo and passengers boarding the Junkers G-24 *Ypiranga* (P-BABA).

(bottom) A graphic shows the aircraft and the coastline between Natal and Porto Alegre and the three days to make the entire trip (3,440 km./2,138 mi.).

CONDOR was now established as a "Brazilian" airline—"Serviço Aéreo Na America do Sul e Para a Europa" ("Air Service in South America and to Europe")—and had major plans with LUFT HANSA to make that statement a reality.

CONDOR became "international" within South America on 29 August 1930 with the opening of service between Rio de Janeiro and La Paz, Bolivia, (covers, opposite page) in coordination with another German-backed company, LLOYD AEREO BOLIVIANO (LAB), then not quite five years old.

An air mail rate change went into effect on 12 September 1930.

| Distance (km) | Each 5 gr.* |
|---|---|
| 500 | 350 rs. |
| 1,500 | 500 rs. |
| 3,000 | 700 rs. |
| 4,500 | 1,000 rs. |
| | (* 12.5 gr. printed matter) |

Four days later CONDOR commenced service between Corumbá, on the border with Bolivia and a terminus of the railroad line from São Paulo, and Cuiabá, 230 kms. further north and the capital of the state of Mato Grosso. A Junkers F 13, piloted by Captain von Clausbruch, was used.[20] A cover marking the event (below) bears the full set of stamps overprinted for the new rates which had gone into effect four days earlier. The cover also bears the spread wing condor logo of the company which is very similar to that of SCADTA. These overprinted stamps are very hard to find on cover, especially commercial use, as they were in use for only ten weeks—the use of CONDOR stamps was terminated on 30 November 1930.

In September 1930 Fritz Hammer was replaced as the Director General of CONDOR. There were other skies for him to conquer.

Through the efforts of CONDOR, the Brazilian government granted approval to LUFT HANSA for its ill-fated, behemoth seaplane, the Dornier DO-X, to carry mail in and from Brazil. The epic flight departed Lake Constance on 5 November 1930 and suffered from continual breakdowns and equipment failures. LUFT HANSA's Captain Friedrich Christiansen, who had assumed command at the Cape Verde Islands, finally reached Fernando de Noronha on 5 June 1931 and made it to Natal the next day. Seven months had passed. The 12-motored craft underwent yet another overhaul and some re-painting. On 17 June, the DO-X left Natal flying south to Rio de Janeiro, making several stops along the way picking up both mail and fuel and several passengers. The flight consumed five days.

16 September 1930: First Flight: Corumbá - Cuiabá
[300 rs. postage + 1,350 rs. air = Unusual rate for 230 kms.]

(top) Mail being "rapidly" transferred ashore at Natal, Brazil from a Dornier Wal to a waiting CONDOR aircraft.
(bottom) 29 November 1930: A final souvenir of the CONDOR stamps on the day before they were abolished.

On 17 July 1931 Captain Fritz W. Hammer arrived in Rio de Janeiro, assumed command of the DO-X, and began preparations for the trip north. On 3 August provisional President Getúlio Vargas was flown over Rio harbor on the final test before the trek north. The *New York Times* reported that the plane would follow the PAN AM route north and "will carry no passengers or mail." This obviously would not be the case—Fritz Hammer would see to that. Three days later the ship left for Bahia carrying 20 passengers, including an avid aviation buff, Clara Adams, the first woman passenger on the *Graf Zeppelin*, west to east, and Dorit von Clausbruch, wife of one of the pilots, and "several thousand pieces of mail."

It was just afternoon on Thursday, 27 August 1931, when the craft landed near Bedloe's Island in New York harbor. The plane was moored at Glen Curtis Airport in Queens and was opened to the public. Tour proceeds were split between the American and German Red Cross. On 3 September most of the crew of the DO-X visited President Herbert Hoover in Washington. Fritz Hammer and the von Clausbruchs made a trip to the Cleveland Air Races. The DO-X returned to Germany, reaching Berlin on 24 May 1932.[21]

The DO-X flight cachet on a CONDOR envelope.

In 1931 CONDOR's service was primarily along the coast, although it eventually developed some spurs inland. To deal with some of the more remote—and less lucrative—portions of the interior, the government established CORREIO AÉREO MILITAR and

The world's largest airplane, the Dornier DO-X, a 12-engined experimental seaplane, on Lake Constance, Germany.

Airplane drawings all to the same scale ~ 1 inch = 30 feet

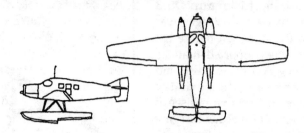

JUNKERS F-13

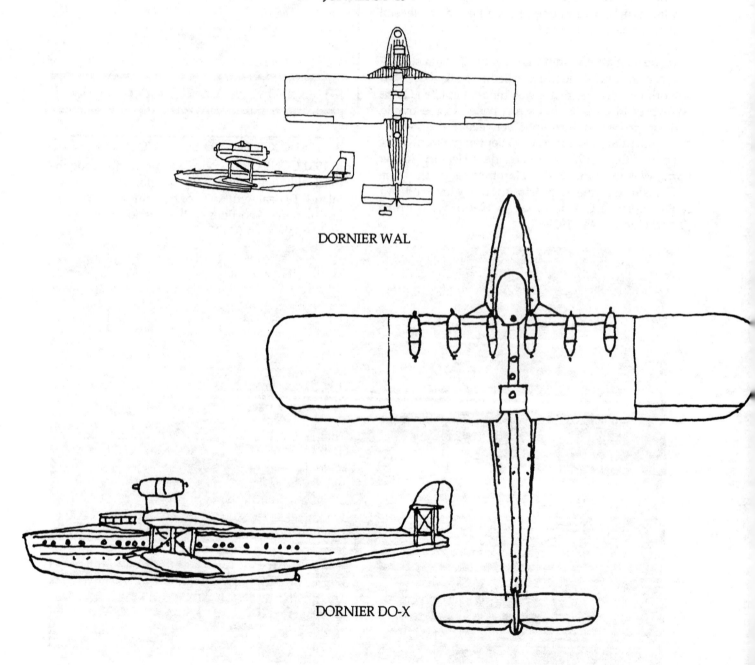

DORNIER WAL

DORNIER DO-X

proceeded over the next five years to develop landing fields, some of which were equipped with radio beacons. Airlines were coming of age in Brazil.

The new image of PANAIR DO BRASIL started to spread itself along the coastal highways paralleling the CONDOR routes. The French government, for reasons still not fully explained, withheld the postal subsidy from AÉROPOSTALE in 1931 and a management/political intrigue ensued.[22] Service along the "line" was interrupted. CONDOR filled the gap.

LUFT HANSA conducted extensive North and Baltic Seas' tests on drag-sail techniques for flying boats landing in the open seas. After the airplane maneuvered onto or above the sail, which was dragged behind the mother ship, the ship's speed was increased causing the sail to rise around the bottom of the airplane, stabilizing it even in rough seas, allowing for transfer/pick up of mail or, eventually, the aircraft itself. This drag-sail principle would eventually be used in the South Atlantic in the CONDOR/LUFT HANSA operations in 1934.

# VIA CONDOR

On 6 November 1931 CONDOR used another new cachet (above) for the first time, marking a flight between São Francisco and Rio de Janeiro, and on 21 December, yet another (below), between Curitiba and Rio de Janeiro.

This cachet (below) was first used, on 30 August 1932, on a flight between Paraiba (now João Pessoa) and Rio de Janeiro.

The *Graf* made nine flights in 1932 with air mail flying time cut to only four days between Germany and Brazil. On 1 July LUFT HANSA chartered Norddeutscher Lloyd's steamer *Westfalen* and modified it with a catapult that had been developed by Heinkel for larger planes. A large crane and drag-sail were subsequently added to the stern. Test trials were started. A new system was born.

Four days after a trial shot towards Bathurst, on 6 June 1933 a LUFT HANSA Dornier Wal, the *Passat*, was launched toward Natal —8.5 tons of metal put into the air at 150 km/hr. The *Graf Zeppelin* was about to have some stronger competition. In October 1933 another test of the *Westfalen*, now outfitted with maintenance and spare parts facilities and fuel storage capabilities, and the "indestructible" Wals was made—from take-off in Africa to landing in Brazil—in 14 hours flying time.

In 1933 the French government regrouped its airlines and AÉROPOSTALE returned under a new banner, that of AIR FRANCE. The *Graf Zeppelin* made nine flights to Brazil between May and November. On 15 July Wiley Post set out in the *Winnie Mae*, a Lockheed Vega, on a seven-day solo-flight around the world. Three days later, AEROLLOYD IGUSSAÚ commenced regular services in Brazil, bringing the number of operating companies there to five.[23] By the end of the year, VIAÇAO AÉREA SÃO PAULO (VASP) was formed, but actual operations would wait until the following year.

On 3 February 1934 a Henkel HE-70—a single-engine, low-wing monoplane, the fastest passenger transport in Europe—left Berlin's Templehof airport and flew, via Stuttgart and Marseilles, to Seville. Mail was transferred to a Junkers JU-52/3m, the tri-motored, all-metal, low-wing monoplane which was destined to become the workhorse for LUFTHANSA (its name now written as one word) and many of the companies operating in South America (as well as others around the world). The mail was carried via Las Palmas to Bathurst. There it was transferred to the *Westfalen* (or rather to the Wal, *Taifun*, waiting on its catapult).

The *Westfalen* left the harbor and, one and one-half days later, fired the *Taifun* toward Natal. Thirteen hours later, the mail was transferred to a Junkers W-34, equipped with floats (pontoons) and off on its way to Rio de Janeiro, courtesy of CONDOR. Waiting at Rio was a CONDOR connecting flight to Buenos Aires. The west-east (return) flight commenced on 7 February at Rio Grande and the mail was back-stamped five (!) days later in Stuttgart.[24] (For illustrations and a first return flight cover, see DEUTSCHE LUFTHANSA, pp. 33-36, front cover and page 2.)

With the arrival of the second converted ship, *Schwabenland*, stationed at the mouth of the Gambia

CONDOR's JU 52/3m *Tupan* in the floating dry dock at Buenos Aires (c. 1933).

CONDOR's JU 52/3m *Caiçara* in the harbor at Rio de Janeiro (c. 1933).

Correio Aéreo: A History of the Development of Air Mail Service in Brazil

River, the *Westfalen* was moved to its position off Fernando de Noronha and simultaneous operations (in opposite directions) were conducted—more efficient use of men and machines.[25]

On 2 May CONDOR/LUFTHANSA applied a rectangular cachet picturing a Wal and the launching ship. A large circular cachet was also used interchangeably on ZEPPELIN and LUFTHANSA flights outbound from Brazil—both serviced by CONDOR—so dates must be verified to determine which service was used across the Atlantic (see DEUTSCHE LUFTHANSA, p. 36).

On 20 April 1934 Argentina had granted CONDOR permission to transport its mail and Uruguay followed within a month. The first CONDOR-ZEPPELIN Brazil - Argentina air mail flight occurred in June 1934, when the *Graf Zeppelin* flew to Buenos Aires (see p. 59). Later that year, the Stuttgart - Bathurst - *Westfalen* - Natal flight on 15 December by LUFTHANSA-CONDOR was marked with an interesting cachet (below)—the usual weekly flight was then carrying mail destined for Christmas delivery—a Wal was shown flying over a branch of a decorated tree, complete with ornament and lighted candle.

In January 1935 Amelia Earhart, "First Lady of the Airways," performed a first flight—Hawaii to the continental United States. In March, Nazi General Hermann Wilhelm Göring transformed the Zeppelin Company into an instrument of the Third Reich and, by the end of the month, LUFTHANSA inaugurated night service, reducing the flying time from Germany to Brazil to three days.

During 1935 AIR FRANCE (from the ashes of AÉROPOSTALE) operated 42 flights across the South Atlantic, starting fortnightly on 1 February. LUFTHANSA operated 80 flights and, after 1 July, through an arrangement with AIR FRANCE, flight schedules were adjusted so that bi-weekly service was available.

On 5 October 1935 CONDOR flew Rio de Janeiro - Porto Alegre - Montevideo - Buenos Aires - Mendoza - Santiago, "over" the Andes for the first time. Actually, the flight should be called "through" the Andes at a narrow pass that in good weather could be traversed by a skilled pilot. Unfortunately, the weather usually wasn't good, although the pass had been equipped with a radio beacon. The airplanes of this period were not capable of climbing to the altitude (7,000 m.) necessary to fly "over" the Andes. The highest point in South America is just north of this point. The JU-52's limit was 5,200 m. Better airplanes were needed.

On 15 February 1936 the Dornier Wal *Tornado* was lost after launching (eastbound) from the *Westfalen*. The *Schwabenland* was replaced by the *Ostmark*, a smaller, but faster—especially designed—catapult ship. This third ship would allow for overhaul and maintenance without interrupting the service. On 19 April the German terminal was changed from Stuttgart to Frankfurt. The larger Dornier Wals, DO-18s, entered service this year. The *Schwabenland* was moved further north and eight survey flights were conducted on the route Lisbon - Azores (sometimes Bermuda was added) - New York during the period 11-26 September. After launching the two Wals, *Aeolus* and *Zephyr*, the ship would steam across the Atlantic to prepare for the return launchings. The *Schwabenland* was joined by the *Friesenland* and by the airplanes *Norwind* and *Nordmeer* on the Northern route.

AIR FRANCE made 104 weekly crossings in 1937. The *Graf* began its last scheduled flight to Brazil on 26 April as the events of 6 May ended the zeppelin era—transatlantic air service was now strictly by heavier-than-air equipment.

In the South Atlantic, the 250th crossing by the LUFTHANSA-CONDOR consortium was marked on 10 June 1937 by a cachet (below), printed in various colors, applied at Bahia, Rio de Janeiro, São Paulo, Santos, Florianópolis and Porto Alegre.

Flying "through" the Andes (c. 1935)

CONDOR's Junkers G-24 *Potugar* (P-BAHA) at a stop along the mail route (c. 1930)

Correio Aéreo: A History of the Development of Air Mail Service in Brazil

Cardinal Pacelli (later Pope Pius XII) deplanes from CONDOR's JU 52/3m *Caiçara* (PP-CAV)
on his visit to Rio de Janeiro in October 1934.

SYNDICATO CONDOR's Junkers JU 52/3m *Caiçara* (PP-CAV) on the "beach."

At the beginning of 1938 LUFTHANSA began its own operations paralleling CONDOR (somewhat akin to PAN AM and PANAIR's operations). LUFTHANSA's aims in South America became more obvious with the establishment of SUCURSAL PERU and the opening of the route (720 miles) Lima - Arequipa - La Paz. Efforts were made to connect the line with SEDTA. If successful, the overall network would have reached within 600 miles of the Panama Canal. SUCURSAL attempted to establish air service to the Galapagos Islands in May 1940—not much economic sense for an island population of about 2,000, but strategically located on the western approach to the Panama Canal.

While LUFTHANSA looked for further long-distance expansion, CONDOR concentrated on Brazil. Service had been opened to Belém with the line from Rio de Janeiro inaugurated on 15 April 1936, marked by a special envelope. CONDOR's thrusts into the interior, relatively remote, under-populated areas of Corumbá and Porto Velho (further north in Rondina) were unusual, unless their proximity to the neighboring countries with "friendly" airlines—Bolivia (LAB) and Colombia (SCADTA)—were considered with "ulterior" motives.

On 27 March 1938 a Dornier DO-18 Wal was catapulted off the *Westfalen* then steaming off the Devon coast of England. It established a long-distance record for a seaplane—5,000-plus miles, non-stop—to Caravelas, Brazil (on the coast about 200 miles north of Vitória). On 6 April the return flight, Rio de Janeiro - Las Palmas, was made.

By the middle of the year LUFTHANSA's first land plane to cross the South Atlantic, a Focke-Wulf FW-200, set a new record (9 hours, 47 minutes) between Bathurst and Natal, and joined CONDOR service. The FW-200 was the first successful four-engine land plane and was destined to replace the JU 52.

The German army invaded Poland on 1 September 1939—World War II had begun. CONDOR assumed all of LUFTHANSA's service in South America. LUFTHANSA's efforts were needed at home. CONDOR continued to expand and solidify its network. Some routes, previously operated by the Brazilian military, were turned over to CONDOR operation, including a line between Belem and Oiapoque, near the border of French Guiana. Service had been opened between Porto Velho and Xapuri (Acre) and then between Porto Velho and Cruzeiro do Sul near the Peruvian border.

In 1939 the Colombian government announced plans to nationalize all air lines within the country. The following year, a new (and still extant) national company was formed: AEROVÍAS NACIONALES DE COLOMBIA (AVIANCA). It absorbed SCADTA and a much smaller line, SERVIÇIO AÉREO COLOMBIANO (SACO). Two German ex-SCADTA pilots organized another small line, AEROVÍAS RAMALES COLOMBIANAS, S.A.(ARCO), which was acquired by AVIANCA less than a year later.

The nationalization movement by the various governments in South America continued as attempts were made to rid the lines of German influence. The United States' concern—soon approaching paranoia—over the "enemy" operating so close to the Panama Canal, obviously, came to bear on some of these decisions. Efforts to "encourage" the transfer to nationals were increased as the United States itself was drawn closer to the war. One recourse which eventually would be used to expedite "cooperation" was the withholding of aviation gasoline, a "weapon of war" which could be—and was—used to terminate airline flights.

Meanwhile, Fritz Hammer had moved to Ecuador where, again with the backing of LUFTHANSA, he established the SOCIEDAD ECUATORIANA DE TRANSPORTES AÉREOS (SEDTA) on 24 July 1937 and began survey flight operations between Guayaquil and Quito (about 160 miles). The company was in obvious competition with PANAGRA and an apparent attempt by the Germans to further establish themselves in South America— LUFTHANSA already had trans-continental connecting service across Bolivia by the German influenced LLOYD AÉREO BOLIVIANO (LAB) and, in 1938, across Peru by DEUTSCHE LUFTHANSA SUCURSAL PERU—and closer to the Panama Canal, to the fear of the U. S. government. Ecuador provided no subsidies for mail or anything else, and the company had to provide its own capital from its own income. This was, in the case of SEDTA, not enough to cover its overhead.

Guayaquil at sea level, Quito at 2,700 meters, mountain passes at 4,200 meters and still active volcanos reaching 6,000 meters in-between, the route presented problems. Adding to these problems was the untimely death of its founder: Fritz Hammer, fellow German pilot Conrad Butscher, and Ecuadorian crewmen Marco Aguirre and Ricard Weiss all perished in the crash of their Junkers W 34 on a peak in the fog-shrouded Andes mountains, not far from Guayaquil. Reported missing on Friday, 4 March 1938, the wreckage was found the next day. Outside the gates of Quito, in a German cemetery surrounded by eucalyptus, the intrepid explorer Fritz Wilhelm Hammer found his rest.

With the advent of the war, most of the German airline influence in South America ended. For SEDTA, the date was 5 September 1941, when already having deprived it of fuel, the Ecuadorian government commandeered its remaining equipment. Like Fritz Hammer, dead at forty-nine, SEDTA's flying days were over.

SUCURSAL PERU was absorbed by PANAGRA in April 1941. LAB was "nationalized" in May with PANAGRA holding a 25% share for "management." SEDTA's gasoline was curtailed in May, but it managed to continue reduced operations until September when the Ecuadorian government suspended them. PANAGRA's line was further extended as a result.

And CONDOR? Restrictions on foreign employees operating in Brazil were established as early as 1931, when the government required that two-thirds of each employee category be nationals. This proved extremely difficult because of the lack of qualified personnel and the replacement process was, therefore, a slow one. In 1936 another decree required 100% nationals and that "naturalized" foreigners could not exceed one-third, a provision apparently aimed at the German operations. The final goal was eventually to require 100% ownership of all "local" air transportation by Brazilian nationals.

As the United States began to exert its influence into the airlines of the Americas by convincing the respective governments of the inherent threat of German dominance within their borders, it was understood that German pilots, mechanics, and, eventually, German equipment would have to go. The obvious difficulty was "what" would replace them. CONDOR had been the service facility for most of the airlines operating in South America and the mechanics remained Germans or "naturalized" German-Brazilians. Very few "true" nationals were trained as pilots or mechanics, and the equipment still depended on Germany for spare parts—parts which were not interchangeable with "American-made" items.

The "Allies" or, more specifically, the United States, eyed the "shoulder" of Brazil as the easy stepping stone for supplying military forces in the Mediterranean and Southern Europe. To accomplish this, the facilities of PAN AM and CONDOR would have to be "developed" but, more importantly in the latter case, "controlled." One of the first steps, then, would be the enforcement of the established regulations that airlines be "nationally" controlled. Pressure was brought to bear on CONDOR. This was somewhat strange, since PAN AM operated 100% control of PANAIR and, even after recapitalization of PANAIR in 1943, still held 50%. Another decree, in October 1939, limited "foreign" companies' operations to within 15 kilometers of the coast. PAN AM's Rio - Asunción line was specifically excluded. The government even helped start a new national airline, NAB (see NAVEGAÇÃO AÉREA BRASILEIRA S/A) in 1940.

Another CONDOR rate schedule (above) envisions a panorama of the harbor at Rio de Janeiro (c. 1935) with planes landing and taking off and and a CONDOR launch heading for shore. The plane at left, by its markings "PP-CAX" would be the Junkers JU 52/3m *Curupira*. CONDOR had several different model hydroplanes in operation at this time (from Don Thomas, *Nostalgia Panamericana*, 1987, courtesy of the author).

Airplane drawings all to the same scale ~ 1 inch = 30 feet.

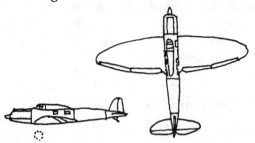

HEINKEL HE 70

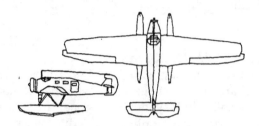

JUNKERS W 34

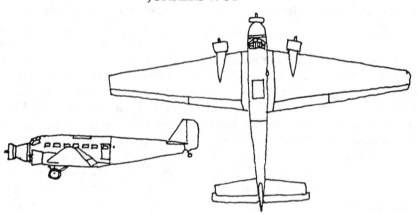

JUNKERS JU 52/3m

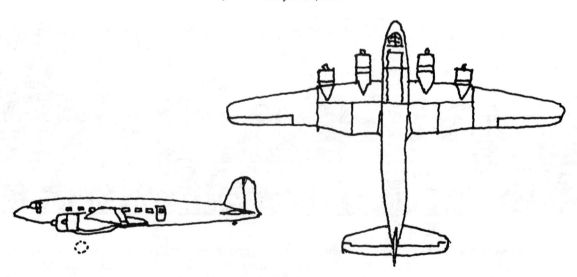

FOCKE-WULF FW 200

"All men of action utilize CONDOR air service. Mail service, South on Monday and Thursday, North on Wednesday, closes at 6 p.m." An advertisement (Herm. Stolz & Company was the SYNDICATO CONDOR agent in Rio de Janeiro), c. 1930, sometimes found inside covers or in mail pouches.

Another development was the improvement in and increased use of land airplanes. In the Douglas DC-3 and Boeing 307 "strato–clipper" type—sealed, pressurized cabins permitting flying above 20,000 feet—land planes, a viable alternative was to be found to the German models. In July 1941 PANAIR was authorized by the government to improve or construct at least eight land plane bases along the "shoulder" from Amapa (north of the Amazon) to São Salvador (Bahia). American capital, equipment, management and technical assistance would be provided, including the training of local personnel. The Roosevelt administration provided "special defense funds" to help finance these operations.

In August 1941 CONDOR's name was changed to SERVIÇOS AÉREOS CONDOR and, under further political pressure, ceased operations at the year's end. The Brazilian government assumed the "assets" of the company (12 JU 52s, 2 FW 200s) and the debt to the "parent" LUFTHANSA (US $2.7 million).[26] After a further naturalization process, services were resumed in April 1942 and, in November, the name was again changed to SERVIÇOS AEREOS CRUZEIRO DO SUL, LTDA., known today as simply CRUZEIRO.

◊

"Compliments" baggage label.

Airplane drawings all to the same scale ~ 1 inch = 30 feet

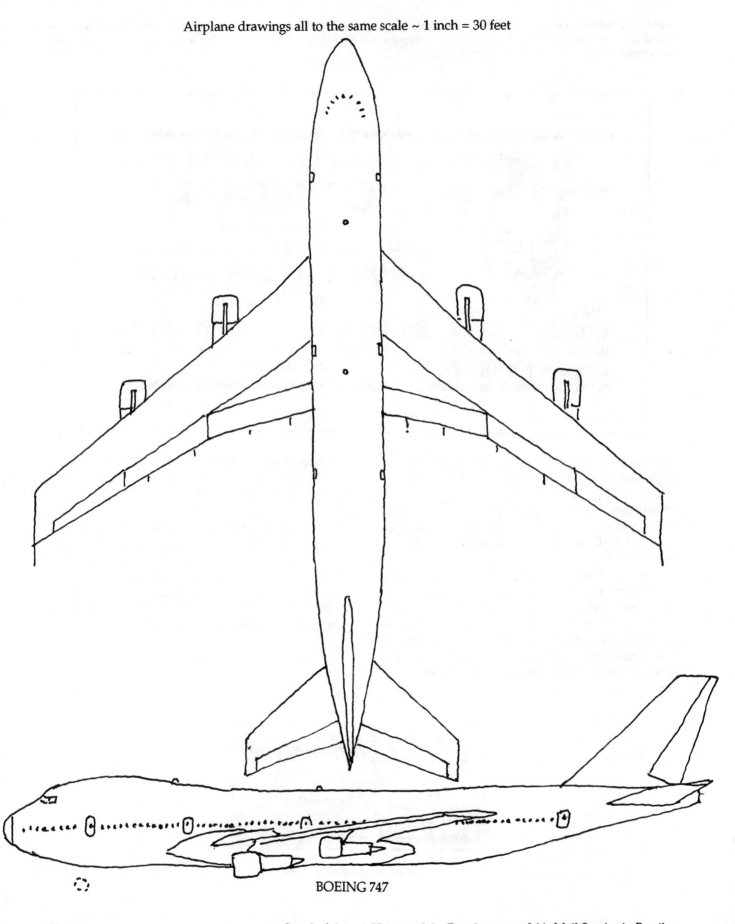

BOEING 747

Correio Aéreo: A History of the Development of Air Mail Service in Brazil

# VIAÇÃO AÉREA SÃO PAULO, S.A.

German interest and influence in airline development, as well as their special interest in South America, has already been discussed throughout this book. The Junkers Company provided relatively small companies with equipment at very favorable terms. These companies, now desirous of obtaining larger multi-engine aircraft but usually unable to meet up-front payment demands—30% cash with order, balance on delivery—of the British and American suppliers, were able to obtain JU 52s, that were to be the mainstay of the early airlines in Latin America, relatively easily.

Buying through LUFTHANSA or CONDOR at prices about 50% less than comparable American models, the companies also received extended payment plans (e.g., four- or five-year pay-backs at monthly amounts determined by the amount of flying time—a sort of early version of the variable rate mortgage). The 17-passenger tri-motored version of the JU 52, the JU 52/3m, first appeared in April 1932 and its all-metal structure, covered in corrugated sheet Duralumin, proved to be very satisfactory in the South American climate. Supplying 30 airlines worldwide, almost 200 were produced between 1932 and 1939—about half still in operation at the end of 1940.

In Curitiba on 28 February 1932 the Mate Leão company started an airline, AEROLLOYD IGUASSÚ S.A., with two Klemm three-seat monoplanes and very little capital. The first test flight was between Blumenau and Joinville on 8 May. Government authorization followed on 30 June and air service was inaugurated between Curitiba and São Paulo on 18 July 1933. AEROLLOYD (as VASP which followed) started service long after the government started issuing airmail stamps so they did not get involved with company produced stamps; however, AEROLLOYD used a cachet similar to CONDOR's pre-stamps (above, right).

In November 1933 a group of private investors in São Paulo joined together to deal with the problem of rapid access to the many small and mid-sized towns throughout the coffee-rich state and they formed another airline, VIAÇÃO AÉREA SÃO PAULO, S.A. (VASP). Scheduled service was started on 16 April 1934 between São Paulo, Ribeirão Preto and Uberaba (cover and cachet, below).

16 April 1934: First Flight: São Paulo - Ribeiro Preto

The next day VASP opened the route—São Paulo - São Carlos - Rio Preto. Increased capital was added by the investors, which now included the City of São Paulo. The following year the state government added to the equity funds and became, eventually, the largest shareholder in the operation; the municipal bank became an investor; and VASP acquired two Junkers JU 52/3ms through the São Paulo office of German importer, Theo. Wille e Cia.

AEROLLOYD IGUASSÚ made several first flights during 1933: Joinville - Curitiba, 16 February; Matinhos - Curitiba, 12 July; São Paulo - Curitiba, 18 July; and São Paulo - Cuiabá, 6 September. In 1934 it opened the line São Paulo - Curitiba - Joinville , and return (cover, below). The cover (opposite, top) from Santa Catharina to Rio de Janeiro, in spite of its markings, was probably carried north of São Paulo by another airline, most likely VASP, since, to my knowledge, AEROLLOYD did not go that far north. On 15 January 1935 AEROLLYD extended to Florianópolis—these were not long flights: Curitiba - São Paulo, 260 mi.; - Florianópolis, 170 mi.

Meanwhile, VASP opened the route—São Paulo - Franca—on 13 September 1935. A first flight was made between São Paulo and Rio de Janeiro on 4 August 1936. Traffic on this route was more than all her other routes combined and made VASP a "major" line.

In March 1937 a red advertising cachet was applied.

# VIA VASP

VASP inaugurated service on 3 September 1937 between São Paulo and Araquari and—São Paulo - Araquari - Goiânia— on 31 July 1938, with—São Paulo - Curitiba—following on 10 October 1938. The first "Rapid Service" on the São Paulo - Rio de Janeiro route was commenced on 20 December 1938 (cachet, right).

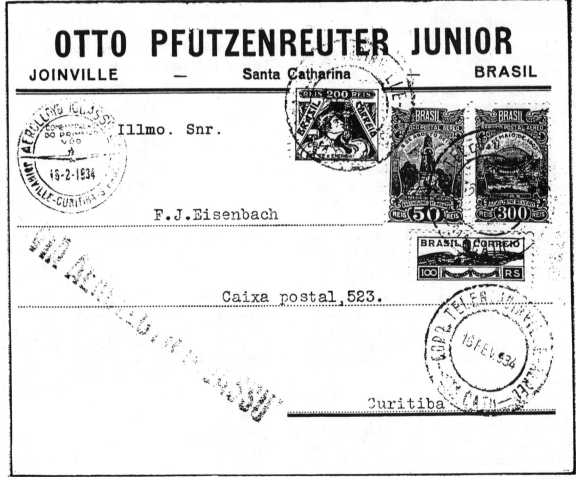

16 February 1934: First Flight: Joinville - Curitiba
200 rs. postage + 350 rs. air mail + 100 rs. required sur-tax

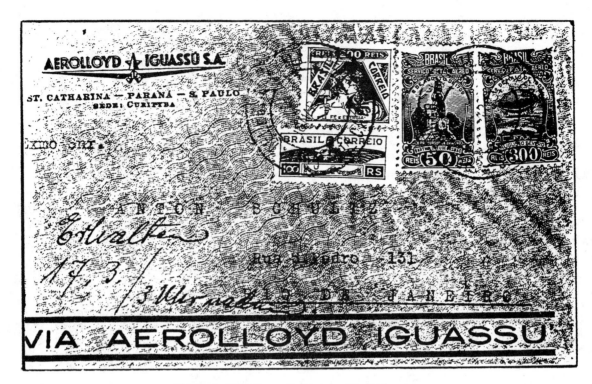

16 March 1934: Santa Catharina - Rio de Janeiro
200 rs. postage + 350 rs. air mail + 100 rs. required sur-tax

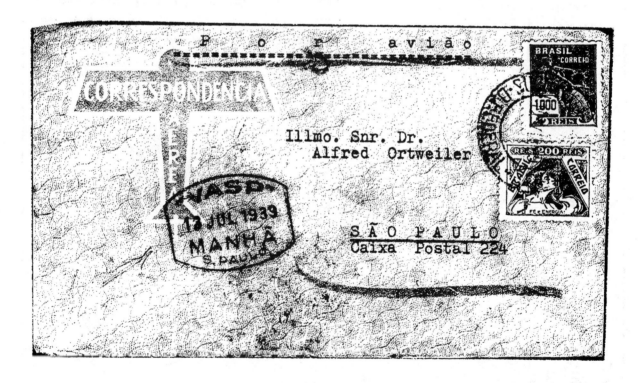

13 July 1939: Rio de Janeiro - São Paulo
1,200 rs. postage/ air mail

AEROLLOYD IGUASSÚ did not have the means to carry out its projected development and was forced into negotiations with VASP. Law No. 4812 of 28 October 1939 authorized VASP to assume AEROLLOYD's contract and the routes it formerly operated. Service was inaugurated from São Paulo to Florianópolis on 30 November (cachet, above left). The first anniversary of the "Rapid Service" was marked by a special cachet (above, center). Another circular cachet was applied during a festival week at the time of the sixth anniversary of VASP, in a curious fashion--in red and black, one on top of the other (above, right).

In 1940-41, the São Paulo National Industries Fair was promoted by a series of cachets applied, in different colors, over an extended period:

7-21 September (red)
22 September-7 October (yellow-green)
8-22 October (blue)
22 October-6 November (violet)
7-26 November (black)
27 November-6 December (red)
7-21 December (dark green)
22 December-1 January (blue)

7 September 1940: Opening Day, National Industries Fair, São Paulo.

7 September 1940: São Paulo - Rio Grande
1,200 rs. postage/air mail

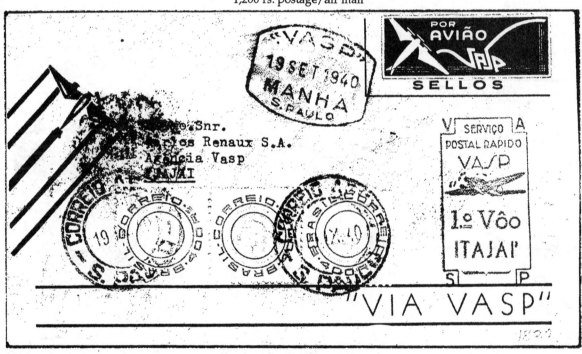

19 September 1940: São Paulo - Itajai
1,200 rs. postage/air mail

A similar appearing cachet was used to commemorate the new service from São Paulo to Itajai, 19 September 1940, applied in green(above) and on opening the line from Rio de Janeiro to Porto Alegre, 28 November, the color of which varied with the city at which it was applied (right).

 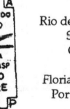

Rio de Janeiro (black)
São Paulo (blue)
Curitiba (violet)
Itajai (red)
Florianópolis (green)
Porto Alegre (blue)

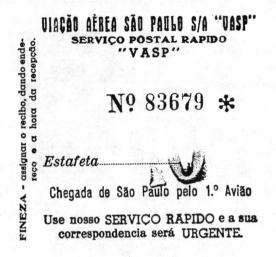

For the "Rapid Service" VASP used a yellow-colored paper sticker (above), usually applied to the back of envelopes, which was used to record the time and date of delivery, something akin to the "Return Receipt Request" form used in the U. S. Because these were fragile and lightly attached, many have been lost over time.

The second anniversary of the "Rapid Service" line between São Paulo and Rio de Janeiro was noted on

20 December (cover, below). The "bird" is a stylized top view of a Junkers JU 52/3m (see VASP label on the cover at bottom of previous page and drawing on page 148).

As the conflict in Europe worsened, it might have been expected that German supported operations in Latin America would have suffered. However, this did not happen, at least initially, as funds, either originating with or funneled through CONDOR were apparently made available to most, if not all, of the German-supported airlines operating at that time. CONDOR's storehouses were well stocked with the spare parts necessary to keep the equipment operating. This position was further strengthened, between March and May 1941, when three German supply ships evaded the English blockade bringing in a quantity of spare engines, more than 20 tons of spare parts, and two complete Junkers JU-52s.[1]

Germany's effort to support the airline activities in South America, while involved in a war at home, dramatically emphasizes the importance she placed on these activities (as well as Latin American public opinion).

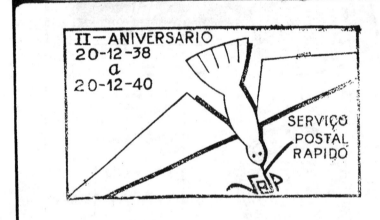

20 December 1940: Second Anniversary of the "Rapid Line": São Paulo - Rio de Janeiro
1,200 rs. postage/air mail

By the fall of 1941, however, the blockade had become increasingly more effective, and certain shortages (particularly spark plugs) started to take their toll. German and other foreign influences in the airlines would soon be reduced and/or eliminated entirely. It is interesting to note that at about the time of the reorganization of CONDOR approximately 62% of its routes were "paralleled by Panair do Brasil or VASP or both."[2]

The demise of the Axis influence in Latin American airline operations has already been discussed. A formal policy was established at the third meeting of the Foreign Ministers of the American Republics held in Rio de Janeiro on 28 January 1942, where it resolved:

> To recommend to each American Republic that in harmony with its national laws, immediate steps be taken to restrict the operation or use of civil or commercial aircraft and the use of aviation facilities to bona fide citizens and enterprises of the American Republics or to citizens or enterprises of such other countries as have shown themselves, in the judgement of the respective countries, to be in full sympathy with the principles of the Declaration of Lima.

The Third Anniversary of the "Rapid Service" had been marked on 20 December 1941 (below, left), and service between São Paulo and Anapolis opened two days later (below, right).

VASP made it through the war by cannibalizing its equipment as spare parts for its fleet of five German-made JU 52/3ms dwindled and replacement sources were eliminated. At war's end however, it turned to DC-3s (C 47s) and acquired at least 16 in the period 1946-1948.

VASP opened routes to Presidente Prudente and Tupa (and various intermediate points) in 1947 and followed in subsequent years to develop routes between São Paulo, Maringa, Londrina and Curitiba.

Expansion during 1955-1960 involved major routes to Corumbá, Cuiabá, Goiânia, and an extension of the Anapolis route to the new capital of Brasília. In 1957 the coastal route was extended northward from Rio de Janeiro to Salvador, Recife, Natal and Fortaleza. Direct flights commenced between both São Paulo and Rio de Janeiro and Belo Horizonte. A multi-stop route north from Brasília to Belem was opened.

Route development and the inter-connecting of the cities serviced was paralleled with the acquisition of new modern equipment, including DC-3s. Turbo-propped Viscount 810s were ordered in 1958 and Caravelle jets in 1962. In the same year (1962), a two-way stock acquisition found VASP acquiring LOIDE AÉREO NACIONAL, S.A. LOIDE had developed from an association with two other post-war airlines, LINHAS AÉREAS PAULISTAS (LAP) and TRANSPORTES AÉREOS BANDEIRANTES (TABA) in 1951. TABA had absorbed NAVEGACAO AÉREA BRASILEIRA, S.A. (NAB). As a result, VASP, at least temporarily, doubled its business. However, a business recession, rampant inflation, major highway improvements (diverting some traffic to the ground), pressure from other airline competition, and labor-management difficulties combined with the political problems of a state government—which controlled the company—being in conflict with the federal government—which controlled the skies—soon found VASP in financial difficulties.

Subsequent changes in state government improved those relations, but the federal government was determined that there would be only one international carrier (VARIG), and that wasteful competition on domestic routes should be minimized or eliminated. At one point, it considered a forced merger of VASP and SADIA while VARIG was involved in absorbing REAL.

VASP continues to operate today with the other three national lines—TRANSBRASIL (formerly SADIA), CRUZEIRO DO SUL (formerly CONDOR) and, of course, VARIG.

◊

# APPENDICES

## A. CROSSING THE SOUTH ATLANTIC

The South Atlantic was first successfully crossed by airplane by Captain Arturo de Sacadura Cabral (1892-1924) and his navigator, Captain Carlos Viegas Gago Coutinho (1869-1959), who flew from Lisbon on 30 March 1922 in a Fairey III D seaplane, *Lusitania*, to Las Palmas, Canary Islands (about 1,000 miles) and then on to the Cape Verde Islands. On their third hop, they crossed to St. Paul's Rock (near the Equator, about 30° west longitude), and demolished their plane in the process. After another plane arrived from Portugal, they continued on to Recife and, finally, to Rio de Janeiro on 17 June 1922.[1] They received an official welcome and a $50,000 prize. In 1915 Cabral had become one of the

first military fliers in Portugal and the first naval flyer. He died in the North Sea while piloting a seaplane to Lisbon. Coutinho had invented the astrolabe for aerial navigation (1921). A Portuguese stamp (above) was one of four issued in 1972 for the 50th anniversary of the flight. The Portuguese airline, TRANSPORTES AEREOS PORTUGUESES (TAP) prepared a cachet, which also included a map of the route, for the same anniversary (left, below).

◊

In 1926 (22 January-10 February) flying from Palos, Spain, the Dornier Wal *Plus Ultra* reached Buenos Aires via Brazil (6,232 miles in 62 hours, 52 minutes flying time). The pilot was Commander Ramon Franco (brother of the Spanish dictator) assisted by Captain Julio Ruiz de Alda.

◊

The "Four Continents Flight" (25,200 miles in 4 months) of General Francesco De Pinedo (1890-1933), Captain Carlo P. Del Prete (1897-1928), and a mechanic named Zacchetti, left Rome, Italy, on 8 February 1927.[2] In an Italian Savoia Marchetti SM.55 seaplane, *Santa Maria*, they crossed from Dakar, South Africa, to Natal, Brazil, via the Cape Verde Islands (2,300 miles of sea in 5 days). De Pinedo continued the flight on to Rio de Janeiro (26 February), Buenos Aires, and Montevideo (13 March), and then north to the United States, reaching Roosevelt Dam Lake, Arizona, where his plane was lost to an accidental fire on 6 April 1927.[3]

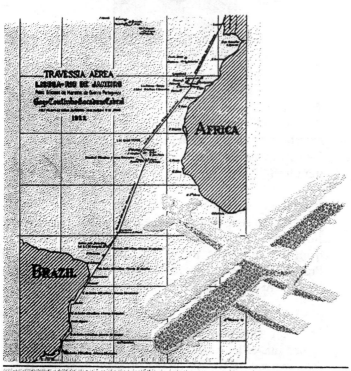

CHEGADA AO RIO DE JANEIRO
EM 17 - 6 - 1922

The Savoia Marchetti SM.55 was an unusual aircraft with its twin-hulls and a tail supported by booms extending aft from the hulls. Twin engines, mounted in tandem (pusher-puller style) were set above the cockpit located in the wing between the hulls. The design allowed easy access to all parts of the aircraft even in flight!

◊

A Brazilian flying quartet—pilot João Ribeiro de Barros (1900-?), navigator Captain Newton Braga, copilot Lieutenant João Negrão and mechanic Vasco Cinquini—left Genoa, Italy on 13 October 1926 in another SM.55, reconditioned to Barros' specifications and re-named *Jahú* after Barros' home town in São Paulo state. The route was via Gibraltar - Porto Praia - Fernando de Noronha - Natal - Recife - Salvador - Rio de Janeiro - Santos - São Paulo, arriving on 28 April 1927. One of a pair of Brazil stamps (below) honoring civil aviation pictures an artist's drawing of the airplane—canvas covered wood—which is now displayed in the Santos Dumont Foundation Aeronautics Museum in São Paulo (see also pp. 174-175).

1977 Brazil issue: 50th anniversary

◊

On 16 March 1927, in an attempt to fly around the world, the Portuguese team of Sarmento de Beires, Jorge de Castilho, Duvalle Portugal (who went only as far as Bolama) and Manuel Gouveia made a successful crossing of the South Atlantic—the first time an aircraft remained airborne over the sea during the whole night. The airplane, a CMASA/Dornier DO Wal, *Argos*, was pictured on a Portuguese stamp.

1982 Portugal issue picturing the *Argos*

◊

Starting out from Le Bourget, Paris, on 10 October 1927 two French pilots, Lieutenants Dieudonné Costes (1896-?) and Joseph Le Brix (1895-1931), in their Breguet XIX, *Nungesser-Coli*, completed the first non-stop (3,420 km/2,125 mi in 19 h 50 min) crossing of the South Atlantic—from St. Louis, Senegal, to Natal, Brazil—and on to Rio de Janeiro and, eventually, continuing on to Buenos Aires (7,705 miles in 72 hours).[4]

◊

Another Italian flight by, now, Major Carlo P. Del Prete and Captain Arturo Ferrarin (1895-?) left Montecelio, near Guidonia, Italy, on 4 July 1928 for a non-stop flight to Touros (near Natal), Brazil, (4,475 miles, 51 hours, 59 minutes) in an SM.64.[5] A world straight-line distance record was set by this flight. The SIAI-Marchetti SM.64 had been specifically designed for endurance flying. A single-engine monoplane, it had twin tail booms and the reversed engine mounting and cockpit below were streamlined for reduced air resistance.

1978 Brazil issue: 50th anniversary

◊

Two well-known Spanish flyers, Captain Ignazio Jiminez and Francisco Iglesias, left Seville on 24 March 1929 in a Breguet airplane, *Jesus del Gran Poder*, and reached Bahia, non-stop, 43 hours and 48 minutes (4,100 miles) later, in spite of bad weather.

◊

1929 was a popular year for crossing "attempts" as no less than seven others were made. The last non-stop flight of the year was made 15-16 December from Seville, Spain, to San Antonio (near Natal), Brazil, by Major Tadeo Larre-Borges (Uruguay) and Lieutenant Leon Challe (France).

◊

The year 1930 saw several more events. France's record-maker Jean Mermoz (1901-36) made the first "commercial" crossing on 12-14 May. Mermoz is also credited with the first passenger aircraft crossing on 28 May 1933.[6]

◊

# B. THE INSTRUCTIONS OF 17 MARCH 1927

The significant date in the history of air mail in Brazil is 17 March 1927. On that day Dr. Victor Konder, Minister of Transportation and Public Works, signed a document entitled "Instructions Approved by Executive Order of this date for the Execution of Transportation of Mail by Air" (*Diario Official*, 19 March 1927, 6463/4).[1]

The entire document, containing 39 paragraphs, is too lengthy for reproduction here, and I will confine the present discussion to sections of particular interest to aero-philatelists. In brief, the Instructions provided for an air mail service to be executed wholly by specifically authorized domestic airlines; these were to be fully responsible for the mail from the time they received the pouches at the dispatching post office to the time of their delivery to the post office at their destination. A scale of air mail rates was fixed, the entire amount of which represented the carrier's compensation, to be collected by the carrier by means of stamps issued by the carriers.

At the same time, and in addition to the carrier's air mail fee, the regular proper domestic postage had to be prepaid as well as a mandatory special delivery fee. The mixed franking found on covers is thus explained. The stamps issued by the carriers were legally authorized; in fact, they were required to be issued by law. These stamps are not listed in Scott's or Stanley Gibbons. I believe, however, that in omitting them the Scott's catalog does not face the realities of Latin American air mail conditions in the late twenties and early thirties. This point will be discussed further below.

It is strange that Scott's lists the first air mail stamps of Colombia—the labels allowed to be used by the airlines but not required to be used—but not the true first air mail stamps of Brazil. The Brazil stamps are known as "provisionals" or "semi-officals"—on what basis I can not determine.

AIR MAIL RATES

The rates for the transportation of mail matter by air are fixed in the Instructions, as follows:

> Sect.2. The rates for the transportation of correspondence by air within the national territory shall be:
> a) For letters, letter cards and postcards, for every 20 gr. or fraction
> 1$300 for a distance up to 500 Km.
> 2$000 for a distance over 500 Km., but less than 1,500 Km.
> 3$000 for a distance over 1,500 Km, but less than 3,000 Km.
> 4$000 for a distance over 3,000 Km., but less than 4,500 Km.
> 5$000 for a distance over 4,500 Km., but less than 6,000 Km.
> b) The same rates shall be in effect for every 50 gr. or fraction in the case of newspapers, printed matter, manuscripts, samples and packages.
> c) Registration and insurance fees, applying to mail both with and without declared valuation and collected by the carriers may not exceed fees provided under current postal regulations.
> d) The official correspondence between departments of the Federal Government shall have a discount of 10% from the above rates.

> I.) Apart from the fees already mentioned in this condition, and which shall be collected for the exclusive benefit of the companies or proprietors, the Post Office shall collect on all mail presented for transportation by air, as revenue of the Union, the rates and fees which are required by the then current postal regulations for mail of the respective class and weight.
> II.) Among the rates and fees referred to in 2-I of this condition, there shall be comprehended the registry fee, which is optional, within the terms of current postal regulations, as well as the special delivery fee which shall be obligatory in order that the air mail shall be dispatched immediately upon arrival, by special messenger.

Sect. 4. The amount of the charges and fees belonging to the Post Office shall be collected by means of postage stamps or postage meters used at the P.O. station.

Sect. 6. The rates and fees belonging to the carriers shall be collected by their agents or representatives, without postal intervention of any kind.

In this connection, let me refer to the annual report for 1927 of the postal administration of Santos. It states that 21 letters with a total weight of 5,270 gr. were dispatched via CONDOR during 1927, the company receiving 59$400 and the post office 22$800.

## AUTHORITY FOR AIRLINE STAMPS

I now turn to the section carrying perhaps the greatest philatelic significance: the authorization for the issue of stamps by the airlines. This section makes two provisions: it orders airlines authorized to operate under these Instructions to issue stamps for the collection of their charges and fees, and provides for the use of provisionals until the time such stamps were available for use. It cannot be stressed too often that:

Sect. 1: The transportation of mail by air shall be carried out....by planes the owners....of which shall be specifically authorized to carry out air transportation in Brazil, *observing all the conditions established in these Instructions...*

controls all the further provisions.

Sect. 5: These charges and fees accruing to the companies shall be collected by special stamps issued by the companies, the designs (of each company) to be well distinguished from those of another (company) and to have been approved by the Director General of Posts, or by means of postage meters belonging to the companies, after the design of the meter impression has been approved by the same authority.

During the first six months counting from the date on which the carrier has been authorized to execute air-mail transportation, cancelers or any other device convenient to the carriers may be used to acknowledge the receipt of their fees.

According to the annual report of the Post Office Department for 1927, the various post offices then authorized to accept and dispatch air mail received from CONDOR a total of 1,985 pieces of mail and dispatched via CONDOR 689 pieces of mail. I assume that these figures include VARIG mail, since it includes mail from cities on VARIG's route after 15 June 1927. Also, as CONDOR issued its stamps on 8 November 1927 and VARIG on 9 November, some part will have been prepaid with stamps. Considering then that many covers will have been lost and that a large number of covers were of a definite philatelic nature, a properly used commercial cover with the prestamp fee cancel will be quite a scarce item.

The use of the CONDOR stamps ceased on 30 November 1930 with CONDOR's entry into the International air mail field, in conjunction with the Zeppelin and Dornier transatlantic services. The use of VARIG stamps was discontinued on 1 July 1934, in accordance with postal regulation (Portaria 527) of 12 April 1934. ETA, the other company to issue stamps under the provisions of Section 5, suspended operations in 1930.

## PROVISIONS FOR FOREIGN MAIL

Most of the other sections of the Instructions deal with technical matters, such as the handling of the mail, accounting and other matters.

Regarding foreign air mail, Sections 34 to 36 give the relevant information.

Sect. 34: The obligations of the carriers having obtained concessions for international air transportation shall be the same as those already defined in these Instructions as well as those established by international conventions.

Sect.35: The rates for international air transportation shall be established for each concession which may be granted for this purpose.

Sect.36: The international postage charges shall be collected in accordance with provisions of the international conventions in force; as for the domestic charges, the provisions already indicated in I and II of Sect. 2 shall be observed.

With time and the experience gathered, the Instructions were modified, the first change being the abolition of the mandatory special delivery fee on 28 February 1928, which led to an increase in the use of the air mail. The major modification occurred in 1933, with the signing of Law 22.673. As a result, special stamps were abolished and changes were made in rates and accounting methods.

◊

# C. THE FIRST AIR MAIL STAMPS

The first air mail stamps of Brazil are not those listed in the Scott and Stanley Gibbons Catalogues. For some unexplained reason they ignore the stamps required to be issued by the "domestic" lines and treat them as "provisional" issues. Unlike the situation in Colombia, where the first two airlines were allowed to issue stamps of their own choice—the first of which were really labels and which, curiously, are officially recognized, but certainly more "provisional" than those of Brazil—the Brazil companies were required by the government to issue and use stamps of approved designs. Most other stamp catalogs recognize these issues. (All stamps are shown enlarged 150% unless otherwise noted.)

## THE INSTRUCTIONS OF 1927

The document (see Appendix B) specifically stated that the transporting agents must issue stamps to collect the fees for services and, in addition, required that government issued postage stamps be used for the normal (surface) delivery portion. The regulations further permit the use of "cancellers or any other device convenient to the carriers" in lieu of stamps during the first six months of the carrier's operation after government approval. The designs of the devices/stamps as well as the rates to be charged were to be approved by the government.

## CONDOR SYNDIKAT

CONDOR SYNDIKAT was the first to take advantage of these regulations and, in compliance with the Decree, utilized a triangular "pre-stamp" in black (see p. 126). It operated, officially, between March and July 1927, and continued some flights—mostly survey flights for new routes, primarily further north on the coast—until November. Pre-stamp covers do exist after July (see p. 128), when it helped start SYNDICATO CONDOR as a "national" line.

## SYNDICATO CONDOR

CONDOR initially issued seven stamps: 500 rs., olive; 700 rs., orange; 1,000 rs., carmine; 1,300 rs., green; 2,000 rs., blue; 3,000 rs., violet; and 10,000 rs., red-orange; printed in Germany by the Reichsdruckerei, Berlin, on paper watermarked with circles and crosses—the same paper used for the official issues of Würtemberg (*Scott* Wmk. 116). The first six values were printed in quantities of up to 200,000 each, but less than 40,000 of the highest value were made. The stamps bear the inscription "SYNDICATO CONDOR" at the top, above the outstretched wings of a stylized bird, super-imposed on the central portion of the Brazilian flag. The stamps were officially issued on 8 November 1927.

Additionally, another 1,300 rs. stamp without the inscription "SYNDICATO CONDOR" was printed in two slightly different shades of green, presumably unintentionally. Some of these stamps would be later over-printed by CONDOR, but initially they served as the basic stamp for VARIG to use, which is the apparent reason for the missing inscription. CONDOR would also have some of these untitled stamps overprinted later for the first Zeppelin flight and for a rate change in 1930.

Basic 1,300 rs. stamps
"SYNDICATO CONDOR" (left) + Untitled (right)

CONDOR did not issue stamps for the mandatory Special Delivery fee, the high cost of which had limited air mail use, and its mandatory use was abolished by the government on 1 March 1928. CONDOR's registration fee was obtained by overprinting 15,000 copies of the highest value (10,000 rs. red-orange) from the original set with a black "R" and "Rs 400" also in black. These were issued on 1 August 1928.

On 9 January 1930 Dr. Victor Konder, Minister for Transportation and Public Works and "father" of commercial aviation in Brazil, was honored on the third anniversary of the New Year's flight when CONDOR issued its only commemorative—featuring his portrait. The stamp was printed by the government Mint, *Casa da Moeda* (House of Money), in Rio de Janeiro in a quantity of 20,000 copies. The stamp was on sale for only three months.

CONDOR had 10,100 copies of its original highest value (10,000 rs. red-orange) stamp overprinted with a more stylized "R" (below), known as the "running R," which was issued on 18 January 1930.

Above: Registration (left), Konder commemorative (right)

13 May 1930: Rio de Janeiro - Porto Alegre
700 rs. postage/registration + 2,000 rs. air + 400 rs. air registration = Correct 20 gr. rate for 1,100 km.

An air mail rate change went into effect on 12 September 1930 which was based on 5 gram units and incremental distances (see table on p. 137).

To accommodate these rates CONDOR had three values of the original issue and the unissued, untitled stamps overprinted on 10 September by Thomas & Paus, Ltd. of Rio de Janeiro: "Rs. 50" on the 700 rs.; "Rs. 200" on the 3,000; "Rs. 350" on the 10,000; and "Rs. 750" on the 1,300 untitled. A graphic design blocks out the original value, a shield on the 50 and 350 and an "Iron Cross"(?) on the other two values. The surcharge values are in different arrangements on each stamp.

Rate change issues

A third registration issue was generated by using the same "running R" this time overprinted on the 1,300 rs. green stamp.

Third registration issue and overprint invert (100)

As with many overprinted stamps, "errors" are bound to occur. The stamps illustrated (above and right) here are the known errors for this issue. The numbers in "( )" are the quantities known.

defect in "s" (?)      double (50)

triple (?)      inverted (150)

error caused by paper fold (?)

Surcharge inverted (100)

The use of these CONDOR stamps ended on 30 November 1930 when the line transferred its activities to true "international service" in consort with LUFT HANSA and ZEPPELIN. Government air mail stamps were put into use.

## VARIG

VARIG had its own version of the triangular "pre-stamp"—the triangle is elongated and inverted, point down (see p. 103). The inscription is similar to CONDOR's.

On 9 November 1927 VARIG released its first stamps—the green untitled issue—overprinted in red, at the top, "V A R I G." In addition to the simply overprinted "V A R IG" on the 1$300 rs., another overprint carried both the company name and an obliterating "$700" over the face value of the basic stamp, also in red.

The first two issues

On 8 March 1928 VARIG added an additional overprint to the 1$300 rs. overprinted stamp: an "R" and "Rs. 400" for *registrado* (registration) and an "E" and "$700" for *expresso* (special delivery).

Registration and special delivery

Then, on 22 May 1928, VARIG issued another overprinted stamp, with the word "VARIG" in smaller type, measuring 9.5 mm in overall width rather than the 12.5 mm of the original issue. The reason behind this variation is not known to this writer.

The "small" overprint issue

The "R" and "E" overprinting was done several times using different plates in different combinations and, eventually, different red ink. As a result there are several different varieties of these stamps with the large letters "moving around" in location. In addition, there are some differences in the letter formation (type style), most notably in the thickness of the stroke of the letter "R" and the "400."

My chart (opposite) attempts to trace the evolution of these stamps. The number above each frame indicates the known quantity, the numbers below the frame are the catalog number from *Catálogo Antunes 83*/Yvert & Teller at left and from RHM, the Brazil specialized catalog at right. On the lines, at left, the number above the line represents the known quantity and the number below, the date of issue. I do not have many of these stamps nor have I seen many of them. Some of the varieties that I do have are shown below for reference.

"R" & "E" variations

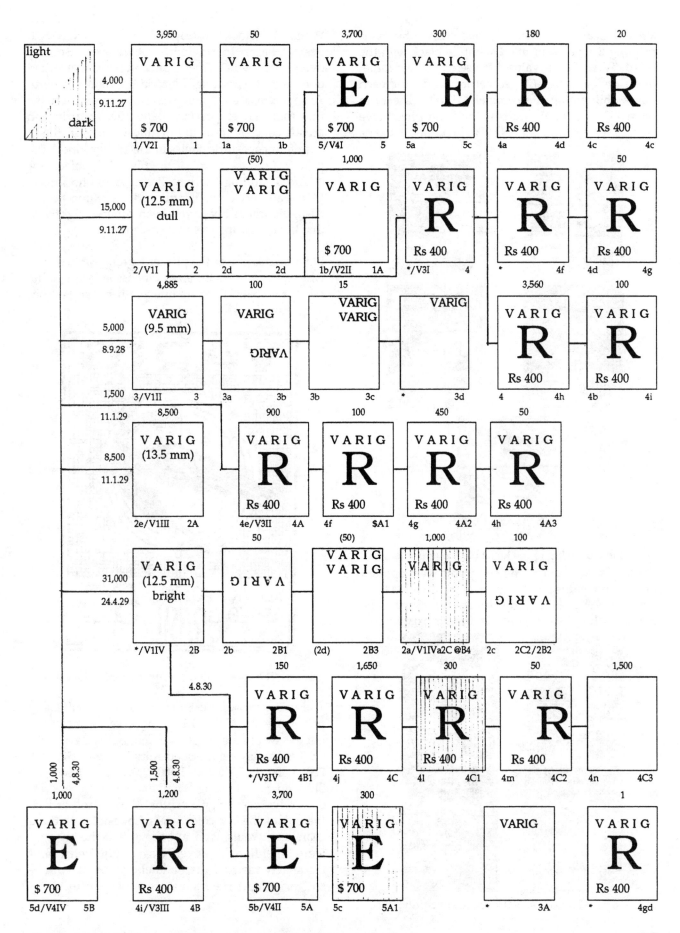

VARIG dealt with the 1930 rate change by overprinting the green untitled stamp in black with the word "VARIG," a value between two horizontal lines, and a different geometric design for each value obliterating the original "1$300." The rates were 350 rs. per 5 gr. units in the "first zone." Five stamps were issued: 50; 350; 700; 1,050; and 1,400 rs.

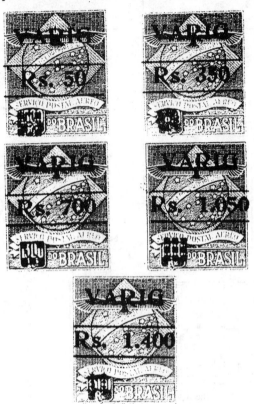

First Zone (up to 500 kms.) black overprints.

For the "second zone" the overprints were applied in red and valued 500; 1,000; 1,500; and 2,000 rs. with different obliterating designs—curiously, the highest value's was a swastika. Inverts exist.

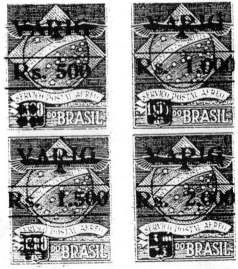

Second Zone (over 500 kms.) red overprints.

When the stock of original stamps (CONDOR design) began to run out—it had been used for overprints several times—the company which had done the overprinting, Livraria do Globo in Porto Alegre, prepared a new design, first used on the first flight envelopes (see page 109) featuring an artist's conception of the mythical Icarus in flight, with four concentric circles in the background.[1] The printer used a more distinguished typeface for "VARIG" adding "Serviço Postal Aereo no Brasil" (Air Mail Service in Brazil) and the value below. Also, the Icarus image has been rotated slightly so that the image appears to be ascending.

Illustrated is one of the printer's proofs, actual size, which is four times the size of the issued stamp. The two "cross-hair" lines are unexplainable and do not appear on the issued stamps.

Icarus: The issue of 1931 (Printer's proof, actual size)

The first series of these new stamps was officially put on sale on 27 April 1931; however, some of the issues saw philatelic use as much as five days earlier. Ten values were issued initially: 50; 350; 500; 700; 1,000; 1,050; 1,400; 1,500; 2,000; and 10,000 rs. Subsequent reprintings were made in different colors. (It has been suggested that the control, or lack thereof, of the ink color was responsible for these changes. I would tend to believe that the changes were intentional. Meyer was a philatelist and assumably realized the philatelic value of "different" printings.) The stamps are very colorful!

On 23 November 1931 the last re-overprint of the originally red "VARIG" issue was done in black with a stylized "R" and "E" for registration and special delivery fees.

Registration and Special Delivery Issues.

These overprinting plates were apparently subsequently used on the new Icarus issue starting on 1 August 1933.

Registration and Special Delivery Issues.

In 1934 the printing of the Special Delivery "E" and Registration "R" stamps resulted in some faulty overprints. VARIG appointed a "committee of examining philatelists" to review the printing and they recommended punching out the faulty stamps to prevent them from becoming "varieties of value to collectors."[2] A punched hole, 16 mm in diameter, through the sheets devalued these stamps (5 per sheet of "E"= 1,990 stamps, 4 per sheet of "R"= 1,596 stamps. The net result was that these stamps became very collectable "varieties of value." The stamps shown here are from the author's collection. On the next page are illustrations of the full sheets.

The punched Special Delivery issue.

The punched Registration issue.

The last printing was issued on 19 June 1934. On 30 June 1934, the VARIG stamps were withdrawn from sale and replaced by stamps issued by the government postal authorities.

Some time later the entire Icarus issue was counterfeited abroad. These stamps are fairly easy to recognize: at least one of the concentric circles touches the back of Icarus' head; there are irregularities in the background grid; and the cancels are unreadable, usually oval, and not to the design of either of the only two official cancels that the company used (see pp. 104 & 107).

Counterfeits.

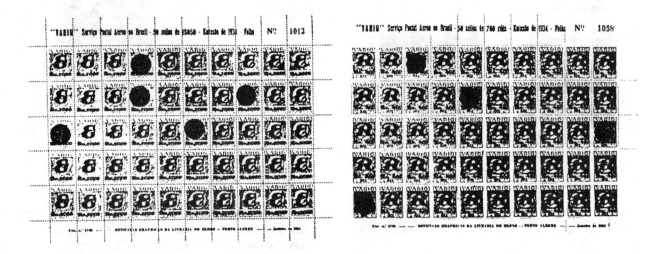

Top: The punched VARIG "Registration" and "Special Delivery" issues of 1934.[3]
Bottom: "In the presence of the Regional Post Office Director, directors of the Rio Grandense Philatelical Society, journalists and personalities, the original plates used for printing the VARIG stamps were destroyed yesterday."[4]

Correio Aéreo: A History of the Development of Air Mail Service in Brazil

## ETA

This company, the third domestic line, was based in Rio de Janeiro and was authorized to operate by governmental decree on 1 March 1929 and to carry mail on 12 June. It prepared stamps—the design of which was produced by the *Casa de Moeda*—which were printed by typography by Tipografia Vilasboas in Rio de Janeiro and issued on 17 June 1929. The design was based on a stylized airplane which formed the letters "ETA." The differences among the stamps are their color, face value(s), and perforations.

The first stamps were printed in a sheet of sixteen—four rows of four copies (4x4) of each value, 200, 1,000, 2,000, and 5,000 rs.—with a large margin at the bottom. Therefore, two stamps of each value are imperforate on one side and the top row of stamps, the 200 rs., are imperforate on the top as well. The stamps utilized a thick, dark gum ("grosso, goma escura desigual").

First issue, full sheet (actual size) without bottom margin

Another value, 300 rs., may have been intended to be included in this sheet, but was not. Instead, it was printed in a smaller sheet of four, two over two (2x2). It was intended to be rouletted and purple dash lines were printed between the stamps in the same purple color ink as the background image. (The "airplane" formed by the letters "ETA" and the values were printed in the same red color on all the stamps.) These stamps were rouletted—rather poorly, making separation difficult—and were then perforated between. Therefore, each of the 300 rs. is imperforate on two edges. RHM lists an issue date of 28 November 1929. The gum is not as dark ("amarela lisa") as the first sixteen-stamp sheet.

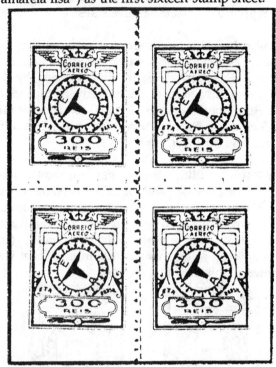

Four-stamp sheet showing the rouletting marks and later perforations

Apparently, at least four of these sheets were printed with the center upside-down, as 16 copies of this invert are known to exist.

Inverted center.

The thick, dark gum of the first printing of the 16-stamp sheet was apparently unsatisfactory, and a second printing was ordered. This time the same sheet format was used, but the former wide bottom margin contained a row of four 300 rs., i.e., a four x five (4x5) sheet. A thin, white gum was used and the sheet perforated. ETA apparently rejected this format and, to save face or more importantly to save his printing effort, the printer simply removed the bottom row. This would leave as the bottom row the 5,000 rs. similar to the first printing. My copy of this sheet has been trimmed, apparently right at the inside of the perforations. Apparently some copies of the trimmed 300 rs. "escaped" destruction. These are perforated on at least three sides.

Finally, the 300 rs. was reprinted in the smaller format (2x2), using the same white gum, and perforated. This issue is easily distinguished by the gum color, if unused, or, more easily, by the lack of rouletting marks or cuts. The 300 rs. paid the rate for 5 grams or fraction thereof (see p. 62). It is difficult to find on cover.

After this printing, the printer apparently took some "artist license" and the ETA "airplane" began to "maneuver." These stamps—quantity printed unknown—have been referred to as the "kamikaze" issues. The maneuvering airplane varies (see below), suggesting that more than one sheet was printed in this modified fashion.

The "maneuvering" airplane or "kamikaze" issues.

## THE GOVERNMENT ISSUES

"International" carriers, and at first there was only one—the French AÉROPOSTALE—were not required or allowed to issue their own stamps, but were required to use stamps prepared by the government to collect air mail fees. This presented a problem as, in 1927, the government had no air mail stamps nor had it produced designs for any.

The solution was to overprint and surcharge the second set of "Official" stamps originally released in November 1913. These 16 stamps all bear the same engraved portrait of President Hermes da Fonseca, but in eight different frames, and were printed by the American Bank Note Company. Hermes Rodrigues da Fonseca (1855-1923) was a military officer and Minister of War in the cabinet of President Affonso Penna (1847-1909). Penna was elected President in 1906 and his portrait appears on the first (1906) "Official" stamp series. Fonseca was President of the Republic of Brazil from 1910 to 1914 and had no connection with air mail service nor with aviation. Apparently, the stamps were used because they were available.

The overprinting by the Brazil mint was in black with the words "SERVIÇO AEREO" obliterating the portrait, and the values were surcharged with new values increasing or decreasing the original. On four of the designs small diamonds or lozenges were used to obliterate the values in the top corners. As often happens in the case of overprints, a variety of "errors" emerged. At least 27 are known; the *Scott Catalogue* lists only a few of them.

Two values of the 1927 issue.

Government postage was also required, but no part of the money collected from the sale of the air mail stamps belonged to the Brazilian Post Office, which was, in effect, C.G.A.'s collection agent. The same arrangement, incidentally, held true for the first "official" airmails of Argentina and a similar situation existed in Chile.

In 1929 the first five specifically designed air mail stamps (50, 200, 300, 500, and 1,000 rs.) were issued by the government. These were followed by three higher values (2,000, 5,000, and 10,000 rs.). These stamps honor Brazil's early pioneers in aviation.

The 50 rs. value pictured a monument to "the flying priest" (*o Padre Voador*), Bartholomeu de Gusmão, whose portrait appears on the 2,000 rs. value. **Bartholomeu Lourenço de Gusmão** was born in Santos in December 1685. At 15 he began a novitiate in the Society of Jesus at the Belém Seminary in Cachoeira, Bahia, but left within a year. He then invented a machine to lift water from a lagoon up a hill to the seminary, a device soon recognized throughout the country. In 1701 he left for Portugal and Coimbra University where he majored in mathematics.

Monument                de Gusmão

Then a priest and chaplain to the royal household in Lisbon, on 8 August 1709 Father Gusmão demonstrated one of his inventions to a select group which included the King and Queen; the Papal Nuncio, Cardinal Conti (later Pope Innocent III); and other members of the Court. This invention was a hot-air balloon constructed of thick paper, patterned after a design of Leonardo de Vinci. The "design" rose to a height of about 13 feet before some of the servants "killed" it for fear of starting a fire.

This was almost 75 years before the Montgolfier brothers, but the Lisbon press called the experiment a failure and ridiculed the priest. An anonymous *Manifesto*, written in non-technical terms with a fanciful and rather ridiculous illustration of *Passarola*, a bird-shaped glider supposedly powered by humans flapping its "wings," was attributed to him. The picture was reproduced throughout Europe and resulted in his loss of prestige in the eyes of the scientific world. Although in 1720 he had been one of 50 members chosen to the Royal Academy of History,

this ridicule was followed by a period of trouble with the Inquisition and a jailing on the charge of sorcery. He escaped and fled to Spain. In poor health and suffering with a malignant fever, he died in Toledo on 18 November 1724, not yet 39. (His younger brother, Alexandre de Gusmão (1695-1753), as minister under Dom João V helped define the borders of Brazil.) A 1944 issue also honored the Padre with an artist's conception of his balloon.

*Padre Voador* and his balloon at court.

**Alberto Santos-Dumont** is probably the most famous name in Brazilian air history. Born 20 July 1873 in Minas Gerais state (Palmrya, now Santos-Dumont),[5] youngest of seven children of a wealthy coffee plantation owner who used the most modern machinery of the day, the young boy had a chance to develop his own mechanical genius, additionally inspired by the novels of Jules Verne. He ventured to Paris and in 1898 in the *Santos-Dumont No. 1*—an 80-foot long cigar-shaped bag of varnished silk filled with hydrogen and powered by a 3.5 horsepower auto engine—he made his first flight (which abruptly ended when he hit a tree).

On 19 October 1901 in the *No. 6* he made the first successful flight from the Parc d'Aérostation (St. Cloud) around the Eiffel Tower and back (about seven miles) within the 30-minute time-limit, winning the Henri Deutsch de la Meurtha (a wealthy member of the Aéreo Club) Grand Prize of 100,000 Ffr. which he divided between the ground crew and the poor of Paris.

On 13 September 1906, not quite three years after the Wright brothers' historic morning at Kill Devil Hills, NC, Santos-Dumont's *14-bis* made its first "hop" of 23 feet at Bagatelle, near Paris. This was technically the first public demonstration of flight. The next month's prize flight of 197 feet was followed on 12 November 1906 with a 722 feet flight which reached an "altitude" of 18 feet and another prize.

Santos-Dumont went on to develop a series of monoplanes called "Dragonflies" which continued to make records. But, when he saw the airplane diverted to a means of destruction at the advent of World War I, he retired from flying, believing he had brought a curse into the world. He returned to Brazil in 1928 and was further depressed when a SYNDICATO CONDOR plane, coming out to salute his return, crashed in Rio harbor. Finally, when the São Paulo revolt utilized air power against his homeland in its ill-fated effort, his remorse overcame him. On 23 July 1932, just after his 59th birthday, he took his own life.

to the Federal Chamber of Deputies in 1893. Interested in aviation, inspired by Santos-Dumont's work, and under the patronage of Brazil President Floriano Peixoto, he commissioned a balloon built in Paris and shipped to Brazil in 1894. After several tests this *Bartholomeu de Gusmão* was retired.

In 1902, with the financial support of friends and relatives, he went to Paris and commissioned a 70,500 cubic foot balloon which he christened *PAX*. At 98 feet long, with a 39-foot maximum diameter and powered fore and aft by "air screws" (not unlike the puller-pusher propeller blades of the Dornier Wal), it was a rather fanciful creation looking a bit circus-like. On 12 May 1902 Severo and his mechanic, Saché, lifted off from Vaugirard in Paris for an unfortunately brief and fatal flight. At an altitude of 1,200 feet a fire started aft of the basket, *PAX* exploded, killing both men instantly.

PAX                Augusto Severo

**João Ribeiro de Barros** was born on 4 April 1900 at Jahú, São Paulo. Interested early in flying and a pilot by age 23, he was especially intrigued by the pioneering work of the Portuguese Captain Sacadura Cabral (1892-1924) and Captain (later Vice Admiral) Gago Coutinho (1869-1959), who made the first East-West aerial crossing of the South Atlantic in March-June 1922.

Airship *No. 6*          Airplane *14-bis*
Alberto Santos-Dumont

**Augusto Severo de Alberquerque Maranhão,** unlike Santos-Dumont, devoted his efforts only to lighter-than-air machines. Born in Macaíba, a little village near Natal, on 1 January 1904 and educated at Recife and Rio de Janeiro's Polytechnical School, he worked as a teacher, an import/exporter, and a newspaperman. On entering politics, he was elected

Barros scouted a crew: São Paulo Public Force Lieutenant João Negrão, copilot; Army officer Newton Braga as observer (navigator); and Vasco Cinquini, mechanic. The four left for Italy and the Savoia Marchetti factory to purchase a seaplane. They acquired an S.55—a design which first appeared in 1924—a strange shaped, canvas-covered, wooden seaplane with the cockpit stuck in the wing between two hulls and below the pusher-puller engine mounted on struts above. This model, as the *Alcyone,* had been unsuccessfully used in an earlier Italian (Count Casagrande) attempted flight. The plane was modified and, in August 1926, renamed *Jahú*, after Barros' home town. Legal formalities, the proverbial "red tape," delayed the expedition. By 13 October 1926 the first leg was under way on the route: Genoa - Gibraltar - Porto Praia - Fernando de Noronha - Natal - Recife - Salvador - Rio de Janeiro - Santos - São Paulo (Santo Amaro). The plane reached its destination on 28 April 1927. Barros received the "Harmon" award, the highest honor given to pilots by the "Ligue Internationale des Aviateurs." Charles Lindbergh received the same distinction for his solo flight 22 days after Barros' flight.

The *Jahú* is displayed in the Santos Dumont Foundation Aeronautics Museum in São Paulo and was pictured on another stamp commemorating the 50th anniversary in 1977 (see p. 160).

The *Jahú*.

## NYRBA SERVICE

In February 1930, anticipating the start of regular air mail service between Brazil and the United States by the New York, Rio & Buenos Aires (NYRBA) airline, the government issued another stamp of 3,000 rs. for this specific purpose. The stamp design features the Statue of Liberty in New York harbor (at left) and Sugar Loaf Mountain in Rio de Janeiro (at right) with an allegorical bird carrying an envelope which reads "VIA AEREA." The design is based on a cachet and multi-colored label used by the company which reads "VIA NYRBA." The label is wider and squatter than the single-colored (violet) stamp.

First flight to the U. S.

NYRBA label.

Ironically, the use by NYRBA was short-lived, the company having lost the transport "war" (and eventually its very life) to PAN AMERICAN. The stamp design, however, continued in use for several years, undergoing several paper/watermark and perforation variations, as well as a value change (surcharge decrease) by overprinting for Zeppelin use with the Second Flight of 1931. Again, as an overprint, several varieties exist. Many catalogs do not recognize this as a "Zeppelin issue." It is interesting to note that this surcharge "2.500 REIS" was done as an "emergency" measure to provide more postage for Zeppelin use. However, many of the 80,000 stamps surcharged were destroyed when the issue was canceled in 1933, making one wonder what the "emergency" really was (see p. 45).

The overprint of 1931.

## ZEPPELIN SERVICE

In May 1930 the *Graf Zeppelin* (LZ-127) made its first trip to South America, or more specifically, Brazil as well as to the United States. SYNDICATO CONDOR, acting as an agent, sold stamps printed in Germany which, as issues of the Zeppelin Company, were not required to be approved by the Brazilian government. Interconnecting flights by CONDOR also bore CONDOR's stamps and government postage. (These Zeppelin issues, which were only valid for this first flight, will be discussed in the following section.)

The Brazilian government in anticipation of further and regularly scheduled flights connecting Europe and Brazil prepared two new Zeppelin stamps in 1931. These were created by using two existing "airship" stamps—overprinting the 200 rs. and 500 rs. values of 1929. They were overprinted "ZEPPELIN" and surcharged "2$500" and "5$000" respectively. These were to pay the *Graf Zeppelin* and CONDOR fees on mail (postcards, 2,500 rs., and letters, 5,000 rs.) returning from Recife. The stamps were in use until 22 March 1932 when they were withdrawn from sale. Remainders were not destroyed, but, later, were sold to collectors. The few full sheets remaining had a control mark, "OUT 1933" (October 1933) printed in red on the back (gum side) which is diamond shaped and extends over two stamps. (It should be noted that when the original stamps were produced the perforation pins were not properly aligned, resulting in perforations that are usually rough or torn, and centering that is often poor.)

The Zeppelin overprints of 1932.

After the Second Flight of 1932, the first two Zeppelin stamps were withdrawn and the government overprinted two definitives for use on the third and following flights. The 5,000 rs. Ruy Barbosa issue of 1929 was changed to read "ZEPPELIN 3$500" and the 10,000 rs. "Allegory of Education" issue of 1928 now read "ZEPPELIN 7$000." It is interesting that although the face value of both stamps was reduced, the Zeppelin rates were increased. In 1931 a postal card cost 2,500 rs. Zeppelin fee plus 400 rs. Brazilian postage. By the Third Flight of 1932, a card cost 3,500 rs. plus 400 rs., letters went from 5,000 rs. plus 400 rs. to 7,000 rs. plus 700 rs. This may reflect inflation (see p. 47).

Ruy Barbosa          Allegory of Education

Neither of the images on these two definitives has anything to do with air transport and it is difficult to determine why they were selected. I can only assume there was sufficient quantity around for a reasonable overprinting quantity.

In 1933 another stamp was issued for the developing air mail services. This design featured the green and gold of the Brazilian flag furled at left with a stylized airplane in flight at right. The issue went through several subsequent printings on different paper (watermarks) and perforation spacings.

Air mail allegory

During and after the Second World War, the air mail issues of Brazil seemed to have little reference to air-related topics. There were some exceptions. In 1944 another issue honored *Padre Voador*, Bartholomeu de Gusmão, with an artist's conception of the original balloon experiment (see p. 173).

In 1947 an issue paid homage to the Santos-Dumont monument in St. Cloud, France, which includes a statue of the legendary Icarus. In 1956, Santos-Dumont's *14-Bis* was the design, in several values and colors, including a souvenir sheet, with the lowest value in a block of four in a different color, for the 50th anniversary of Santos-Dumont's heavier-than-air flight. In 1959, Air Week's 25th anniversary was commemorated with another issue picturing Icarus, and a Caravelle jet aircraft celebrated the inauguration of jet service by VARIG in Brazil.

The issuance of air mail stamps by the government ended in 1966. It is interesting to note that many subjects of aeronautical interest have appeared on regular commemorative issues of Brazil, just as many of the air mail issues after 1940 related to subject matter that, in most cases, isn't even remotely related to the subject of flight.

THE POSTAL TAX ISSUE

Government Decree 22.620 of 5 May 1933 required the use of a special tax stamp on all correspondence sent within South America, to the United States or to Spain. The purpose of the stamp was to raise funds for airport construction. The stamp pictures the upper portion of the statue of Icarus erected as a memorial to Santos-Dumont in St. Cloud, France, which was destroyed during World War II. The stamp's obligatory use was 1 October 1933 to 31 May 1934. It was then allowed to be used as normal postage until 31 August 1934.

Postal Tax issue

On 14 November 1947 another semi-postal tax stamp was issued in honor of Air Week. Its use was not obligatory and the funds raised were intended for the Civil Aviation Fund. Its theme was also Icarus, a painting "Icarus Awakening" by Lucilio Albuquerque, and was printed in a triangular format.

Semi-postal Tax issue (actual size)

THE 1930 ZEPPELIN STAMPS

I have discussed the government issued stamps, including the stamps the government issued for Zeppelin flights. However, the first flight of the *Graf Zeppelin* to Brazil, in May 1930, was not included in the government-issued stamps.

This may be attributed to the fact that this was a period of time that the political situation in Brazil was, at best, unstable. Although the presidential election of 1 March 1930 was relatively peaceful, the smoldering tempers flared, resulting in the assassination of one of the candidates, João Pessôa, on 25 July, and, finally, a revolution in October which brought Getúlio Vargas to power. It also may be that the government treated the Zeppelin service as experimental and/or under the agency of SYNDICATO CONDOR which did, in fact, service the

interconnecting flights within Brazil and continued to do so after the government produced air mail stamps for future services.

It may also be that the government didn't want to influence the design (which it didn't) under the 1927 rules or treated the entire issue as "foreign" even though SYNDICATO CONDOR, which handled both the sales of the stamps and the interconnecting service in Brazil and other lands they serviced (included in the basic stamp fee), was under the Instructions of 1927.

In any event, three stamps were printed in Berlin, by the Reichsdruckerei (German national printing plant), the same source for the stamps of SYNDICATO CONDOR. The original stamps were in three different values and three different colors: 5,000 rs., green; 10,000 rs., red; and 20,000 rs., blue. The design consisted of the value in the upper corners, on either side of a top-centered "1930"; the words "PREMEIRO VOO COMMERCIAL" (First Flight Commercial), above the wings of the CONDOR logo; below, the starboard side view of the *Graf Zeppelin* over a stylized ocean with a three-masted sailing ship below the nose; and, at the bottom, the words "BRASIL-EUROPA" (see quote on p. 40). Interestingly, the design makes no mention of either company by name.

One of the first three issues

These stamps were intended to pay for the Zeppelin Company services within and from Brazil and corresponded to the rates in the United States (60¢, $1.20, and $2.40) respectively: between Rio de Janeiro and Recife, between Rio de Janeiro and Lakehurst, and between Rio de Janeiro and Europe via Lakehurst. Postcards would be carried at half the rate for letters. Foreign mailers, for the most part stamp collectors, could secure these services, and the stamps, from agents of LUFTSCHIFFBAU ZEPPELIN or SYNDICATO CONDOR (see advertisement on page 41). As with the other air mail stamps, senders were required to pay the normal postage

1.

2.

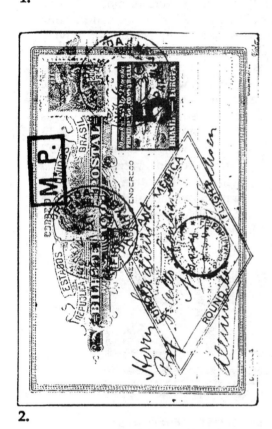

3.

4.

5.

6.

Correio Aéreo: A History of the Development of Air Mail Service in Brazil

rate using the regular government (non-air mail) issued stamps which accounts for the additional franking on covers or cards of the period. It should be noted that these stamps were prepared for this flight only—the only flight to/from Brazil in 1930.

In addition to the basic issue, copies of all three values were overprinted in black "Graf Zeppelin" in the center under the image of the airship, and then "U.S.A." over the word "EUROPA." The quantity of the lower two values was about double that of the highest value.

The "Graf Zeppelin" surcharge stamps

One of the "Graf Zeppelin U. S. A." overprints

The 20,000 reis was apparently the least popular ($2.40 was a lot of money in 1930 in this country, let alone Brazil), and a quantity (about 10,000) of the highest value was surcharged in black revaluing in about equal quantities to the other two values with the words "Rs. 5$000" and "Rs. 10$000" in the center and two black rectangles obliterating the original values in the top corners. The exact date of this action is a matter of dispute among cataloguers.

One of the surcharge devaluation stamps

In addition, about 5,000 copies of the basic CONDOR stamp, the 1$300 green, also printed by the same agency, were overprinted/surcharged in black "Graf Zeppelin Rs. 5$000" in the center and a black rectangle was used to obliterate the original value. The stamp saw limited use and copies on cover or card are difficult to find. Some 1,600 copies of the basic 1$300 were overprinted/surcharged "Graf Zeppelin Rs. 10$000," but these were never "officially" issued.

Meanwhile, a local hand-struck surcharge, a large black "5," was added to the center of some copies of the otherwise non-overprinted 20$000 rs. value. This was done in Parahyba (now spelled Paraíba), then the capital of the state of the same name. The city's name has been changed to João Pessoa, in honor of its former Governor and minority Vice-Presidential candidate who was assassinated in Recife in 1930.

Parahyba is located on the coast a short 70 miles north of Recife. Recife is the capital of the state of Pernambuco. (The city and the state shared the later name in earlier times, including the period under discussion here.) Recife had facilities for the airship, i.e., a mooring mast, that was not available at Rio de Janeiro. It would not be until 1936 that an actual hangar was available, built in Rio de Janeiro.

The so-called "Parahyba 5"

Pictured opposite page are examples of the "rarity":
1. 22 May, Parahyba to Parahyba do Norte (Ernest Oehken), sold in 1980 Köhler auction for 45,000 DM;
2. 25 May, Parahyba to Saxony, Germany (Prof. Otto Leonard), sold in 1984 Feldman auction for 36,000 SFr;
3. 25 May, Parahyba to Bremerhaven, Germany (Capt. Wilhelm Petermoller), sold in 1977 Munich auction for 39,000 DM;
4. 25 May, Parahyba to Monte Carlo, started in 1980 Corinphila auction at 15,000 Sfr;
5. 28 May, Recife to Neuruppin (Mr. Breithaupt) with added franking, started in 1967 Frankfurt auction at 9,000 DM;
6. 28 May, Recife to Friedrichshafen (Mr. Flemming), sold at 1968 Stanley Gibbons auction for £1,600.

On 27 April 1985 at the W.R. Weiss auction at the Collector's Club in New York a "sound" unused copy was offered. The late Anthony DeBellis, an avid collector of Brazilian air mail material and former President of the Brazil Philatelic Association, and I attended the inspection of lots and the auction. Philatelist and writer Ernest A. Kerr arrived too late for the inspection but indicated that he had "seen nine of these stamps" in his career. There was a question about the shape of the "5" as illustrated in the catalog (previous page), which Mr. Weiss explained that the printer used a "separation technique" to print the illustration in blue and black and, apparently in the process, the shape was "modified." The catalog description included the statement "for use on mail to prepay the motor fee to the aerodrome."[6] The stamp opened at $15,000 and was sold to an agent on the floor for $16,000. I am not aware of any subsequent auctions for this issue on or off cover. Records of previous sales are available. Pictured on page 178 are some examples which are described at the bottom right of page 179.

It should be noted that four of these pieces were posted at Parahyba—the first, six days after the counter sale of the originals started. One piece is addressed to "Parahyba do Norte" a town which in fact is one and the same as Parahyba (named after the river that runs through it); the "do Norte" was often added to avoid confusion with the town of Parahyba do Sul near Petropolis (also named after the river which runs through it, from São Paulo state into Rio de Janeiro state. Commander Breithaupt, a former Zeppelin commander, was a passenger on the 1930 flight. Flemming was a WW I commander of zeppelins and later became commander of the *Graf Zeppelin*.

The strangest aspect of this stamp is the secrecy and lack of authentic information about it. Various collectors and writers have tried to unearth the truth and the whereabouts of the existing copies. In the 1950s, the late, great, Brazilian authority, Werner Ahrens, testified to nine examples—"two unused copies, four postcards from Paraíba, two postcards and a fragment from Recife"—five of which he had seen, including an unused copy "completely glued down on brown paper."[7]

It is interesting to note that, to my knowledge, two copies of this "rarity," on or off cover, have never appeared at the same time or place. It has never been clear why this surcharge was necessary or whether or not it was ever officially sanctioned.

What is known is that it was done and, apparently, some 13 copies survive. However, the existence of such stamps was not made known until noted in the Sieger *Zeppelin Post Katalog* in 1937. The first illustration did not appear until 1939. Lehmkuhl proposes that a solitary employee acted on his own and produced the stamp to fill an order for the lower value. He recorded the deed, including sending three copies to Recife. It is from these records that Sieger learned of their existence and these were the records later studied by Ahrens.[8] Lehmkuhl states that only nine copies are currently accounted for: the six shown here, the Weiss stamp, an unused copy stuck to black paper, and a used copy on a piece of brown envelope. Where are the other four? Forgeries exist.

◊

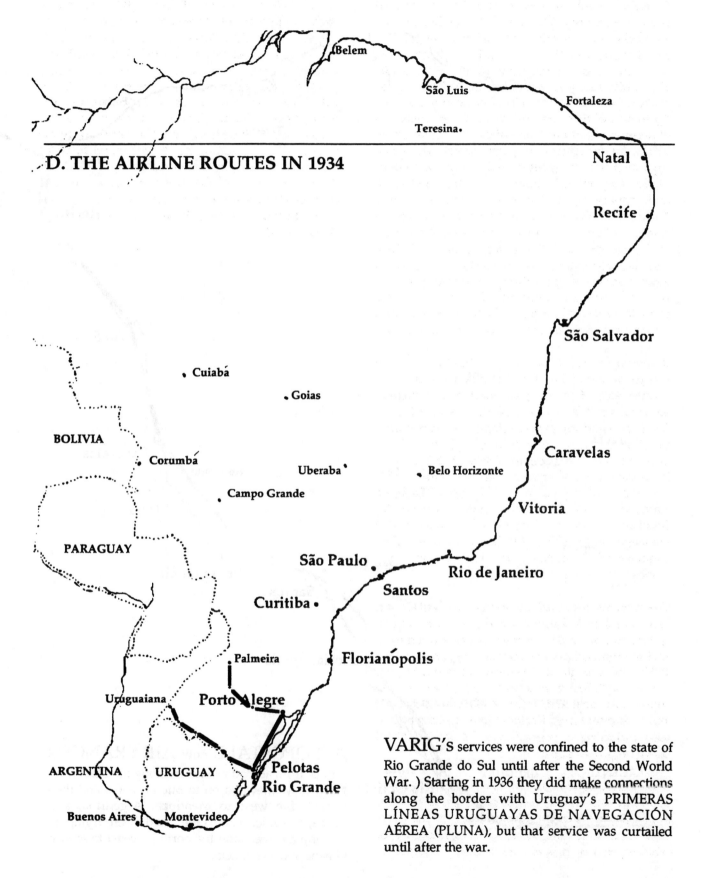

# D. THE AIRLINE ROUTES IN 1934

Belem

São Luis

Fortaleza

Teresina.

Natal

Recife

São Salvador

. Cuiabá

. Goias

BOLIVIA

. Corumbá

Uberaba

Belo Horizonte

Caravelas

. Campo Grande

Vitoria

PARAGUAY

São Paulo

Rio de Janeiro

Santos

Curitiba .

Florianópolis

Palmeira

Uruguaiana

Porto Alegre

ARGENTINA

URUGUAY

Pelotas

Rio Grande

Buenos Aires

Montevideo

VARIG's services were confined to the state of Rio Grande do Sul until after the Second World War. ) Starting in 1936 they did make connections along the border with Uruguay's PRIMERAS LÍNEAS URUGUAYAS DE NAVEGACIÓN AÉREA (PLUNA), but that service was curtailed until after the war.

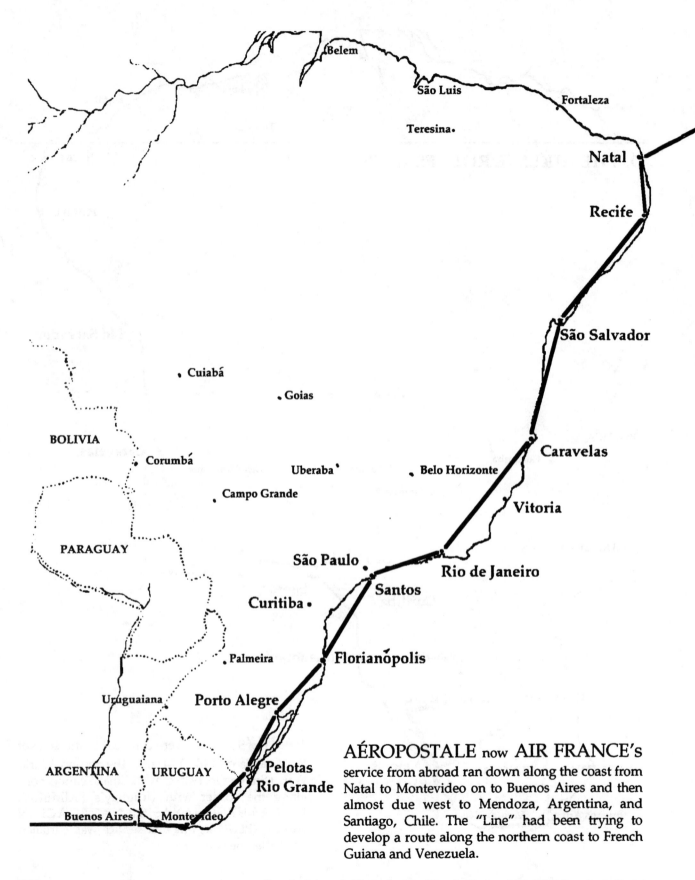

Belem

São Luis

Fortaleza

Teresina

Natal

Recife

São Salvador

Cuiabá

Goias

BOLIVIA

Corumbá

Uberaba

Belo Horizonte

Caravelas

Campo Grande

Vitoria

PARAGUAY

São Paulo

Rio de Janeiro

Santos

Curitiba

Florianópolis

Palmeira

Porto Alegre

Uruguaiana

ARGENTINA

URUGUAY

Pelotas

Rio Grande

Buenos Aires

Montevideo

**AÉROPOSTALE** now **AIR FRANCE's** service from abroad ran down along the coast from Natal to Montevideo on to Buenos Aires and then almost due west to Mendoza, Argentina, and Santiago, Chile. The "Line" had been trying to develop a route along the northern coast to French Guiana and Venezuela.

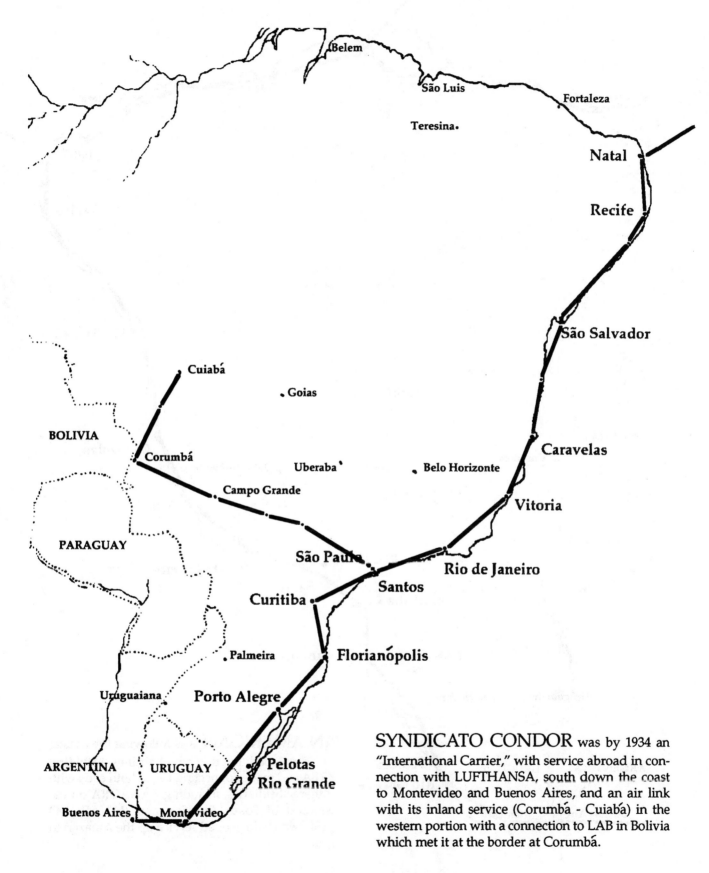

**SYNDICATO CONDOR** was by 1934 an "International Carrier," with service abroad in connection with LUFTHANSA, south down the coast to Montevideo and Buenos Aires, and an air link with its inland service (Corumbá - Cuiabá) in the western portion with a connection to LAB in Bolivia which met it at the border at Corumbá.

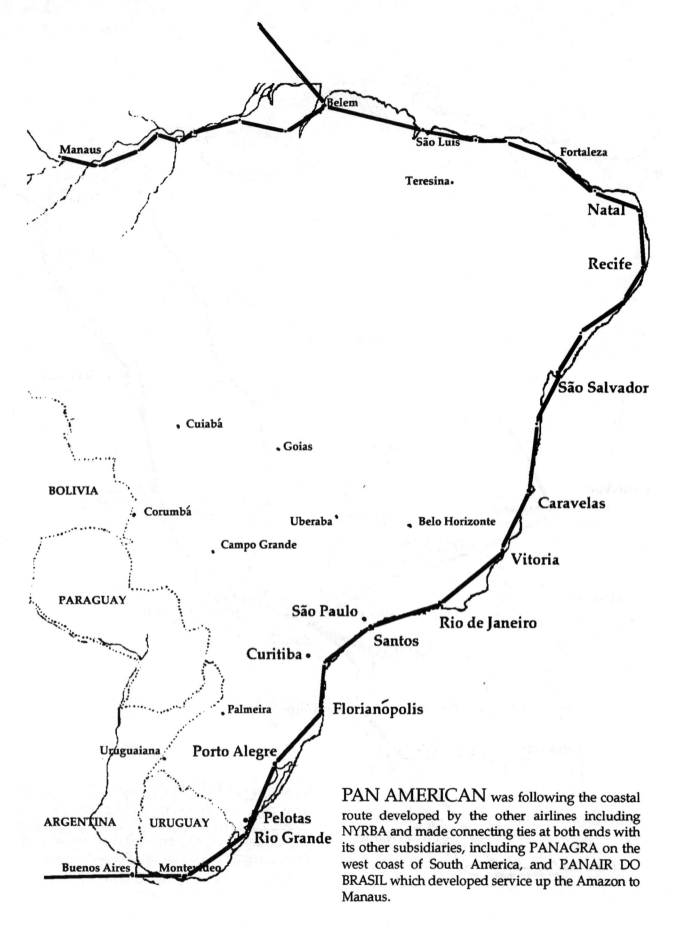

Manaus

Belem

São Luís

Fortaleza

Teresina.

Natal

Recife

São Salvador

Cuiabá

Goias

BOLIVIA

Corumbá

Uberaba

Belo Horizonte

Caravelas

Campo Grande

Vitoria

PARAGUAY

São Paulo

Rio de Janeiro

Santos

Curitiba

Florianópolis

Palmeira

Uruguaiana

Porto Alegre

ARGENTINA

URUGUAY

Pelotas

Rio Grande

Buenos Aires

Montevideo

PAN AMERICAN was following the coastal route developed by the other airlines including NYRBA and made connecting ties at both ends with its other subsidiaries, including PANAGRA on the west coast of South America, and PANAIR DO BRASIL which developed service up the Amazon to Manaus.

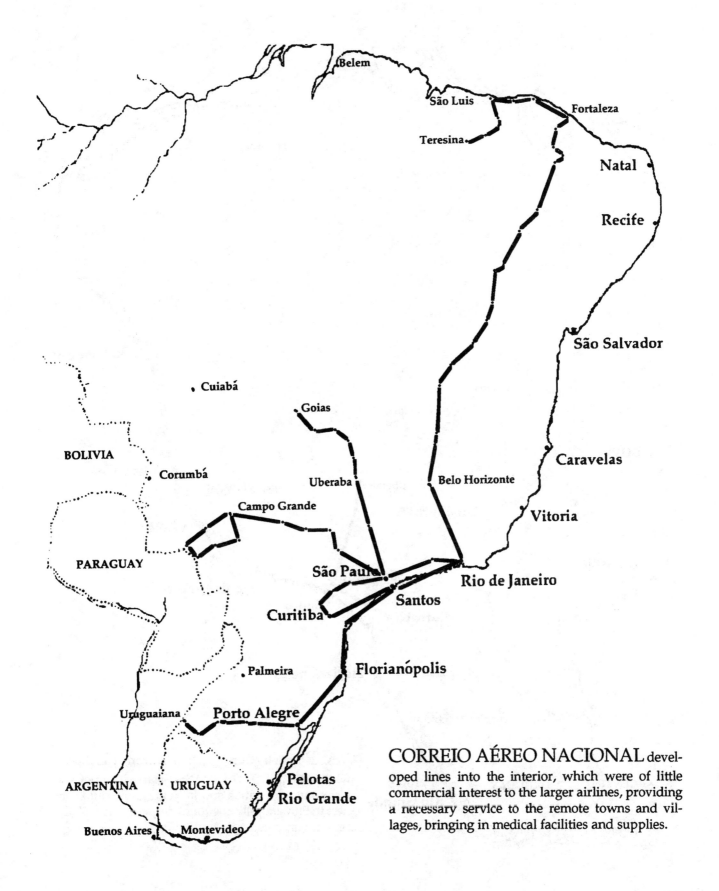

Belem

São Luis

Fortaleza

Teresina

Natal

Recife

São Salvador

Cuiabá

Goias

BOLIVIA

Caravelas

Corumbá

Uberaba

Belo Horizonte

Campo Grande

Vitoria

PARAGUAY

São Paulo

Rio de Janeiro

Curitiba

Santos

Florianópolis

Palmeira

Uruguaiana

Porto Alegre

ARGENTINA    URUGUAY

Pelotas
Rio Grande

Buenos Aires    Montevideo

**CORREIO AÉREO NACIONAL** developed lines into the interior, which were of little commercial interest to the larger airlines, providing a necessary service to the remote towns and villages, bringing in medical facilities and supplies.

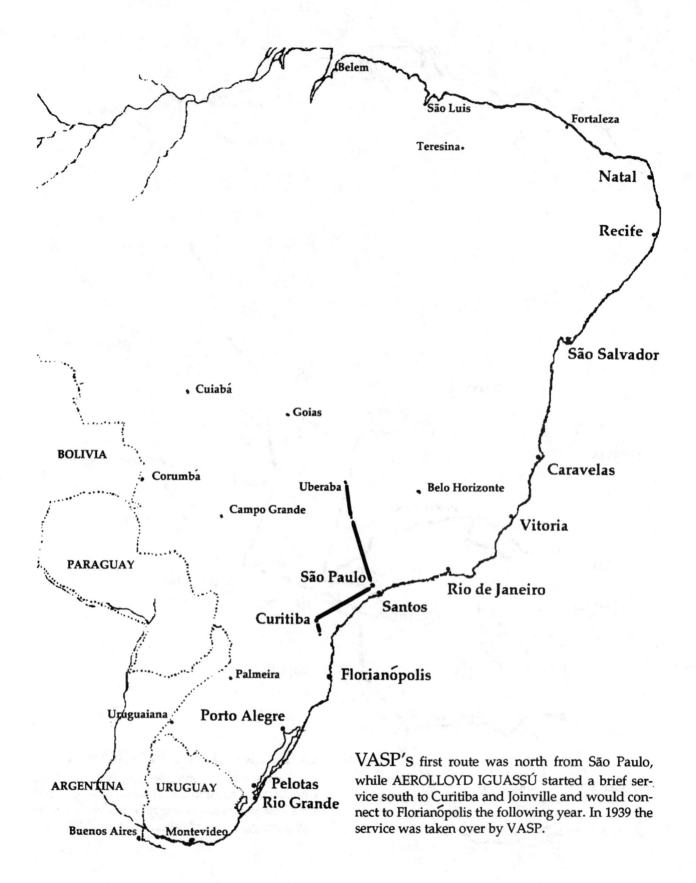

Belem

São Luis

Fortaleza

Teresina.

**Natal**

**Recife**

**São Salvador**

. Cuiabá

. Goias

**BOLIVIA**

. Corumbá

**Caravelas**

Uberaba
. Belo Horizonte

. Campo Grande

**Vitoria**

**PARAGUAY**

**São Paulo**

**Rio de Janeiro**

**Curitiba**
**Santos**

. Palmeira
**Florianópolis**

Uruguaiana
**Porto Alegre**

VASP's first route was north from São Paulo,
while AEROLLOYD IGUASSÚ started a brief service south to Curitiba and Joinville and would connect to Florianópolis the following year. In 1939 the
service was taken over by VASP.

**ARGENTINA**  **URUGUAY**
**Pelotas**
**Rio Grande**

Buenos Aires  Montevideo

Correio Aéreo: A History of the Development of Air Mail Service in Brazil

# E. BRIEF CHRONOLOGY OF EARLY AIR MAIL RELATED ACTIVITIES

| Year | Month | Brazil aviation | World aviation |
|------|-------|-----------------|----------------|
| 1911 | Sep | | First official air mail flight in U. S. |
| 1913 | Jan | Military School of Aviation founded | |
| 1914 | Aug | | Beginning of World War I |
| 1916 | Aug | Naval School of Aviation founded | |
| 1918 | Aug | | First scheduled air mail service in U. S. |
| | Nov | | Armistice signed |
| 1919 | Sep | | C.C.N.A. founded in Colombia |
| | Dec | | SCADTA founded in Colombia |
| 1920 | Jul | | First two Junkers F 13s arrive in Colombia |
| 1921 | Jan | Otto Meyer emigrates to Brazil | Von Bauer involved with SCADTA |
| | Apr | | LATÉCOÈRE forms C.G.E.A. |
| 1922 | Jul | | Von Bauer becomes Director of SCADTA |
| | | | Allies impose "Nine Rules" on Germany |
| 1924 | May | LATÉCOÈRE advance party survey flights | CONDOR SYNDIKAT formed in Berlin |
| | July | | First night mail in U. S. |
| | Oct | | ZR-3 arrives in U. S., named *Los Angeles* |
| 1925 | Jan | Civil Air Navigation Regulations | |
| | | LATÉCOÈRE flies Rio to Buenos Aires | |
| | Feb | | Kelly Air Mail Act (CAM) in U. S. |
| | Mar | LATÉCOÈRE flies Rio to Recife | |
| | Aug | | Two Wals arrive in Colombia |
| | | LATÉCOÈRE forms C.B.E.A. | SCADTA Trans-Caribbean flight to U. S. |
| 1926 | Jan | | LUFT HANSA founded |
| | May | | Air Commerce Act in U. S. |
| | Oct | VARIG founded | |
| | Nov | "Luther flight" | |
| 1927 | Jan | *Lagôa dos Patos* demonstration flight | |
| | | Directory of Military Aviation founded | |
| | Mar | Instructions for Transportation of Mail by Air | PAN AMERICAN formed |
| | Apr | | Bouilloux-Lafont purchases C.G.E.A. |
| | | C.G.E.A. becomes C.G.A. (AÉROPOSTALE) | |
| | May | | Charles Lindbergh solos across the Atlantic |
| | Jun | VARIG authorized to operate | |
| | Jul | | CONDOR SYNDIKAT officially terminates |
| | Aug | SYNDICATO CONDOR born | |
| | Oct | | First non-stop crossing of South Atlantic |
| | Nov | CONDOR-VARIG first flight | |
| 1928 | Jan | CONDOR authorized to operate | |
| | Mar | AÉROPOSTALE starts air/ship service | U. S. Foreign Air Mail Act (FAM) |

| | | | |
|---|---|---|---|
| | Aug | ETA founded | |
| | Oct | | *Graf Zeppelin* flight to U. S. |
| 1929 | Jan | | Admiral Byrd over "Little America" |
| | Mar | | NYRBA incorporated |
| | Jun | ETA first flight | NYRBA surveys U. S. to S. A. route |
| | Oct | | Stock market crashes in New York |
| 1930 | Feb | NYRBA first international flight | NYRBA first international flight |
| | | ETA embattles NYRBA at Rio de Janeiro | |
| | | AÉROPOSTALE establishes CAB | |
| | Mar | CONDOR-LUFT HANSA air-sea service | |
| | Apr | CAB flies Recife to Natal | |
| | May | Mermoz and *Comte de la Vaulx* cross Atlantic | |
| | May | *Graf Zeppelin* flight to Brazil | *Graf Zeppelin* flight to U. S. |
| | Jul | *Comte de la Vaulx* lost on return to Europe | |
| | Sep | | NYRBA transferred to PAN AMERICAN |
| | Oct | PANAIR DO BRASIL formed from NYRBA | |
| | | ETA ceases operation | |
| | Dec | | Italo Balbo mass flight to Brazil |
| 1931 | | Three flights by *Graf Zeppelin* | |
| | Feb | AÉROPOSTALE loses subsidy | |
| | | Army forms CAM | |
| | Jun | CAM first survey flight | |
| 1932 | | Nine flights by *Graf Zeppelin* | |
| | May | | Amelia Earhart solos across the Atlantic |
| 1933 | | Nine flights by *Graf Zeppelin* | |
| | Jan | *Arc-en-Ciel* crosses Atlantic to Natal | |
| | Jun | | LUFT HANSA catapult experiments |
| | Jul | | Wiley Post solos around the world |
| | Aug | AÉROPOSTALE absorbed by AIR FRANCE | French government forms AIR FRANCE |
| | Oct | *Graf Zeppelin* "Century of Progress" flight | *Graf Zeppelin* "Century of Progress" flight |
| 1934 | | Twelve flights by *Graf Zeppelin* | |
| | Feb | CONDOR-LUFTHANSA catapult service | |
| | | Navy forms CAN | |
| | Apr | VASP starts service | |
| 1935 | | Sixteen flights by *Graf Zeppelin* | |
| | Mar | | DZR formed |
| | Nov | | First scheduled air mail across the Pacific |
| 1936 | | Twenty Zeppelin flights | |
| | Apr | *Hindenburg*'s first flight from Brazil | |
| | Dec | Zeppelin hangar finished at Santa Cruz | Mermoz and *Croix-du-Sud* lost in Atlantic |
| 1937 | | Three Zeppelin flights | |
| | May | | *Hindenburg* destroyed at Lakehurst |
| 1938 | | | U. S. Civil Aeronautics Act (CAB) |
| 1939 | Aug | LUFTHANSA ends service to Brazil | |
| | Sep | | Beginning of World War II |
| | | | LATI formed |
| | Dec | LATI first flight | |
| 1940 | Feb | NAB formed | |
| 1941 | Jan | Ministry of Aeronautics created | |
| | | CAN and CAM joined as NACIONAL | |
| | May | NAB authorized to operate | |
| | Dec | | LATI ends operations |

◊

# NOTES

## INTRODUCTION

### CORREIO AÉREO

1. Without real support or encouragement from the U. S. government, the Curtiss company was active in Latin America. In São Paulo, salesman Orton W. Hoover, who had been in Brazil before the First World War, gave demonstration flights and helped to establish a state government aviation school. In 1922 he moved his efforts to Rio de Janeiro and sold equipment to the Brazilian military.

2. The first CAMs (Contract Air Mail) for routes designated CAM 6 and 7 were let to the Ford Motor Company which inaugurated service on 15 February 1926.

3. It should be noted that Brazil had not ratified the International Convention of Air Navigation (1919), the Ibero American of Madrid (1926), Pan American of Madrid (1926), or the Pan American of Habana (1928), therefore foreign aircraft could enter Brazil and fly over national territory only under permit previously obtained from the Ministry of Communications and Public Works. It is also noted that the "official" decree usually followed—often much later—the actual introduction of aircraft and/or services.

4. Colombia-German Air Transport Society. SCADTA was not the first airline in Colombia. CAMPANIA COLOMBIANA DE NAVEGACION AEREA (CCNA) preceded it on 16 September 1919 (now recognized in Colombia as National Aviation Day) and had received air mail rights two days before SCADTA was born. CCNA suffered many equipment problems and accidents and was substantially out of business by the end of 1922. Its greatest contribution, at least to philately, was the production of the first Colombian air mails—patterned after the colorful advertisements of the Curtiss Aircraft Company. The first experimental mail flight in South America was in Chile, on 1 January 1919, from Valparaiso to Santiago by a pilot named Figueroa. It should also be noted that the Colombian government did not require that the airline companies issue stamps, but at the same time they offered no subsidies. Consequently, the airlines issued stamps to provide necessary income.

5. The person primarily responsible for the promotion and development of German interests in South America, Fritz W. Hammer, is discussed under SYNDICATO CONDOR.

6. There were earlier efforts. R. E. G. Davies, *Airlines of Latin America since 1919* (Washington: Smithsonian Institution Press, 1984), 335 lists no less than six individuals or companies which received certificates of airline operation in 1918-19 before the enactment of any regulations, including one British (Handley Page Ltda). One Italian group was active but did not receive authorization. However, none of these ever operated any service and any remaining equipment was turned over to the government by 1920. This study does not include balloon ventures or the work of Alberto Santos-Dumont, Brazil's aviation pioneer, since most of his efforts were in aircraft development, all of it abroad and not related directly to airlines or air mail.

## THE AIRLINES

### COMPAGNIE GÉNÉRALE AÉROPOSTALE

1. For an extensive, illustrated study, see Gerard Collot and Alain Cornu, *Ligne Mermoz, Histoire Aérophilatelique, Latecoere, Aeropostale, Air France, 1918-1940* (Paris: Editions Bernard Sinais, 1990).

2. Davies, *Airlines of Latin America since 1919*, 336.

3. Phillips, *Illustrated Catalogue of First Air Mails* (Newport, England: Phillips, 1938), 1016. Three Breguet 14s were involved, "stopping at São Paulo, Florianópolis and Porto Alegre. Two only continuing

to Pelotas, Montevideo and B.A. thus effecting the First Air Mail between the two largest capitals in S. America." "Early Foreign Flights, Brazil, No. 1," in Joseph L. Eisendrath, ed., *American Air Mail Catalogue*, 5th ed., vol. 1 (Washington: American Air Mail Society, 1974), 121.

4. Recife is the capital of the state of Pernambuco and was formerly known as Pernambuco, and it appears that way in various catalogs and texts. The name Recife is used to describe the city throughout this document. Pernambuco was derived from an Indian term, *paranambuco* (broken sea). Recife is Portuguese for "reef."

5. "Early Foreign Flights, Brazil, No. 2," in *American Air Mail Catalogue*, 5th ed., vol. 1, 122.

6. Karlheinz Wittig, *Brasilien Erstflüge bis 1949*, (Lohmar, Germany: Verlag Karlheinz Wittig, 1991), 15. The south-bound return flight is incorrectly listed as Bahia - Pernambuco in "Early Foreign Flights, Brazil, No. 3c," in *American Air Mail Catalogue*, 5th ed., vol. 1, 122.

7. In 1925 *The Aircraft Yearbook* described it as providing "irregular" service between Recife - Maccia - São Salvador - Caravelas - Vitoria - Rio de Janeiro - Paranagua - Florianópolis - Porto Alegre.

8. R. E. G. Davies, "Marcel Bouilloux-Lafont— Where is the Glory?" *Bull's Eyes*, 23(3): 6 (1992). R. E. G. Davies, *Rebels and Reformers of the Airways*, (Washington: Smithsonian Institution Press, 1987), 286.

9. See Appendix B for a partial translation.

10. The first Brazil air mail stamps were made by overprinting the "Official" issues of 1913 (see Appendix C).

11. Later arrangements would be made with Chile and Paraguay (1928), Venezuela (1929), and Bolivia and Peru (1930).

12. A complete trip by steamship took 16 days, and the trip from New York to Buenos Aires took 20—a considerable commercial disadvantage, since French merchants could now send and receive a reply before the U. S. dispatches even arrived.

13. *Jane's All the World's Aircraft* (London: Sampson Low, Marston & Co., 1927).

14. Davies, *Airlines of Latin America since 1919*, 360. AÉROPOSTALE leased six ships from the French Navy—the two mentioned, plus *le Révigny*, *l'Épernay*, *le Reims* and *le Belfort*. These were replaced by the end of 1930 with specially-designed ships: *Aéropostale I, II*, etc. In addition, four supply vessels were utilized: *le Bemtévi*, *le Becfigue*, *le Cicogne* and *le Phocée*.

15. The 1928 *Aircraft Yearbook* describes COM-

PANHIA AERONAUTICA BRASILEIRA as AÉROPOSTALE's service in Brazil, employing "525 French planes, 13 pilots, many mechanics and 120 other persons", established with a capital of $494,000. Davies, *Airlines of Latin America since 1919*, 345, "On 13 December 1927—a month after Aéropostale had launched its service—the Brazilian *Diario Oficial* announced the establishment of the Companhia Aeronáutica Brasileira to provide ground installations and services and to construct landing fields at points serviced by Aéropostale."

16. The aircraft was named in memory of the president of the Fédération Aéronautique Internationale who died in an airplane crash in the U. S. in 1929.

17. An extensive discussion of the career of Marcel Bouilloux-Lafont, and the rise and fall of his AÉROPOSTALE, may be found in R. E. G. Davies' 1981 article, "Marcel Bouilloux-Lafont—Where is the Glory?" reprinted in *Bull's Eyes*, 23(3): 5-11 (1992), 23(4): 4-6 (1992), & 24(1): 5-11 (1993) and in a revised form as "Marcel Bouilloux-Lafont: The Shattered Dream," in Davies, *Rebels and Reformers of the Airways*, pp. 283-298.

18. There is apparently some disagreement as to passenger service prior to World War II. Some authors indicate that the *Arc-en-Ciel* was the first to carry passengers. Others indicate that *no* passengers *only* mail, was carried on any aircraft prior to the War.

19. Alberto Santos-Dumont is probably the most famous name in Brazilian air history. A brief biography is included in Appendix C.

## CORREIO AÉREO NACIONAL

1. "The idea of military mail service was first conceived by a group of War Ministry officials, notably Eduardo Gomes, Lemos Cunha, and Casimiro Montenegro, with tacit support from the Minister of War." Davies, *Airlines of Latin America since 1919*, 383.

2. Brig. Eduardo Gomes as "initiator, inspirator and stimulator" was declared "Patron of the National Air Mail" by the National Congress, 12 December 1972, Law. No. 5,866.

3. Phillips, *Illustrated Catalogue of First Air Mails*, 1147.

4. "From July—November 1932 the Paulista Revolution affected the figures." Phillips, *Illustrated Catalogue of First Air Mails*, 1147.

5. See Bruce B. Powell, "Brazilian Civil Censorship During World War II," reproduced in *Bull's Eyes*, 16(1): 10-13 (1985) & 16(2): 5-7 (1985). See also John

Paul do Rio Branco, "Postal Services of the Brazilian Expeditionary Force," *Bull's Eyes*, 20(4): 7-11 (1989).

6. Centro de Relações, *CAN* (Rio de Janeiro, Públicas da Aeronáutica, 1976), 17-18.

7. Paulo Magalhães, quoted in Lt. Brig. Nelson Freire Lavenère-Wanderly, "50th Anniversary of the National Air Mail," *Edital*, No. 11 (Brasília, Brazil: ECT, 1981).

## DEUTSCHE LUFTHANSA A.G.

1. This was a development of the first all-metal aircraft, the J 1, a military plane of 1915. In September 1919 the plane set an altitude record—carrying eight people to 22,150 feet—which was unofficial because Germany had not been admitted to the International Aeronautics Federation. Two were imported to the U. S. in May 1920 as model JL-6 and displayed at the Pan-American Aeronautical Congress in Atlantic City. The U. S. military ordered six of the planes.

2. Of 132 airlines operating world-wide at the time, Germany controlled 62.

3. Until 1934 LUFTHANSA was not written as one word, as it is today.

4. Previously mail was carried on scheduled passenger flights.

5. Britain had apparently granted landing rights to the Germans in an attempt to give some competition to the French that they themselves were unable to provide.

6. R. E. G. Davies, *Lufthansa: An Airline and its Aircraft* (New York: Paladwr Press, 1991), 38.

7. A special fee—3$500 rs. or RM 1.25—for the catapult service was added to the normal rate.

## DEUTSCHE LUFTSCHIFFBAU ZEPPELIN G.m.b.H.

1. The development of zeppelins has been the subject of many books and numerous articles, both in and out of the philatelic press, therefore, I will attempt to limit my discussion as it relates to Brazil and her air mail service.

2. Aktiengesellschaft zur Förderung-der Motorluft-schiffahrt. The literal translation sometimes varies.

3. Construction of airship facilities was begun in several of these major cities.

4. A new number was assigned to each new design whether or not an airship was constructed.

5. Three out of four airships had been lost to accidents.

6. DLR combined with several other lines to form AERO UNION in 1921, and then with DEUTSCHER AERO LLOYD in 1924. See Davies, *Lufthansa: An Airline and its Aircraft*, 19, for an incredible genealogy chart of the German air industry.

7. The Allies were also demanding a large amount of money in compensation for the seven sabotaged airships. The U. S. had yet to get an airship.

8. Britain's R.34 had made the first North Atlantic crossing by an airship on 2 July 1919.

9. See Henry Cord Meyer, "How Philatelists Kept the Zeppelin Flying," *The American Philatelist* 65(9): 796-798 (1979).

10. Donald J. Lemkuhl, *The Zeppelin Stamps* (Winter Park, FL: Winter Park Stamp Shop, 1992), 22.

11. Most literature, advertisements and catalogs relating to the zeppelins refer to Recife, the capital of the State of Pernambuco, as Pernambuco, as it was known at the time (1930). The name Recife is used to describe the city throughout this book. Pernambuco was derived from an Indian term, *paranambuco* (broken sea). Recife is Portuguese for "reef."

12. Reproduced from William A. M. Burden, *The Struggle for Airways in Latin America* (New York: Council on Foreign Relations, 1943), 18.

13. See Lemkuhl, *The Zeppelin Stamps*, 32, for a further discussion.

14. For a detailed account of the first zeppelin flight to South America, see Mason S. Curran, "The 'Triangle' Flight of the Graf Zeppelin, Spring 1930," *The Airpost Journal*, 52(8): 252-259 (May 1981).

15. A special connecting flight, which left Berlin the day after the *Graf* departed for Seville, brought additional mail some with the marking "Anschlussflug zur Sudamerikafahrt 1930 des luftschiffs Graf Zeppelin" (connecting flight to the 1930 flight to South America of the airship Graf Zeppelin). Mail was also posted on board and franked with CONDOR's stamps for further posting at Recife or Rio de Janeiro (see cover page 44). These stamps were available only in Berlin.

16. See SYNDICATO CONDOR; the stamps paid for both services.

17. Interestingly, the Zeppelin Company used a different flight number every time the airship took off, e.g., the 1930 flight includes flight numbers: 62-Friedrichshafen to Seville, 63-Seville to Recife; 64-Recife to Rio de Janeiro, 65-Rio de Janeiro to Recife; 66-Recife to Lakehurst, 67-Lakehurst to Seville and, finally, 68-Seville to Friedrichshafen—seven flights of record where most people think of one. The *American Air Mail Catalogue*, 5th ed., vol. 1, 280-285, records these as Z106, Z107, Z108, Z109 and Z110, all with subdivisions depending on origin and destination.

18. For a detailed account of all of the *Graf Zeppelin*'s flights to South America, see Walter Curley's *The Graf Zeppelin's Flights to South America* (Weston, MA: Cardinal Spellman Philatelic Museum, 1970).

19. LZ.128 was outmoded before it left the drawing board.

20. Lemkuhl, *The Zeppelin Stamps*, 54.

21. Ibid., 57.

22. Ibid.

23. Hugo Fraccaroli, "Cachets used for 'Graf Zeppelin' and 'Hindenburg' flights in Brazil," *Brasil Filatelico* (December 1941), reprinted in *Bull's Eyes*, 10(1), 6, (1979).

24. Bureau of Civil Aeronautics, "Civil Aeronautics in Brazil," 1935, reprinted in *The Pan American Union*, April 1936.

25. One of the interesting features of the facility was the docking tower, built by C. Haushahn G.m.b.H. of Stuttgart, with two platforms of variable (telescopic) height to accommodate the two different size airships. The zeppelin was held, by its beak, by hydraulic claws and supported at the rear by a railroad car. In order to enter or leave the hangar, it used its own motors or was moved manually.

26. Eckener had been "demoted" to Chairman of the Board when the government took control.

27. Francisco D. R. Pfaltzgraff, "50th Anniversary of the Bartolomeu de Gusmão Airport," *Edital*, No. 24 (Brasilia, Brazil: ECT, 1986).

28. Henry Cord Meyer, *Airshipmen, Businessmen, and Politics, 1890-1940* (Washington: Smithsonian Institution Press, 1991), 120.

29. For an interesting, illustrated, documentary account of the life of the company and the airships, in English, by one who was there between 1934 and 1938, see Harold G. Dick, with Douglas H. Robinson, *The Golden Age of the Great Passenger Airships: Graf Zeppelin & Hindenburg*, (Washington: Smithsonian Institution Press, 1985).

## EMPRESA DE TRANSPORTES AÉREOS LTDA

1. The Klemm was manufactured in Germany by Leichtflugzeugbau Klemm G.m.b.H., and the L-25 model was a two-seater, low-wing craft with a 20 hp. Mercedes-Benz engine. It was slightly smaller than the Ryan NYP.

2. ETA did not provide same-day, round trip service.

3. Writing in his memoirs, *A Dream of Eagles* (Boston: Houghton Mifflin, 1973), O'Neill refers to ETA as "AERONAVES ETA, S.A." This is the only place I have seen this reference to the name of this company.

4. A. H. Davis, "A Romance of the Air Mail," *The Air Mail Collector*, II:18, 3, (April 1930).

## LINEE AEREE TRANSCONTINENTALI ITALIANE

1. For a more complete discussion of LATI, see Richard Beith, *The Italian South Atlantic Air Mail Service, 1939-1941* (Chester, England: Richard Beith Associates, 1993).

2. Beith, *The Italian South Atlantic Air Mail Service, 1939-1941*, 8.

3. Henry Ladd Smith, *Airways Abroad* (Washington: Smithsonian Institution Press, 1991), 67-68.

## NAVEGAÇÃO AÉREA BRASILEIRA S/A.

1. Davies, *Airlines of Latin America since 1919*, 443.

## NEW YORK, RIO & BUENOS AIRES LINE INC.

1. Ralph O'Neill's 1973 memoirs, *A Dream of Eagles*, makes an intriguing story. O'Neill died, 23 October 1980, at the age of 83.

2. Ford had operated private, daily parcel service between Detroit and Chicago since 3 April 1925, using Ford mono-planes. Ford was actively engaged in aircraft construction—the most famous, the Ford Trimotor, first flew in June 1926.

3. Between February 1926 and April 1927, 12 lines started operations as feeders to the Post Office Department's own transcontinental service.

4. Billy Mitchell had been court-martialed in 1925 for his outspoken efforts to promote air power.

5. The reference was obviously to a stay of execution at a time when the death penalty was not only in effect, but used, sometimes indiscriminately.

6. Newspaper reports, in the middle of January 1928, about a joint sales mission to South America by Consolidated and Curtiss, represented by Captain Leigh Wade and Lieutenant Jimmy Doolittle, probably convinced Boeing.

7. Aircraft facilities were minimal at this time and gasoline/landing services were obtained from AEROPOSTALE and CONDOR agents.

8. The line was affectionately termed the "Near Beer" line by its staff, attempting to make the acronym palatable, while alluding to the imitation brew of Prohibition.

9. This plane-type was used by Lindbergh, on a flight to Panama some months earlier, and also used

by Lindbergh's employer, PAN AMERICAN, on some of its routes.

10. Ford Trimotors could not climb the 20,000 foot Andes Mountains, but a pass at 16,000 feet had been discovered. Even then the plane encountered rough air, snow and ice, and the passengers were supplied with individual oxygen tubes.

11. A. H. Davis provided early reports of air activity from Brazil in 1930 to *The Air Mail Collector* (the precursor of *The Airpost Journal*).

12. PANAGRA was a joint effort of PAN AMERICAN and the W. R. GRACE shipping line.

13. For an illustrated, detailed account of this historic event see Julius Grigore, Jr., *NYRBA's Triple Crash Covers, Outlaw Flight and its Postal Markings* (Balboa: Julius Grigore, Jr., 1991).

14. One of the difficulties of reading—and, presumably, writing—news reports of this period was the practice of naming the aircraft after cities along the route. Thus we have the *Porto Alegre* waiting in Rio de Janeiro and the *Bahia* coming from Bahia, but in the *New York Times'* accounts the aircraft names are neither italicized or in quotes.

15. Eisendrath, ed., *American Air Mail Catalogue*, 5th. Ed., Vol. 4, 2072.

16. A northbound plane would leave the same day as a southbound plane—flying only in daylight—and the pilots would remain where they were when they transferred their loads, waiting for the return load several days later.

17. Reproduced from Burden, *The Struggle for Airways in Latin America*, 25. The same picture, enlarged, appeared on the cover of the "Rotogravure Picture Section G" of the *New York Times*, Sunday, 15 November 1929.

18. Under FAM terms, all monies paid to the airlines by the foreign governments went to the U. S. Post Office to offset the U. S. subsidy.

19. NYRBA's lower rates would siphon mail from PAN AMERICAN, but, alternatively, not provide a reasonable revenue to the U. S. Post Office.

20. "In the award and interpretation of the contracts herein authorized, the decision of the Postmaster General shall be final, and not subject to review by any office or tribunal of the United States except by the president and the federal courts." *Foreign Air Mail Act*, 8 March 1928.

## PAN AMERICAN AIRWAYS, INC.

1. Smith, *Airways Abroad*, 10. This is the only reference I have found indicating any suggestion of Dr. von Bauer's flight experience.

2. For an extensive, well-documented study of the U. S. attitude during this period, see Wesley Phillips Newton, *The Perilous Sky: Evolution of United States Diplomacy toward Latin America, 1919-1931* (Coral Gables: University of Miami Press, 1978).

3. PAN AMERICAN, INCORPORATED was financially supported by the same group that would eventually form NYRBA.

4. This was the service formerly operated by AEROMARINE.

5. PAN AMERICAN agents would secure exclusive landing rights in various countries *before* routes and/or bids for services were announced, making competitive bidding impossible.

6. For further discussion of this concept, see Newton, *The Perilous Sky: Evolution of United States Diplomacy toward Latin America, 1919-1931.*

7. R. E. G. Davies, *A History of the World's Airlines* (London: Oxford University Press, 1964), 356.

8. PAN AM would establish two subsidiaries for this route to ferry airplanes to Allied forces in Africa and beyond—PAN AMERICAN AIRWAYS AFRICA and PAN AMERICAN AIR FERRIES—both of which would be absorbed into the U. S. Air Force.

9. The aircraft actually departed Miami on 6 December, the day before Pearl Harbor.

10. It is interesting to note, in all of these cachets, how the aircraft changed in design, type and size as PAN AM continued to improve its equipment. PAN AM started with Sikorsky S-38s and the Commodore 16s obtained from NYRBA. The Lockheed Electras and the venerable workhorse, Douglas' DC-3, appeared in use in 1937, and were eventually supplanted by the Constellation and Super-Constellation for international flights.

11. CRUZEIRO is more fully discussed under SYNDICATO CONDOR.

12. For an excellent, delightfully illustrated account of the overall history of this company, see R. E. G. Davies, *PAN AM: An Airline and its Aircraft* (New York: Orion Press, 1987).

13. An interesting account of Juan Trippe's career can be found in Robert Daley, *An American Saga* (New York: Random House, 1980).

14. The *New York Times*, January 9 (1991), D6.

## EMPRESA DE VIAÇÃO AÉREA RIO GRANDENSE

1. Some of this biographical material originally appeared in the *Boletim Informativo Museu Varig* (Porto Alegre, Brazil: Museu Varig, 1979) and in John Paul do Rio Branco, "VARIG-CONDOR: The Early Years," *Bull's Eyes*, 20(3): 15-20 (1989).

2. Quoted in "VARIG: A company history 1927-1977," a synopsis prepared by the company for their 50th anniversary.

3. The actual exemption, State Law No. 413, was not promulgated until 1 December 1926.

4. The other nine were Jose Bertaso, Charles Freb, Arthur Bromberg, Rodolfo Ahrens, Adroaldo Mesquita da Costa, Emilio Gertum, Waldemar Bromberg, Jorge Pfeiffer and Ernesto Rotermund. Of 600,000 Germans in Brazil in 1927, 360,000 lived in Rio Grande do Sul.

5. The CONDOR SYNDIKAT was established in Berlin in May 1924 (see p. 121) to promote aircraft sales and airline development in South America. It was represented in Brazil by Herm Stoltz and Company of Rio de Janeiro (see SYNDICATO CONDOR).

6 The actual arrangement between Meyer's VARIG, LUFT HANSA and the CONDOR SYNDIKAT (and its offspring SYNDICATO CONDOR) was, perhaps purposely, somewhat obscure. For a discussion of this subject see John Paul do Rio Branco, "VARIG-CONDOR: The Early Years."

7. Konder would promulgate Brazil's first "Regulations" for governing the airmail on 17 March 1927. See Appendix B.

8. Authorization was for a period not to exceed one year (Notice No. 60/G).

9. VARIG stated that this flight also carried "mail for publicity purposes."

10. Quoted in "VARIG: A company history 1927 - 1977."

11. Berta died in 1966 and was succeeded by Eric de Carvalho.

12. Many of these early flights were conducted as joint operations by CONDOR and VARIG, with CONDOR supplying the airplane, crew, and technical advice, inspection and maintenance services. Initial postal markings are CONDOR's or simply inscribed *Atlântico*. This changed in the succeeding months as VARIG assumed its own identity.

13. The first meeting discussed the proposed statute of the company, prepared by Dr. Adroaldo Mesquita da Costa and Carlos Maria Bias. For the second, general meeting, Jose Bertaso and Theofilo de Barros acted as Secretaries.

14. Quoted in do Rio Branco, "VARIG-CONDOR: The Early Years."

15. SYNDICATO CONDOR had received permission to operate on 20 August 1927. It did not formally incorporate until 1 December 1927, and was not formally "officially authorized" until 20 January 1928.

16. Davies, *Airlines of Latin America since 1919*, 343-344. The flight took two hours for the first part, 20 minutes for the second, at an altitude of between 60 and 150 feet above the lagoon. The fare was 220 rs. one way, 360 rs. round trip.

17. Note the boxed "EXPRESSO" marking. Article 2d II of the Decree of 17 March required that mail carried be subject to a special delivery fee. The 27-28 March flight (described previously) was exempt from this provision (for some unknown reason). This requirement was abolished on 29 February 1928.

18. The fact that VARIG used only two cancellations is very helpful in identifying forgeries which, especially after the stamps were "removed" from circulation, abound (see Appendix C).

19. The *Gaúcho* is aptly named, as it is a Brazilian term used to designate the residents of the state of Rio Grande do Sul. The Dornier Merkur/Sea, used by LUFT HANSA on the Berlin to Moscow route, was modified as a float plane. Slightly larger than the Junkers F 13, its single engine could develop more horsepower and handle six passengers instead of four.

20. Werner Ahrens, "VARIG, Brazil's First Airline," trans. Alfred J. Hillel, *The Aero Philatelist Annals*, III(3): 5 (1955), acknowledges this date but indicates, without further explanation, that the flight actually took place on 5 August.

21. Ibid., 7.

22. VARIG may have been forced to suspend operations after the Revolution for a period of two years, while the new government was organizing and establishing the office of the Director of Aviation. However, VARIG covers, including first flights, exist from this era.

23. The single-engined seaplane in the center left, below the drawing of the *Atlântico*, is mis-labeled a "Junkers F 13." It is, instead, by both design and identity markings, the Dornier Merkur, *Gaúcho*. On an F 13, the wing is below the fuselage.

## SYNDICATO CONDOR LIMITADA

1. The Contract would last 11 years and included the right to set airmail rates, print and sell their own stamps. There was no government subsidy.

2. Newton identifies the full name as Dr. Peter Paul von Bauer Chlumeck'y in *The Perilous Sky, 26*. Von Bauer was born in Brünn (Mähren) and studied at the Darmstadt Maschinenbau in 1906-07. He studied Physics at the University in Munich and Chemistry in Heidelberg. He died in Emmersdorf, near Klagenfurt in southern Austria, 8 August 1965.

3. The idea for the SYNDIKAT has been credited to Fritz Hammer. See Newton, *The Perilous Sky*, 69. The choice of the name CONDOR remains a mystery as it is the name of a large vulture native to the Andes, but not to Germany or, later, Brazil. It may relate more to earlier activity in Bolivia (LAB) or Colombia (SCADTA).

4. See Newton, *The Perilous Sky*.

5. Claude Dornier died in Zug, Switzerland, 5 December 1969, at the age of 85.

6. The most famous of these was the *Plus Ultra* flown by Ramon Franco across the South Atlantic in 1926 (see Appendix A).

7. Joachim Wachtel, *The Lufthansa Story* (Cologne: Lufthansa German Airlines, 1980), 45.

8. Henry Harley Arnold, *Global Mission* (New York: Harper & Brothers, 1949), 115-116.

9. Wachtel, *The Lufthansa Story*, 45.

10. Ibid.

11. CONDOR is not the first "official" airline. VARIG was officially registered on 1 May 1927 and received authorization to operate on 10 June 1927.

12. "At the suggestion of Commander Hammer, a system for the payment of airmail fees was provided, which had already proved its worth in SCADTA's operations in Colombia." Ahrens, "VARIG, Brazil's First Airline," 4.

13. The Junkers G 24, following Junker's success with the F 13, was an all-metal, three-engined monoplane (the first in civil aviation), had a crew of three and could carry nine passengers. With a range of 800 miles it could be (and was) outfitted with wheels or pontoons.

14. Notice 620/G provided this extension to CONDOR SYNDIKAT, not SYNDICATO CONDOR. How and/or by whom the flights were operated remains a mystery. Wittig, *Brasilien Erstflüge bis 1949*, 19, indicates that the SYNDIKAT ceased operating on or after 8 November 1927.

15. Enrique Olaya Herrera, ally of Dr. von Bauer, ended his tour as Colombia's Minister to Washington, by becoming President of his own country—a post he would hold for the next four years (1930-1934). It is interesting to note that during his term of office (1931) Juan Trippe of PAN AMERICAN had obtained a major share holding role in SCADTA, a fact which was not made public until several years later.

16. An article on the history of the lake appeared in *The American Philatelist*, May 1983.

17. It was 675 feet long, 84 feet wide, and carried a total of 1,315 passengers and a crew of 630. It is unclear to this writer when the appelation "Süd"

(South) is added to the Hamburg-Amerika name (see poster p. 55) or if it was applied by the company or authors trying to distinguish between North and South Atlantic services.

18. Years later, near the end of World War II, the *Cap Arcona* was anchored in the Bay of Neustadt (Schleswig-Holstein) near Lübeck. Its cargo was 2,700 inmates from the Hamburg concentration camp and over 500 guards. On 3 May 1945 R. A. F. aircraft bombed the ship, sending it and most of its cargo to the bottom. The "Queen of the South Atlantic" was no more.

19. It was 20,576 gross tons. Originally launched in March 1914, the *Cap Polonio* was intended as the flagship for the run between Hamburg and Rio de Janeiro. Modified for war use, transferred to the British as reparations in 1919, and then sold back to the original owners in 1921, she was refitted as a luxury liner and recommissioned in February 1922. After more than a decade of success for the line, she was scrapped at Bremerhaven in 1935.

20. The aircraft *Pirajá* "had already been transferred to Corumbá, via Buenos Aires and Asunción, during the emergency of the Paraguay-Bolivia war, and Condor enterprisingly found good use of the aircraft without bringing it back to Rio de Janeiro." Davies, *Airlines of Latin America since 1919*, 381.

21. The full story of the DO-X has been told in other publications, including a long series in *the Air Post Journal* and "The Dornier Do X (1929-1933)" in R. E. G. Davies *Fallacies and Fantasies of Air Transport History* (McLean: Paladwr Press, 1994). It is not the intent to repeat it here.

22. See Davies, *Airlines of Latin America since 1919*, and Davies, *Rebels and Reformers*.

23. AIR FRANCE, PANAIR, CONDOR and VARIG were the other operating companies.

24. The service operated on the first and third weeks westbound, and the second and fourth weeks eastbound (see p. 36).

25. All of these flights were not totally successful—the CONDOR plane, *Tapajoz*, crashed in Rio's harbor, 5 May 1934.

26. I do not know if this debt was ever satisfied.

## VIAÇÃO AÉREA SÃO PAULO, S.A.

1. Burden, *The Struggle for Airways in Latin America*, 66.

2. Ibid, 76.

# APPENDICES

## CROSSING THE SOUTH ATLANTIC

1. The date of accomplishment is listed as 31 May 1922. John P. V. Heinmuller, *Man's Fight to Fly* (New York: Funk & Wagnalls, 1944), 312.

2. No official mail was carried on the ocean portion of the flight. Dr. Perham C. Nahl, ed., *American Air Mail Catalogue*, 5th ed., vol. 4, 1545. "Trans-Oceanic Record Flights, No. 1050,"

3. Many rumors developed over the cause of the disaster, including possible sabotage. Heinmuller, *Man's Fight to Fly*, 35, argues quite convincingly for a poorly discarded cigarette during a refueling operation.

4. The aircraft *Nungesser-Coli* was named after Charles Eugène Jules Marie Nungesser (1892-1927), a French World War I ace, and François Coli (?-?), who took off westward from Paris on 8 May 1927 in an attempt to fly the Atlantic (before Lindbergh) to New York City. Contact was lost and they were presumed lost at sea in spite of early French newspaper accounts that they had landed successfully. All that remains of the attempt is the undercarriage which they ejected on takeoff; it is in the Musée de l'Air, Paris. Twelve days later, Charles Lindbergh (1907-1974), made the trip successfully in the opposite direction.

5. Nahl, ed., *American Air Mail Catalogue*, 5th ed., vol. 4, 1546. "Trans-Oceanic Record Flights" lists a flight, No. 1051, on 12 April 1927, from Rome to Brazil with pilots "Franchetti and DelPrete," indicates that no mail was carried across the ocean, but was carried between Montevideo and Paraguay, backstamped 15 May 1927. I have not found any corroboration of this flight and the names and timing are similar to de Pinedo's "Four Continents Flight." It may be possible that these covers are a result of the earlier flight, but I cannot explain the backstamp dates.

6. The first solo flight across the South Atlantic by a woman was executed on 11-13 November 1935 by New Zealand's Jean Batten, flying a Percival Gulf from Lympne, Kent, England to Natal, Brazil, via Thies, Senegal.

## THE INSTRUCTIONS OF 1927

1. The translation of this information by Alfred J. Hillel, originally appeared in *The Bull's Eye*, publication of The Friends of Brazilian Philately, (II: 2, 1954).

It was reproduced slightly altered in *Bull's Eyes*, (22:1, 1991). It has been modified again in this current work. The rates listed here are slightly different from those in the table on p. 127, which were taken from Werner Ahrens, "The Air Post Stamps of the Condor Syndicate," translated by Alfred J. Hillel, *The Bull's Eyes*, 1(4) 30-33 (1954).

## THE FIRST AIR MAIL STAMPS

1. Icarus, of Greek mythology, was something of a favorite subject for several government issued stamps as well as for VARIG.

2. See Henry M. Goodkind, "Why the holes on these VARIG company stamps," *Aero Philatelist Annals* 1(4): 117-121 (19540.

3. Illustrations of the full sheets reproduced from the *Aero Philatelist Annals*, 1:4, (1954).

4. Illustration reproduced from the VARIG Annual Report 1982 which reproduced it from "Historical and descriptive catalogue of VARIG stamps," compiled by the Philatelical Union of Porto Alegre and published 20 September 1935. I believe the personnel to be (front row, l. to r.) Frederico Barata, Carlos Thompson Flores Neto, Henrique Bertaso, Frederico Bordini, Benjamin Camozato and Ruben Berta.

5. This is as listed in the Encyclopedia Britannica. In his introduction to Alberto Santos-Dumont, Air Marshal Sir Peter Wykeham indicates that the birthplace was "at Cabangu, in the João Aires district of Brazil." *My Airships*, (New York: Dover Publications Inc., 1973, vi). The current town of Santos-Dumont in Minas Gerais is about 100 miles north of Rio de Janeiro.

6. This comment is also made in Dona

7. Werner Ahrens, Ward Ryan, trans., "The Paraiba Zeppelin Provisional," reprinted in *Bull's Eyes*, 10(3): 3-5 (1979).

8. Lemkuhl, *The Zeppelin Stamps*, 29.

◊

# SELECT BIBLIOGRAPHY

Ahrens, Werner. "VARIG, Brazil's First Airline." Translated by Alfred J. Hillel. *Aero Philatelist Annals* 3/3 (1955): 3-16.

———. "The Air Post Stamps of the Condor Syndicate." Translated by Alfred J. Hillel. *The Bull's Eye* 1/4 (1954): 29-33.

———. "The Paraiba Zeppelin Provisional," Translated by Ward Ryan. *Bull's Eyes* 10:3 (1979): 3-6.

Angelucci, Enzo, and Paolo Matricardi. *World Aircraft Origins-World War I*. Chicago: Rand McNally, 1979.

———.*World Aircraft 1918-1935*. Chicago: Rand McNally, 1979.

———.*World Aircraft, Commercial 1935-1960*. Chicago: Rand McNally, 1979.

Arnold, Henry Harley. *Global Mission*. New York: Harper & Brothers, 1949.

Baldwin, N. C. *Bridging the Atlantic*. Sutton Coldfield: Francis Field, 1945.

Beaubois, Henry. *Airships,: An Illustrated History*. New York: Two Continents, 1973.

Beith, Richard. *The Italian South Atlantic Air Mail Service, 1939-1941*. Chester: Richard Beith Associates, 1993.

Brooks, Peter W. *Zeppelin: Rigid Airships, 1893–1940*.Washington: Smithsonian Institution Press, 1992.

Burden, William A.M. *The Struggle for Airways in Latin America*. New York: Council on Foreign Relations, 1943.

Collot, Gerard, and Alain Cornu. *Ligne Mermoz, Histoire aérophilatélique, Latecoere, Aeropostale, Air France, 1918-1940*. Paris: Editions Bertrand Sinais, 1990.

Cooke, David C. *The Story of Aviation*. New York: Archer House, 1958.

Curley, Walter. *The Graf Zeppelin's Flights to South America, 1930-1937*. Weston: Cardinal Spellman Philatelic Museum, 1970.

Daley, Robert. *An American Saga: Juan Trippe and his Pan Am Empire*. New York: Random House, 1980.

Davies, R. E. G. *Airlines of Latin America since 1919*. Washington: Smithsonian Institution Press, 1984.

———. *A History of the World's Airlines*. London: Oxford University Press, 1964.

———. *Fallacies and Fantasies of Air Transport History*. Rockville, Md.: Paladwr Press, 1994.

———. *Lufthansa: An Airline and its Aircraft*. Rockville, Md.: Paladwr Press, 1991.

———. *Pan Am: An Airline and its Aircraft*. New York: Orion Press, 1987.

———. *Rebels and Reformers of the Airways*. Washington: Smithsonian Institution Press, 1987.

de Leeuw, Hendrick. *Conquest of the Air*. New York: Vantage Press, 1960.

Dick, Harold G., with Douglas H. Robinson. *The Golden Age of the Great Passenger Airships Graf Zeppelin & Hindenburg*. Washington: Smithsonian Institution Press, 1985.

Duggan, John, and Jim Graue. *Commercial Zeppelin Flights to South America*. Valleyford, Wa.: JL Diversified, 1995.

Eisendrath, Joseph L., ed. *American Air Mail Catalogue*. 5th Ed., Vol. 1. Cinnaminson, N.J.: American Air Mail Society, 1974.

Fraser, Chelsa. *Heroes of the Air*. New York: Crowell, 1940.

Gooch, William Stephen. *Winged Highway*. New York: Longmans, Green and Co., 1938.

Goodkind, Henry M. "Brazil – Why the Holes on These VARIG Company Stamps?" *Aero Philatelist Annals* 1:4 (1954): 117-121.

Grey, C. G., ed. *Jane's All the World's Aircraft*. London: Jane's, 1919-1936.

Grigore, Julius, Jr. *NYRBA's Triple Crash Covers, Outlaw Flight, and its Postal Markings*. Balboa: Julius Grigore, Jr., 1991.

Haberer, Erich. *Katapultpost-Katalog, Teil 2: Südamerika, 50 Jahre Lufthansa im Südatlantikdienst*. Weil der Stadt, Germany: Haberer, 1984.

Heinmuller, John P. V. *Man's Fight to Fly: Famous World Records and a Chronology of Aviation*. New York: Funk & Wagnalls Company, 1944.

Jackson, Robert. *Airships*. New York: Doubleday, 1973.

Labrousse, Pierre. *Répertoire des Traversées Aériennes de L'Atlantique Sud par L'Aéropostale et Air-France 1930-1940*. Paris: Larbousse, 1974.

Lana, Robert E. *The Mass Flights of Italo Balbo*. Mineola, N.Y.: The American Air Mail Society, 1996.

Leary, William M. *Aerial Pioneers: The U. S. Air Mail Service, 1918-1927*. Washington: Smithsonian Institution Press, 1985.

Lehmkuhl, Donald J. *The Zeppelin Stamps*. Winter Park, Fl.: Winter Park Stamp Shop, 1992.

Lissitzyn, Oliver James. *International Air Transport and National Policy*. New York: Council on Foreign Relations, 1942.

Mance, Brig. Gen. Sir Osborne. *International Air Transport*. London: Oxford University Press, 1944.

Meyer, Henry Cord. *Airshipmen, Businessmen and Politics, 1890-1940*. Washington: Smithsonian Institution Press, 1991.

Meyer, Rolf Harald. *Catálogo de Selos do Brasil 1995, Volume II-1890 a 1966*. São Paulo: Editora RHM, 1995.

Mondey, David, ed. *The International Encyclopedia of Aviation*. New York: Crown, 1977.

Muller, Frank. *Catalogue des Aérogrammes du Monde Entier*. Paris: Muller, 1950.

Myers, Bernard. *Statistics for Selected World Air Carriers*. Washington: Civil Aeronautics Board, 1945.

Nahl, Dr. Perham C., ed. *American Air Mail Catalogue*. 5th Ed., Vol. 4. Cinnaminson, N.J.: American Air Mail Society, 1981.

Newton, Wesley Phillips. *The Perilous Sky: Evolution of United States Aviation Diplomacy toward Latin America, 1919-1931*. Coral Gables: University of Miami Press, 1978.

O'Neill, Ralph, with Joseph F. Hood. *A Dream of Eagles*. Boston: Houghton Mifflin, 1973.

Phillips. *First Illustrated Complete Catalogue of the First Air Mails of Brazil, Green List No. 555*. Newport, England: Phillips, 1944.

Roadcap, Roy R., ed. *World Airline Record*. Chicago: Roadcap & Assoc., 1972.

Smith, Henry Ladd. *Airways Abroad: The Story of American World Air Routes*. Washington: Smithsonian Institution Press, 1991.

Thomas, Don. *Airline Artistry*. Dunedin, Fl.: W. Donald Thomas, 1992.

————. *Nostalgia Artistica*. Dunedin, Fl.: W. Donald Thomas, 1993.

————. *Nostalgia Panamericana*. Dunedin, Fl.: W. Donald Thomas, 1987.

————. *Poster Art of the Airlines*. Dunedin, Fl.: W. Donald Thomas, 1992.

Wachtel, Joachim. *The Lufthansa Story*. Cologne: Lufthansa German Airlines, 1980.

Wittig, Karlheinz. *Brasilien, Erstflüge bis 1949*. Lohmar, Germany: Verlag Karlheinz Wittig, 1991.

William Kriebel has collected Brazil philately since 1949. He has been the editor of the *Bull's Eyes*, Journal of the Brazil Philatelic Association, since July 1980 and the editor of the *Souvenir Card Journal*, publication of the Souvenir Card Collectors Society, since January 1993. He has contributed a column to the *Jack Knight Air Log* since April 1994. He is a member of the American Philatelic Society and the American Air Mail Society. He has exhibited his collection of air mail material, some of which is used to illustrate this book, and won national awards.

Bill is a practising Registered Architect and an Instructor in the Department of Design at Drexel University in Philadelphia.

# INDEX

◊

# About the American Air Mail Society

GENERAL INFORMATION - The American Air Mail Society, organized in 1923, is one of the oldest and largest aerophilatelic societies in existence. AAMS members collect everything from the balloon posts of the siege of Paris to more modern airpost items, such as jet and rocket mail, contract air mail covers, transoceanic and foreign flight covers.

Dues are kept as low as possible and there are many privileges and services for members. It is not necessary that you be an advanced or wealthy specialist to attain membership, or to enjoy aerophilately to the fullest. The only requisites are that you have an impeccable character and have air mail collecting as an interest. Our members believe it to be an honor and a privilege to be affiliated with the group and often gather at stamp shows.

As a cooperative group organized solely to assist airmail collectors, the AAMS and all of its departments and services are not operated for profit.

THE AIR POST JOURNAL - This official monthly journal has been published by the AAMS since 1931. The *APJ* is a copiously illustrated magazine that is sent to each member for the duration of his or her membership. It covers the entire field of aerophilately and reports on new airmail stamp issues and new flights that occur throughout the world. AAMS membership news appears regularly as well.

CATALOGS AND HANDBOOKS - The AAMS has been the world's largest and most successful publisher of airmail literature. *The American Air Mail Catalog* has been published since 1935. Now in its fifth edition, a sixth is under preparation. Other handbooks treat a variety of specialist air mail topics. Now available are books on the siege of Paris in 1870-71, Newfoundland airmails, U. S. pioneer air mails and on many other subjects as well. AAMS members are entitled to a 20% discount off the usual price of these handbooks.

MEMBERSHIP SERVICES - Airmail stamps, covers and literature may be sold through the Sales Department or Auction Department. Exchanges with other AAMS members may be arranged through two (2) free members' want or exchange ads in *APJ*.

The AAMS provides for groups of collectors to form AAMS chapters that study special airmail topics. Some of these groups issue a newsletter as well.

A free translation service of many modern languages' is available to all members.

The AAMS sponsors many awards for exhibits of airmail stamps and covers at regional, national and international stamp exhibitions. Certificates, medals and special awards are presented to airmail exhibits as decided by the show's judges.

ANNUAL CONVENTIONS AND MEETINGS - Two national meetings a year make it possible for members and friends to meet face-to-face and discuss their collecting interests. These meetings vividly display the simplest axiom of aerophilately—airmail stamps and covers remain the vehicles of our collecting interests, but the friends we make are the hobby's richest reward.

For information about any aspect of the American Air Mail Society write to:

## THE AMERICAN AIR MAIL SOCIETY
## P.O. BOX 110
## MINEOLA, NY 11501-0110 U. S. A.